BIHAR TOURISM
RETROSPECT AND PROSPECT

About the Authors

Dr Udai Prakash Sinha (*b.* 1956) is Professor of Economics, T.M. Bhagalpur University, Bhagalpur. He has authored many books including *Planned Development of Resources in a Developing Region* (1985), *Socio-Economic Dimensions of Integrated Development in India* (1991) and *IRDP for Weaker Sections* (1996). He is editing 'Journal of Economic Issues' since 2000 published by Planning Forum, and Anga Economic Society, University Department of Economics, T.M. Bhagalpur University, Bhagalpur. He has also completed two UGC Major Research Projects and contributed more than 50 research papers to reputed national and international journals of Economics and other social-sciences. 28 Research Scholars have already been awarded Ph.D. degree under his able guidance. Micro-level planning and the regional economics are the areas of his interest and research.

Dr Swargesh Kumar, M.A, Ph.D. is Project Fellow in UGC sponsored Research Project, Dept. of Economics, T.M. Bhagalpur University, Bhagalpur and published number of Research Papers in reputed journals. He has presented paper and participated in National Seminar/ Conference regularly. He is member of IEA and BEA.

Bihar Tourism
Retrospect and Prospect

U.P. Sinha
Swargesh Kumar

CONCEPT PUBLISHING COMPANY PVT. LTD.
NEW DELHI-110 059

ISBN-13 : 978-81-8069-799-9

First Published 2012

Published and Printed by

Concept Since 1974

Concept Publishing Company Pvt. Ltd.
A/15-16, Commercial Block, Mohan Garden
New Delhi-110059 (India)
T: 25351460, 25351794, *F*: 091-11-25357109
E: publishing@conceptpub.com, W: www.conceptpub.com
Editorial Office: H-13, Bali Nagar, New Delhi-110 015, India.

Cataloging in Publication Data--*Courtesy:* D.K. Agencies (P) Ltd. <docinfo@dkagencies.com>

Sinha, Udai Prakash, 1956-
Bihar tourism : retrospect and prospect / U.P. Sinha, Swargesh Kumar.
p. cm.
Includes bibliographical references and index.
ISBN 9788180697999

1. Tourism—India—Bihar. 2. Tourism—Government policy—India—Bihar. 3. Tourism—India—Bihar—Marketing. I. Kumar, Swargesh, joint author. II. Title.

DDC 338.47910954123 23

Preface

Tourism today is the world's largest and fastest expanding industry. The vastness of its market, its unpredictability, the diversity of the product itself and above all, the financial and sociological rewards to be gained have made this industry one of the most fiercely competitive industry in the world.

Tourism presents an unparalleled challenge (at the same time opportunity also) to the economics of developing world. Its effect on creating jobs and reducing unemployment is particularly praiseworthy on the industry and commercial endeavours of the country as a whole. The curiosity to know and see the world is bereft of communication network, it is a matter of great pride, privilege and personal courage to be a voyager. It is also being recognized as an industry. It is also an activity that promotes goodwill and fellowship around the world and is great educational asset. It is no less an economic activity and its industry ranking is the second in the world next to oil industry. It is an inseparable combination of economics and sociological issues. It has a tremendous potential for earning foreign exchange, generating employment, increasing tax revenue and promoting business activities like transport, fruit production, agriculture crafts, hotel industry, entertainment and productive services.

The study area—Bihar is a land affluent in natural beauty, whispering forests, sparkling lakes, forts and palaces, holy rivers, holy shrines and natural hot springs emerging from a backdrop of eternal snow.

A magnetic destination attracting throngs of tourists every year with tremendous potential of growth in number and quality, Bihar is one of the eastern states in the Indian union. It is endowed with immense tourism potential and is surrounded by the states of West Bengal, Jharkhand and Uttar Pradesh on its three sides. In the north, it touches the international boundaries of Nepal. Bihar was in days gone by, the arena on which great empires rose and fell.

Bihar, as of today after bifurcation, is still studded with monuments of its past glory-monuments that bear the memory of Jain Mahavir—24th Tirthankar of Jainism and Lord Buddha—founder of the Buddhism. Simultaneously, it also bears deep wound-marks on it caused by several foreign intruders. The ruins of Nalanda and Vikramshila bear the testimony of our being on the zenith of culture and civilization some 2550 years ago. This is the land on which Bhagwan Buddha and Mahavir started their religious orders.

The present work is a modest attempt to highlight the "Tourism Development and Marketing of Tourist Services in Bihar". An attempt has also been made to suggest feasible and practicable plan for tourism development in the country. There are ten chapters in this work which taken together encompass the various factors of development and marketing of tourist services in Bihar.

Udai Prakash Sinha

Swargesh Kumar

Contents

Preface 5

List of Tables 8

List of Figures 10

1. Introduction 13
2. An Overview of the Study 46
3. Tourism in India 76
4. Profile of Bihar 99
5. Tourism and Tourist Places in Bihar 135
6. Tourism and Hospitality in Bihar 179
7. The Competitive Environment of Tourism in Bihar: Fairs and Festivals 193
8. Marketing of Tourism in Bihar 208
9. Tourism Planning and Policy of India vis-à-vis Bihar 222
10. Conclusions and Suggestions 263

Questionnaire 272

Plates 281

Index 289

List of Tables

1.1	The Main Tourist Generators, 1961	22
1.2	International Tourist Arrivals, 1950-1976	23
1.3	International Tourist Arrivals, 1965-1976	24
1.4	International Tourist Destinations 1999	26
2.1	Foreign Tourist Arrivals to India	64
2.2	India's Share in World Arrivals	65
2.3	Foreign Exchange Earnings by India from Tourism	65
2.4	India's Share in World Foreign Exchange Earnings	66
2.5	India's Rank in Arrivals and Earnings	66
2.6	Foreign Exchange Earnings per Tourist Arrival—India and World	68
2.7	Domestic Tourist Visits in India	68
2.8	Share of Tourism Sector in India in GDP of the Nation	69
2.9	Employment Generation through Tourism in India	70
3.1	Trends in Foreign Tourist Arrivals in India in the Eighties	79
3.2	Relative Share of India in Global Tourist Arrivals in the Eighties	80
3.3	Trends in Foreign Tourist Arrivals in India in the Nineties	81
4.1	Population Growth	106
4.2	Population of Major District in Bihar	108
4.3	Major Cities/Districts in Bihar	109
4.4	Bihar State Domestic Product	113
4.5	Literacy Rate from 1951-2001	115
4.6	Religion in Bihar	130
5.1	Number of Tourists in Bihar	136
6.1	Marital Status and Age of Tourists	181

6.2	Age and Gender of Domestic and Foreign Tourists	181
6.3	Domestic Tourist Traffic (2005)	183
6.4	Foreign Tourist Traffic (2005)	184
6.5	Tourist Statistics of Bihar (January to December, 2006)	186
6.6	Tourist Statistics of Bihar (January to December, 2007)	187
6.7	Tourist Statistics of Bihar (January to December, 2008)	188
6.8	No. of Domestic and Foreign Tourists in Bihar (2000-2009)	189
6.9	Budget: Allocation and actual expenditure on Tourism Sector in Bihar	189
8.1	Earnings from Tourist in Bihar (2001-04)	213
8.2	Expenditure of Tourists in Bihar	214
8.3	Population of Souvenir and Handicraft Shops (2005)	215
8.4	Average Employment in Accommodation Units	216

List of Figures

1.1	The Main Tourist Generators, 1961	22
1.2	International Tourist Arrivals, 1950-1976	23
1.3	International Tourist Arrivals, 1965-1976	25
1.4	International Tourist Destination (1999)	27
1.5	Features of Tourists	29
1.6	A Model of Incubating Tourism Entrepreneurs in India	37
2.1	Foreign Tourist Arrivals to India	64
2.2	India's Share in World Arrivals	65
2.3	Foreign Exchange Earnings by India from Tourism	66
2.4	India's Share in World Foreign Exchange Earnings	67
2.5	India's Rank in Arrivals and Earnings	67
2.6	Foreign Exchange Earnings per tourist Arrival—India and World	68
2.7	Domestic Tourist Visits in India	69
2.8	Share of Tourism Sector in India in GDP of the Nation	69
2.9	Employment Generation through Tourism in India	70
3.1	India's Major Tourist Circuits	76
3.2	Trends in Foreign Tourist Arrivals in India in the Eighties	79
3.3	Relative Share of India in Global Tourist Arrivals in the Eighties	80
3.4	Trends in Foreign Tourist Arrivals in India in the Nineties	82
4.1	Tourist Map of Bihar	99
4.2	Population Growth	107
4.3	Population of Major Districts in Bihar	108
4.4	Gross State Domestic Product	113
4.5	Literacy Rate from 1951-2001	116

4.6 Religion in Bihar 130
5.1 Number of Tourists in Bihar 136
5.2 Major Tourist Places in Bihar 137
5.3 Tourist Places in Patna City 138
5.4 Tourist Places in Nalanda 142
5.5 Tourist Places in Gaya 147
5.6 Tourist Places in Muzaffarpur-Vaishali 149
5.7 Tourist Places in Bhabua, Rohtas and Aurangabad 152
6.1 Annual Tourist Composition 180
6.2 Month-wise Trend in Tourist Traffic in Bihar (2005) 185
6.3 No. of Domestic and Foreign Tourists in Bihar (2000-2009) 190
6.4 Bidget: Allocation and actual expenditure on Tourism sector in Bihar 190
7.1 Strategic Drift 193
8.1 Earnings from Tourists in Bihar (2001-04) 213
8.2 Expenditure of Tourists in Bihar 214
8.3 Population of Souvenir and Handicraft Shops (2005) 216
8.4 Average Employment in Accommodation Units 217

1

Introduction

The Nature and Extent

Tourism has been a major social phenomenon of the societies all along. It is motivated by the natural urge of every human being for new experience, adventure, education and entertainment. The motivations for tourism also include social, religious and business interests. The spread of education has fostered a desire to know more about different parts of the globe. The basic human thirst for new experience and knowledge has become stronger, as communication barriers are getting overcome by technological advances. Progress in air transport and development of tourist facilities have encouraged people to venture out to the foreign lands.

Tourism today is not only an entertainment activity, but is also being recognized as an industry. Tourism also is an activity that promotes goodwill and fellowship around the world and is a great educational asset. It is no less an economic activity and its industry ranking is the second in the world, next to oil industry.

Tourism is an inseparable combination of economic and socio-cultural issues. It has a tremendous potential for earning foreign exchange, generating employment, increasing tax revenue and promoting business activities like transport, fruit production, agriculture, crafts, hotel industry, entertainment and productive services.

Meaning and Concept of Tourism

The origin of the word 'tourist' dates back to A.D. 1229. It has come from the word 'tour', a derivation of the Latin word *tornus*, meaning a tools for describing a circle or a turner's wheels. In the first half of the seventeenth century, the term was used for travelling from place to place, a journey, an excursion, a circuitous journey touching the principal parts of a country or region.

The *19th-century Dictionary* defines 'tourist' as a "person who travels for pleasure of travelling, out of curiosity, and because he has nothing better to do". The term 'tourist', the *Oxford English Dictionary* tells us, was used as early as the year 1800. According to the *Dictionnarie Universal*, the 'tourist' is a person who makes a journey for the sake of curiosity, for the fun of travelling; or just to tell others that he has travelled.

The term 'tourist' in the sense of a pleasure tour is, however, of recent origin. In the words of Jose Ignacio De Arrillaga, "tourism in its first period was considered as a sport or rather as a synthesis of automobiles, touring, cycling, camping, excursions and yachting. In the early nineteenth century, the term 'tourist' assumed a meaning of one who makes a tour or tours, especially 'one who does this for recreation or who travels for pleasure, object of interest, scenery or the like'."

Tourism can be defined as the act of travel for the purpose of recreation, and the provision of services for this act. It is a service industry, comprising a number of tangible and intangible components. The tangible elements include transportation systems—air, rail, road, water and now, space; hospitality services, accommodation, foods and beverages, tours, souvenirs; and related services such as banking, insurance and security. The intangible elements include: rest and relaxation, culture, escape, adventure, new and different experiences.

Travel and tourism is major industry in the world and is at the top of the league of invisible earners of foreign currency. Many sovereignties, along with their respective countries and states, depend heavily upon travel expenditures by foreigners as a source of taxation and income for the enterprises that sell services to these travellers. Consequently, the development of tourism is often a strategy employed either by a non-governmental organization or a governmental agency to promote a particular region for the purpose of increasing commerce through exporting goods and services to non-locals.

During recent years, the tourism industry has witnessed unprecedented growth. Increasing consumer demand for educational and participatory travel experiences has resulted in a variety of specially niche markets such as ecotourism, cultural-heritage tourism, and agrotourism. New paradigms link strategic tourism planning with sustainable development.

The leisure and tourism industry is one of the leading global economic activities, a multi-billion-dollar industry with 700 million international travellers per year around the world. Tourism is a motor for employment and income creation and, especially in poor countries, a vehicle for development. But today it is not sufficient to simply create employment without regard for the quality of jobs and the social and environmental effects of tourism in vulnerable areas. A growing number of organizations, including the tourism industry leadership, are increasingly conscious of the risks and are adopting a more responsible attitude.

Thus, tourism in its purest sense, is essentially a pleasure activity in which the money earned in one's normal domicile is spent in the places visited. According to 'Dictionnaire Universal', the term 'tourism' means organized touring. There is no universally accepted definition of tourism and even now the term is defined by different authors in various ways. R.de Meyer defines tourism as "a collective term for human movement and its attendant activities caused by the exteriorization and fulfillment of the desire to escape that is, more or less, latent in everybody". This definition received the first prize from the Academic International de Tourism at Monte Carlo in 1952. But it seems to lack the precision and is not very useful for analytical purposes. Bernecker provided a more workable definition of tourism. According to him,

"Tourism is the sum of the relations and services connected with a temporary and voluntary change of residence for non-commercial or non-professional reasons". On analyzing this definition, it is found that the 'change of residence' of a tourism must be: (i) voluntary, (ii) of a temporary nature and (iii) for a non-commercial or non-professional purpose.

It may be noted, however, that the above definitions define tourism in the narrow sense of 'pleasure travel' only and, therefore, do not include travel for business, religious purposes, education or culture, sometimes, there is a need to define tourism in a wider sense. Obviously, all forms of travel are not tourism. A person coming daily to the place of work in the city is not a tourism. But, if on any weekend, the same person takes his children to the city museum or zoo, he will be regarded as a tourist. By the same logic, a student going abroad to pursue higher studies is not a tourist. He is more likely to have a student visa rather than a tourist visa and his period of stay will usually continue up to the completion of his studies. But the same student may turn into a tourist when he spends his holidays by visiting the places of interest in the host country. Even a person attending a summer school away from his usual place of residence would not be a tourist in the narrow sense, since the purpose of his temporary change of residence is not pure recreation. But in many studies relating to international tourism, students from abroad are regarded as foreign tourists. Similarly, a journalist going to cover the Olympic Games should not be termed as a tourist in the narrow sense, although such visitors are on par with other tourists from the consideration of foreign exchange earned by the host country. Nowadays, business officials travelling internationally are also called 'business tourists' although they are not tourists according to the above definitions.

Another feature of tourism that is not adequately brought out is how long should be the duration of stay of a tourist. As a usual practice, a stay of at least 24 hours is considered necessary to distinguish a tourist from a day-tripper. For statistical purpose, a fortnight minimum is commonly accepted for domestic tourism, but stays of only 24 hours are universally recognized in the case of international tourism. There is hardly any justification for adopting two different criteria for international tourism (IT) and domestic tourism (DT). Realizing the growing importance of collecting tourist statistics, the League of Nations in 1937 defined the term 'foreign tourist' as "any person visiting a country, other than that in which he usually resides, for a period of at least 24 hours". According to this definition, following persons were to be considered 'tourists':

(i) Persons travelling for pleasure, for domestic reasons, for health, etc.,
(ii) Persons travelling to meetings or in a representative capacity of any kind (scientific, administrative, diplomatic, religious, athletic, etc.),
(iii) Persons travelling for business purposes,
(iv) Persons arriving in the course of a sea cruise even when their stay is for less than 24 hours.

Taking all these considerations into account, it is not difficult to see why the most popular and widely accepted definition of tourism is the one defined by the World Tourism Organization (WTO). According to this definition, "A tourist is a person who travels to a place other than his usual place of residence and stays at hotels or other accommodation establishments run on commercial basis (or in any rent-free places) for a duration of not less than 24 hours and not more than six months at a time, for any of the following purposes:

- Pleasure (holiday, leisure, sports, etc.),
- Pilgrimage, religious or social functions,
- Study and health,
- Meetings,
- Business.

Unless otherwise mentioned, the above definition of tourism in the wider sense has been used in this book.

Tourism is people-oriented. It is concerned with the people who desire going away from their own homes on short-term temporary visits. A visitor is any person who visits a country other than that in which he has usual place of residence, for any reason other than following an occupation remunerated from within the country visited. Tourism arises out of visits of tourists and flourishes when the number of tourists increases. A tourist is a temporary visitor who makes at least one overnight stay by staying for at least 24 hours in the country that he visits. The WTO has categorized the term 'visitor' into two: (i) tourists and (ii) excursionists. All those visitors who stay for less than 24 hours in the country visited are commonly called 'excursionists'.

In 1942, two Swiss Professors Walter Hunziker and Kurt Krapf technically defined 'tourism' as "the totality of the relationships and phenomenon arising from the travel and stay of strangers, provided the stay does not imply the establishment of a permanent residence and is not connected with a remunerated activity". According to this definition, the three essential characteristics of tourism are:

- Tourism involves travel by non-residents,
- Stay of a temporary nature in the country visited, and
- The stay is not connected with any remunerated activity.

Importance

Tourism's importance, as an instrument for economic development and employment generation, particularly in remote and backward areas, has been well recognized the world over. It is the largest service industry globally in terms of gross revenue as well as foreign exchange earnings. Tourism can play an important and effective role achieving the growth with equity objectives which we have set for ourselves.

Tourism is one economic sector in India that has the potential to grow at a high rate and can ensure consequential development of the infrastructure of the destinations. It has the capacity to capitalize on the country's success in the services sector and provide sustainable models of growth.

It has potential to stimulate other economic sectors through its backward and forward linkages and cross-sectoral synergies with sectors like agriculture, horticulture, poultry, handicrafts, transport, construction etc. Expenditure on tourism induces as chain of transactions requiring supply of goods and services from these related sectors. The consumption demand, emanating from tourist expenditure, also induces more employment and generates a multiplier effect on the economy. As a result, additional income and employment opportunities are generated through such linkages. Thus, the expansion of the tourism sector can lead to large scale employment generation and poverty alleviation. The economic benefits that flow into the economy through growth of tourism in shape of increased national and State Central, State and local tax receipts can contribute towards overall socio-economic improvement and accelerated growth in the economy.

Tourism is overwhelmingly an industry of Private Sector Service Providers, although the public sector has a significant role to play in infrastructure areas either directly or through Public Private Partnership mode. It is a multi-sectoral activity characterized by multiple services provided by a range of suppliers. It is quite similar to manufacturing industry, where the supply chain is as important as the end product. The related sectors include airlines, Surface transport, hotels, basic infrastructure and facilitation systems, etc. Thus, the growth of tourism cannot be attained unless the issues related to all the sectors are addressed simultaneously.

Another important feature of the tourism industry, which is of particular significance to India, is its contribution to national integration and preservation of natural as well as cultural environments and enrichment of the social and cultural lives of people. Over 382 million domestic tourists visiting different parts of the country every year return with a better understanding of the people living in different regions of the country. They have a better appreciation of the cultural diversity of India. Tourism also encourages preservation of monuments and heritage properties and helps the survival of arts forms, crafts and culture.

It is also important to note that tourism has become an instrument for sustainable human development including:

- Poverty Elimination,
- Environmental regeneration,
- Job creation, and
- Advancement of women and other disadvantaged groups.

The Emergence

The first fifty years of the twentieth century made tourism a major worldwide industry. The emergence of the middle class in Europe along with the technological, political and social events of the day gave a great thrust to tourism. A large number of people were moving out both for leisure and business purposes. This period saw the mass movement of people annually from their home location to another country for a temporary stay for a few days or a week. This mass movement of tourists was, however, prodominant between Europe and America as the conditions of travel between the two continents were perfect. A fairly good infrastructure was already in existence. The necessary elements for travel like time, money and motivation were present. In addition to international movements there was also growth in domestic tourism. The invention of the motor car in Europe and USA, as also technological advancements in rail transport together with construction of networks of highways, gave a boost to domestic tourism.

Although the annual migration of people began rather more than a century ago, the present-day exodus especially in relation to international tourists is essentially a post-World War-II phenomenon. The period between the two world wars can also be associated with the great movement of people for the purposes of tourism as a result of development of various modes of transport, especially the motor car and the aeroplane. The encouraging trend, however, received a setback as the Second World War intervened.

Tourism is sensitive to world economic and political conditions. It can occur on a large scale where the great majority of people enjoy some prosperity and security. Tourism and holiday-making, on global as well as national scale, is manifestation of prosperity and peace. As a great number of people in many countries have higher living standards, they can afford to set aside a proportion of their incomes for holidays and recreation.

Air travel blossomed during the post-World War-II period resulting in rapid development of tourism. As the world began to setlle down after the years of readjustments immediately after the War in 1945, there had been a rapid increase in both domestic and international tourism. The United Nations reported that in the ten-year period between 1955 and 1965, the number of tourist arrivals in some sixty-five countries increased three times from around 51 million to over 157 million. This, however was only a beginning.

In the 1960s, USA, Germany, UK, France, Canada, Belgium, Luxembourg, The Netherlands, Italy, Switzerland, Sweden, Denmark and Austria represented the twelve main tourist generating countries. These twelve countries accounted for some three quarters of all international tourist arrivals in the world. The first two—USA and Germany—accounted for more than one-third of the world tourist arrivals. The reason for this are very clear. These were the countries which enjoyed prosperity and higher standard of living—the two main factors conducive to growth of tourism. The development in the means of speedy transport and communication was also witnessed in these countries more significantly. This rapid increase in tourism in the above countries was therefore the outcome of such factors as prosperity and higher standards of living leading to increased leisure, improved education and, above all, the rapid strides they made in speedy transport and communications.

The trend in the growth of international tourism continues since the mid-1960s. The growth continues to be determined by the living standards in the developed countries. The widespread introduction of holidays with pay to large majority of people is yet another important factor responsible for growth of tourist traffic. Tables 1.1-1.3 and Figures 1.1-1.3 show the international tourist arrivals and the annual percentage of growth in recent years.

Table 1.1 : The Main Tourist Generators, 1961

Countries	*Total World Arrivals Generated (millions)*	*World Arrivals Generated per 1000 population*
USA	21.7	112
UK	7.5	138
France	10.0	204
Germany	21.6	318
Belgium	6.7	340
Luxembourg	NA	NA
Netherlands	4.1	332
Italy	3.1	61
Switzerland	2.2	369
Sweden	1.4	185
Denmark	1.4	287
Austria	2.1	287
Total	**85.6**	**181**

Source : International Union of Official Travel Organisations (IUOTO).

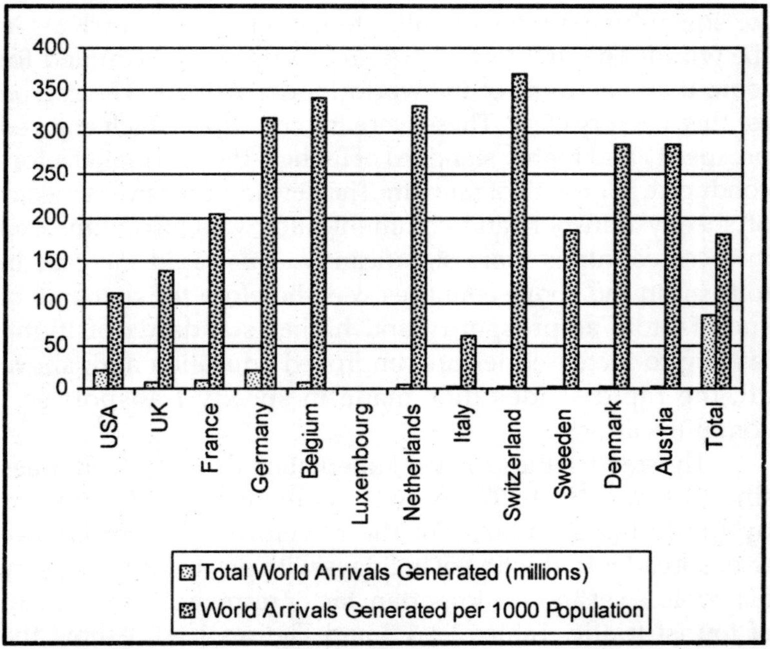

Fig. 1.1 : The Main Tourist Generators, 1961

Table 1.2 : International Tourist Arrivals, 1950-1976

Year	*Arrivals (in millions)*	*Index (1950 = 100)*	*Annual percentage of growth*
1950	25.3	100	—
1960	72.2	281	—
1961	75.3	298	5.8
1962	81.4	322	8.1
1963	93.0	368	14.2
1964	108.0	427	16.1
1965	115.2	456	6.9
1966	130.8	517	13.2
1967	139.5	551	6.6
1968	139.7	552	0.1
1969	154.1	609	10.3
1970 (R)	168.4	666	9.3
1971 (R)	181.5	717	7.8
1972	198.0	783	9.1
1973	215.0	850	8.6
1974	209.0	826	-2.8
1975	213.0	841	1.9
1976 (x)	219.0	841	2.8

Source : World Tourism Organization, 1977.
Note : R, revised figure ; X, estimated.

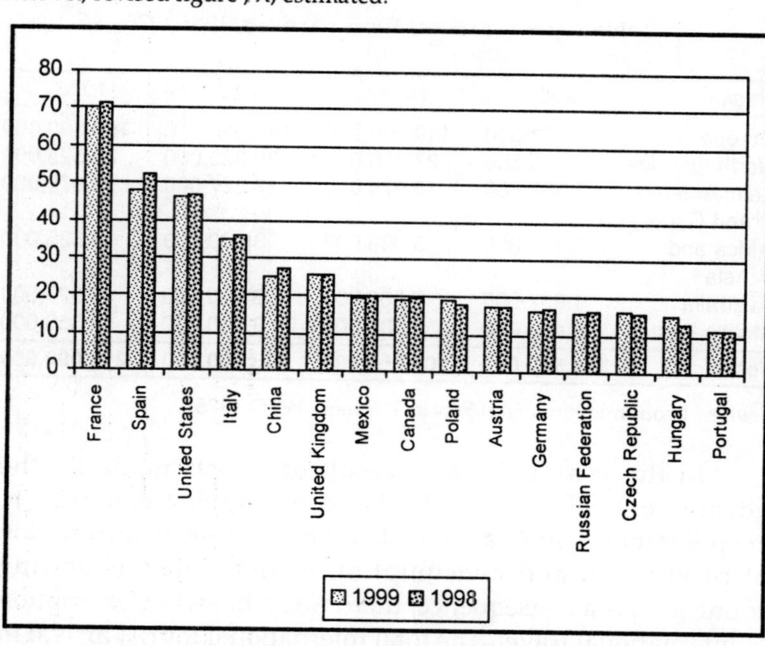

Fig. 1.2 : International Tourist Arrivals, 1950-1976

In 1976, there were nearly 220 million international tourist arrivals in the world (see Table 1.2). This is an increase of more than 90 per cent over 1965. During 1965-1976, which was a period of intensive economic development in most industrialized countries, international tourism grew at an average rate of over 7 per cent annually. During this period, most of the developing countries were also able to benefit from the growing trend in the developed countries to consume tourist products. As mentioned elsewhere, tourism and its development are closely related to consumers' purchasing power and, in turn, to any domestic or international economic fluctuations. In the year 1974, the world economy was seriously affected by the energy crisis which occurred at the end of 1973. As a result, there was inflation which was responsible for the lower purchasing power. Tourism, like all other sectors of production and consumption, suffered the economic consequences of that crisis. Table 1.2 clearly shows this. The total international tourist arrivals in 1974 dropped by over two per cent in relation to 1973.

Table 1.3 : International Tourist Arrivals, 1965-1976

Region	*1965*	*1974*	*1975*	*1976*
Europe	83,731,600	149,000,000	151,500,000	155,300,000
North America	19,335,300	27,926,000	29,323,000	30,525,000
Latin America and Caribbean	3,867,600	18,074,000	17,677,000	17,675,000
Africa and Asia	2,145,800	3,000,000	3,500,000	3,625,000
Australia	1,997,000	7,000,000	8,000,000	8,525,000
Middle East	3,403,600	4,000,000	3,000,000	3,350,000
Total	**114,500,000**	**209,000,000**	**213,000,000**	**219,000,000**

Source : Economic Review of World Tourism, WTO 1978.

In the year 1975, as a result of efforts made by the governments of industrialized and developing countries to keep inflation within acceptable limits, there was resumption of production and consumption in the main generating countries. As a consequence, there was a likewise resumption of international travel. The total international tourist arrival in

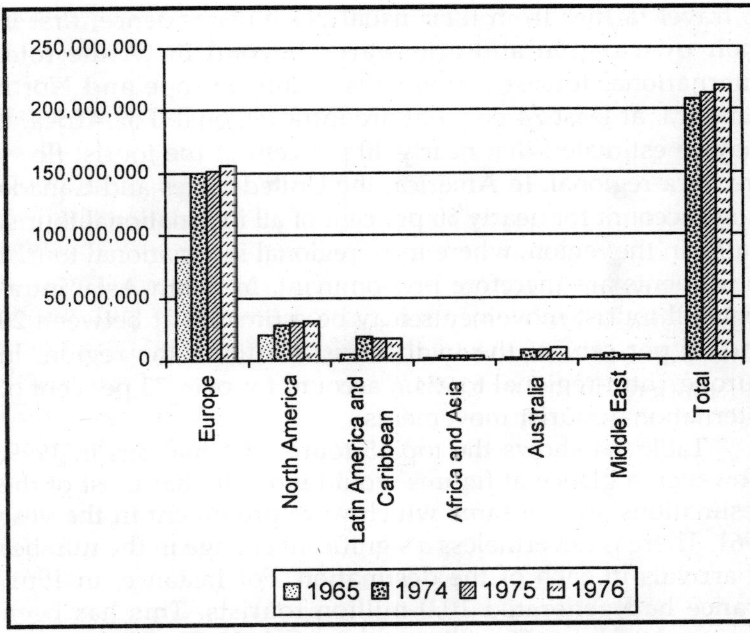

Fig. 1.3 : International Tourist Arrivals, 1965-1976

1975 amounted to roughly 213 million. The total number of international tourist arrivals in 1976 was estimated at between 218 and 222 million, which is a rise of between 2 and 4 per cent over 1975. According to the most recent estimates produced by the Secretariat General, World Tourism Organization, international tourist arrivals in 1999 were estimated to total 700 million, an increase of manifolds over 1978.

Europe and North America continue to be the principal generating as well as receiving areas of international tourism, accounting for 70 per cent and 20 per cent respectively, of the international tourist arrivals. Table 1.3 shows this continuous trend of increase in international tourist arrivals in these areas since the year 1965. It may be stressed here that intra-regional tourism—between countries of the same region—has an appreciable influence on the distribution of world arrivals. Thus, while domestic tourist movements tend to increase more and more, holiday-makers and tourists tend at the same time to travel farther from their usual place of residence, first in their own region and afterwards beyond it. Of the total international tourist movements within Europe and North America, at least 74 per cent are intra-regional. For Africa, it may be estimated that nearly 40 per cent of the tourist flows are intra-regional. In America, the United States and Canada alone account for nearly 50 per cent of all international tourist traffic in the region, where intra-regional international tourist movements are therefore predominant. In South Asia, intra-regional tourist movements may be estimated at between 20 and 30 per cent of the total tourist traffic in the region. In Europe, intra-regional tourism account for over 73 per cent of international tourist movements.

Table 1.4 shows the top 15 tourist destinations in 1999. However, a glance at figures would indicate that most of the destinations are the same which were prominent in the year 1961. There is nevertheless a significant change in the number of arrivals in each of the destination. For instance, in 1961, France had generated 10.0 million tourists. This has been increased to almost 72 million in the year 1999. The big surprise, however, is China which received 27 million tourists in 1999.

Table 1.4 : International Tourist Destinations (1999)

Rank	*Country*	*International tourist Arrivals (million)*		*Percentage charge*	*Market Share*
		1999	1998	1999	1999/98
1	France	70.0	71.4	2.0	10.7
2	Spain	47.7	52.0	8.8	7.3
3	United States	46.4	47.0	1.3	7.1
4	Italy	34.8	35.8	2.9	5.3
5	China	25.1	27.0	7.9	3.8
6	United Kingdom	25.7	25.7	0.0	3.9
7	Mexico	19.8	20.2	2.0	3.0
8	Canada	18.8	19.6	3.8	2.9
9	Poland	18.8	17.9	- 4.5	2.9
10	Austria	17.4	17.6	1.6	2.6
11	Germany	16.5	17.1	3.5	2.5
12	Russian Federation	15.8	16.4	3.9	2.4
13	Czech Republic	16.3	16.0	- 1.8	2.5
14	Hungary	15.0	12.9	- 13.8	2.3
15	Portugal	11.3	11.6	2.7	1.7

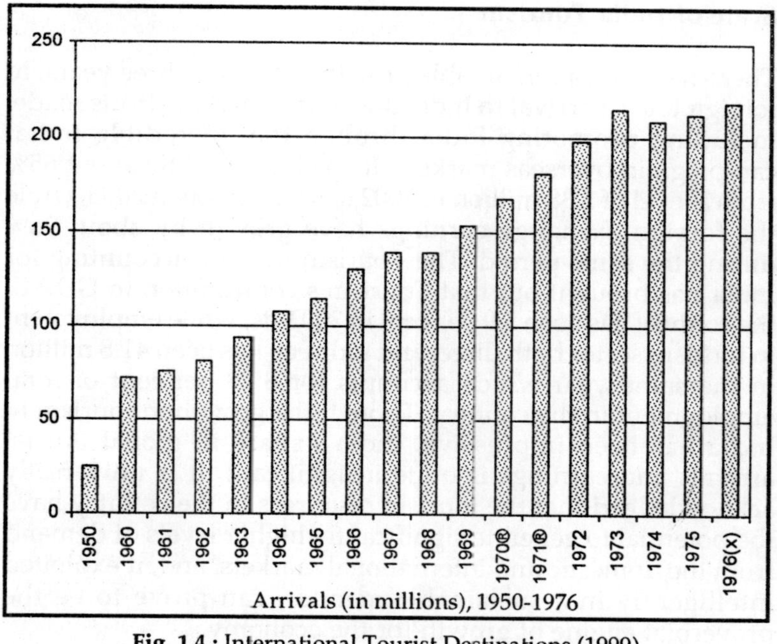

Fig. 1.4 : International Tourist Destinations (1999)

The values shown in Table 1.4 and Figures 1.1 and 1.2 are based upon preliminary data estimated for the full year supplied to World Tourism Organisation (WTO) secretariat by the tourism authorities of the countries and territories concerned. Most countries do not have the figures available for the whole year. However, experiences from the earlier years have shown :

Scale of Global Tourism

According to the World Tourism Organisation (WTO), the year 2005 saw more than 800 million international tourist arrivals, and the tourism receipts were of the order of US $ 682 billion. The World Travel and Tourism Council (WTTC) for 2016 forecasts that travel and tourism will generate 234 million direct and indirect jobs world-wide, accounting for 8.7% of the global employment, and it will contribute up to 10.3% of the global GDP. According to the same estimate, the global travel and tourism activity is expected to increase by 4.7% between 2007 and 2016.

Scale of India Tourism

There has been a remarkable growth in the last three years, in foreign tourist arrival to India due to the various efforts made, including promoting India through the 'Incredible India' campaign in overseas markets. It has increased by about 65% from a level of 2.38 million in 2002 to 3.92 million in 2005, while the foreign exchange earnings have growth by about 96% during the same period. The Tourism satellite accounting for India has brought out that Tourism's contribution to GDP of the country has been 5.9 per cent in 2003-04, while employment in tourism sector both direct and indirect, has been 41.8 million in the same year which accounts for 8.78 per cent of total employment in the country. Though the growth in tourism in India has been impressive, India's share in global tourist arrivals and earnings is quite insignificant. It is universally acknowledged that the tourism resources in the country have the potential to generate significantly higher levels of demand from the domestic and international markets, and, if exploited intelligently in a sustainable manner, can prove to be the proverbial engine of growth for the economy.

Tourism after World War-II

Tourism became a global phenomenon with a very high potential for development after the World War-II. Being amongst the world's fastest growing industries, today it occupies an important place as the world's second largest industry coming next to oil industry. Globally, its earnings over US$ 3.5 trillion generated by over 500 million international travellers, which are expected to rise to US$ 660 million by the year 2020 A.D. Tourism is an industry without smoking chimneys; it involves learning with no requirement of classrooms; it forges human understanding and promotes goodwill and harmony without legislation and rigid formality.

Types

The various definitions of tourism mentioned above have noted that there are different motives of tourists and there are different types of tourist behaviour. It is, therefore, often necessary to make a distinction between different types of tourism for analytical purposes. For instance, tourism is usually classified into two broad categories, namely, international tourism and domestic tourism.

Tourists may often move in formal and informal groups. There are different types of group tourists. There are exclusive groups like married couples, particularly honeymooners, family groups, friends circles, etc. Recently, cooperative holidays are also enjoyed by a group of workers belonging to a common business establishment. Secondly, there are those who may form their groups in the course of the journey itself. For instance, pilgrims may start their journey separately but the difficult terrain and the strain of the journey may often bring them together. Lastly, there are those group tourists who have been brought together by the tour operators. A single tourist could be a social drifter or any army personnel in search of drugs, sex or other excitement. He could also be a high business executive or a government official who has come to the tourist spot to shed his inhibitions. A great majority of them would, however, behave like any other tourist. Figure 1.5 gives a better idea about the tourist features.

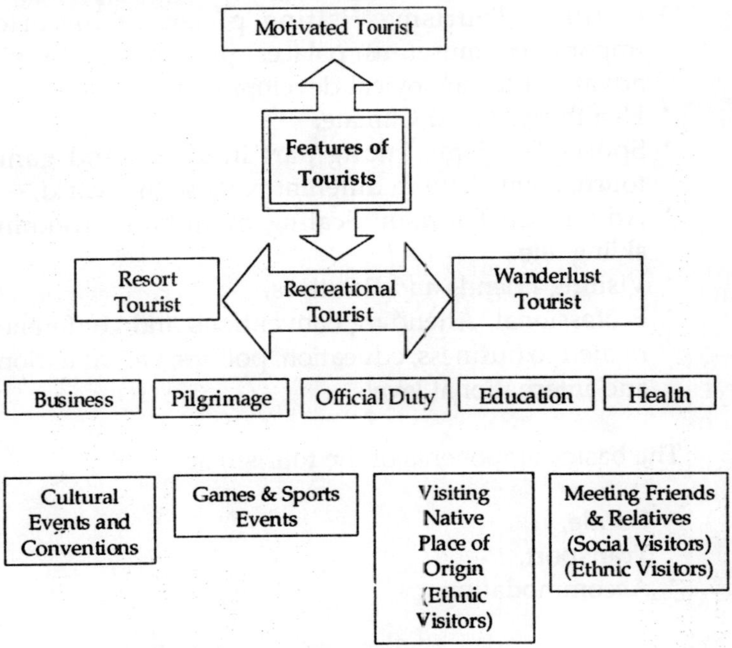

Fig. 1.5 : Features of Tourists.

From the motivational point of view, a distinction can be made between a Recreational and a Motivated Tourist. The primary urge of the first type of tourist is travel for pleasure with its entertainment value or creation as an end in itself. The primary urge of the motivated tourist may be altogether different. To him, travelling for pleasure is there, but not as the primary motive. The basic motivation for travel are:

- Physical,
- Cultural,
- Interpersonal,
- Status and Prestige.

This can be further broken down into:

- Pleasure Tourism: For fun and having a good time,
- Leisure Tourism: Getting relieved of the stress and strain of modern urban living,
- Religious Tourism: Pilgrimage to religious places,
- Cultural Tourism: Visiting places of historical importance, museums, palaces, paintings and seeing advanced technological developments,
- Health and Good Climate,
- Sports Tourism: Taking part in sports and games tournaments held in different parts of the world,
- Adventure Tourism: Scaling mountains, trekking, skiing, etc.,
- Visiting Friends and Relatives,
- Professional: Attending conventions and conferences related to business, education, politics, etc., at national and international levels.

The basic components of the tourism are:

- Locale,
- Transport,
- Accommodation,

- Support Industries, and
- Human Resources

The geographical components of the tourism are:

1. Accessibility and Location,
2. Space,
3. Scenery
   (i) Land forms, e.g. mountains, canyons, coral reefs, cliffs, etc.,
   (ii) Water, e.g. rivers, lakes, waterfalls, geysers, glaciers, seas,
   (iii) Vegetation, e.g. forests, grasslands, moors, deserts, etc.
4. Climate: Sunshine, clouds, temperatures, rain and snow,
5. Animal life,
   (i) birds, game reservations, zoos,
   (ii) Hunting and fishing.
6. Settlement Features,
   (i) Towns, cities and villages,
   (ii) Historical remains and monuments,
   (iii) Archaeological remains,
7. Culture, e.g. way of life, traditions, folklore, magic, arts and crafts.

Tourism in its broadest sense can do more to develop understanding among people, provide jobs, earn foreign exchange and raise living standards than any other economic force known. It plays an important role in education and sports and also helps in national integration. Tourism performs a vital role in promoting international understanding, business relationships and the world peace.

As per the recommendations of the World Tourism Organization made in 1993, tourism has three different features, namely—

(i) Domestic Tourism,
(ii) Inbound Tourism, and
(iii) Outbound Tourism.

Domestic Tourism involves the 'residents of the given country travelling within the country'. **Inbound Tourism** refers to the 'non-residents travelling in the given country', and **Outbound Tourism** refers to the 'residents of a given country travelling in another country'. These three bring forth further three combinations. **Internal Tourism** is concerned with domestic tourism and outbound tourism; **National Tourism** means domestic tourism and outbound tourism, and **International Tourism** stands for inbound and outbound tourism.

Non-Tourism Category

The categories of the travellers that do not come under tourism area: border workers, temporary and permanent immigrants, nomads, transit passengers, refugees, members of the Armed Forces, representatives of consulates and diplomats.

Leisure Tourism and Business Tourism

The purposes of tourism can be broadly categorized as: (i) Leisure Tourism and (ii) Business Tourism.

- For spending holidays,
- For participating in sports and cultural events,
- For study and research purposes,
- For religious purposes,
- For health reasons,
- For visiting friends and relatives,
- For seeing art, culture, ancient monuments of archaeological interest,
- For knowing the country's history and traditions. Business tourism includes travel for following purposes:
- For attending business meetings,
- For visiting exhibitions and trade fairs,
- For attending conferences and conventions.

Role of State and Tourism Industry

Tourism has now become a key sector affecting all aspects of a nation's life. Government must take appropriate measures for creating a suitable framework for the promotion and development of rural tourism.

Tourism sector is expanding fast and becoming highly diversified. Consequently, it calls for equally vast and diversified units of supply. Increased tourist traffic among the countries call for new marketing, promotional and balanced development activities require planning and effective legislation. The financial and technical resources are also required for successful promotional and development strategy in rural tourism.

The state simultaneously plays the roles of policy-maker, entrepreneur, coordinator and stimulator. Tourism can be best fostered if it is integral part of a balanced economic and social development programme. It may also be helpful in earning foreign exchange.

The development of tourism infrastructure is a primary responsibility of the government but the role of private sector cannot be ignored in rural tourism.

Rural tourism can help a community become more attractive and prosperous. It become so because the community acquires the capacity to draw and satisfy visitors who spend money. Visitors who enjoy and appreciate a community are likely to spend money, will recommend it to friends and come back again. That's the formula for success: *get them to stop, to stay (as long as possible), to spread the word and to return.*

Tourists travel for spending their leisure time or for business activity. The organization and business concerns that provide the required services to the tourists make up what is known as the 'tourism industry'. As the tourists are away from their homes on short-term and temporary visits, it is imperative on the part of the tourism industry to cater to the tourists' requirements right from planning their tour till they reach back their homes with satisfaction and pleasant memories. For providing all the required services to the tourists, the following three sectors are the employees therein broadly which constitute the tourism industry :

- Travel and Transport,
- Catering and Accommodation,
- Leisure, Recreation and Business Facilities.

The term 'tourism' refers to both 'inbound' and 'domestic' tourism. Inbound tourism refers to tourists who are not resident of India and foreigners visiting India. Domestic tourism is concerned with residents of India, who may travel for pleasure (holiday, sports, leisure, etc.), pilgrimage, religious and social occasions, business meetings, conferences, health and study purposes.

India has an infinity of attractive features that would be of great interest to all kinds of tourists—the historical researcher, the businessman, the pleasure seeker, the culture tourist or the casual vacationer. Tourists, in general, get fascinated by its long history, ancient culture and traditions, a rare intermingling of religions, languages, climates, wildlife, monuments, hill resorts, beaches and many wonderful aspects that point out India's essential unity in diversity.

Today, tourism is being accorded much importance as the largest industry capable of generating tremendous economic development in many countries of the world. As a foreign exchange earner, it helps in improving the balance of payments position by narrowing trade deficit. During the year 1995-96, foreign exchange earnings from tourism amounted to Rs. 91.86 billions compared to Rs. 73.66 billions in 1994-95. But still India's share continues to be 0.37% of the world's tourism and its receipts amount to 0.51% of the world receipts.

As far as domestic tourism is concerned, in the year 1996, about 23 million domestic tourists visited various interesting parts of India, getting a glimpse of the great traditions and enjoying the diverse cultural heritage.

Policy, Potential and Prospect

New tourism paradigm strongly advocates super-segmentation of tourism market realizing the negative aspects of mass tourism culture of the early years of modern tourism development (1960-85). The growing realization is that despite having tremendous multiplier effects on income and employment generation, tourism may pose threats to the ecological balance and can easily destroy traditional value system of aboriginal communities, tourism Policy of India, 2002 strongly advocates this segmentation, and the Ministry of Tourism and Culture has already declared ecotourism, cultural-tourism and heritage-tourism as special segments. The policy also envisages that a well coordinated public and private sector participation would bring forth the described rate of tourism sector development in the country.

In this context, it becomes pertinent to sort out a national strategy for safeguarding traditional heritage and ethical values, at the same time rejuvenating the country's tourism sector to Rural tourism may be a better choice in this regard.

Potential

India has a tremendous rural tourism potential with a variety of cultural aspect and production systems. This variety is sufficient to attract tourists in its original form. But, the major problem lies in the infrastructure sector including transportation, communication, accommodation and above all linkages among different places of interest. The final disadvantage lies in the creation and development of a strong entrepreneurial class for tourism enterprise. It should be noted that to preserve the original flavour and essence of rural tourism, development of indigenous entrepreneurship may be a wiser step.

Primary phase

Indian tourism as an enterprise is still at its infancy. So, it is urgently felt that the process of incubating the entrepreneurs is the most preferred line of action.

A well designed tourism entrepreneurship development programme should consider the following initial activities :

1. Arousing the need of developing tourism entrepreneurship in terms of prospective income generation, growth of employment opportunities and conservation of available natural and man-made tourism resource of the region. This can be done through local publicity in print and visual media, festivals and fairs of indigenous culture and traditional products.
2. Declaring the tourism potentialities of the region as place of interest and importance by the competent authority and guideline should be prepared for this purpose.
3. Policy to attract specified category of tourists satisfying their requirement is said to be a major step in the formulation of an entrepreneurship development programme. This is a preferred action to boost certainty in the growth of entrepreneurship. This may be contradictory to the popular belief of attracting tourism exodus. Attracting a specified category of tourism represents promoting one or a few favourable tourism clusters like ecotourism, rural tourism, etc. Indian Tourism Policy has already taken such a step by initiating the promotion of ecotourism as a major segment of Indian tourism.
4. Upgradation of the existing tourism infrastructure like transport and communication, accommodation, etc.
5. Creation of human resource development programmes at all levels of education and training. From the secondary level of education there should be optional courses on tourism development and management, forest and environmental studies, etc. Entrepreneurship Development Programmes of the institutions like SISI, IIE should introduce special entrepreneurship drive in tourism sector development.

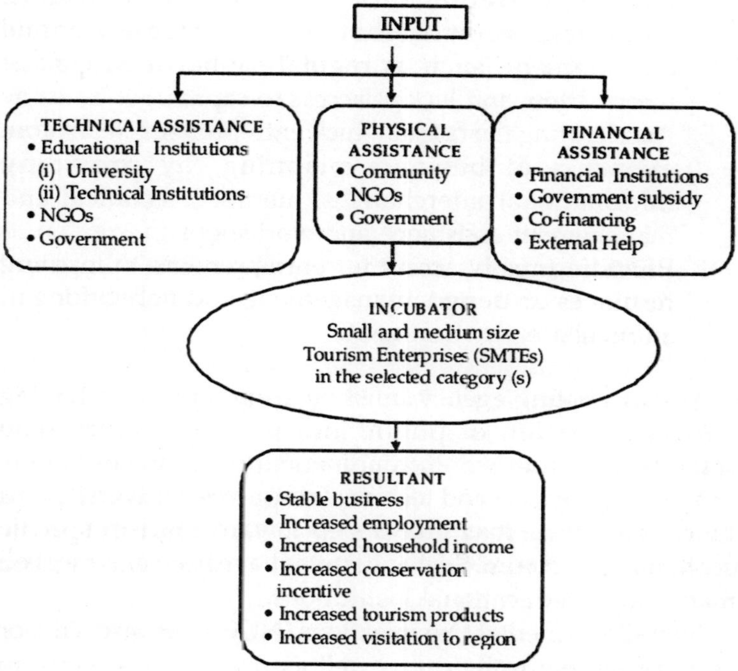

Fig. 1.6 : A Model of Incubating Tourism Entrepreneurs in India.

Secondary phase

The Secondary phase stage Indian tourism entrepreneurship development is to provide business incubation. The incubator helps in property development/management as well as small business development/management. It provide a micro-environment for an enterprise whose activities accelerate the process of enterprise development and increase the likelihood of business growth. In the process, the following stage are generally observed :

1. Conserving entrepreneurs's most scarce and precious resource, time and money, through cost-sharing, time-saving and capital-conserving access to affordable space, service and equipment—all in fixable and timely ways tailored to entrepreneurs's needs.

2. Helping entrepreneurs overcome constraints to enterprise growth that arise macro-economic environment, such as regulatory barriers, lack of information, and lack of access to capital.
3. Accelerating the rate at which entrepreneurs learn core elements of business planning, by providing informational interchanges, mentors, technical and management assistance and workshops.
4. Providing ready access for entrepreneurs to learning resources on design, management, and networking in an incubator environment.

The incubating agency must be an organization having equal participation of public and private sectors. The development of tourism entrepreneurship lies in the inputs like financial, physical and technical resources. University and technical education may take a step toward tourism specific educational curriculum. Such initiatives have been experienced in many Indian educational institutions.

Non-Govermental Organisations (NGOs) are also a major force in providing technical as well as physical assistance to the incubator, they can adopt the participatory process of tourism community education through public interactions in different forms like seminars, workshops, short training programmes and festivities. Moreover, they can provide assistance in selecting potential tourism resources of the region.

Central Government is the final policy-maker regarding the incubator. However, in certain areas the respective state governments must take individual interest. Some of such sectors are :

1. Development of general and tourism-based infrastructure.
2. Developing 'hospitality service' under Tourism Development Corporation (TDC) and making scope for private sector's participation declaring special incentive policy.
3. Maintenance of law and order to private security to the tourism as well as the tourist sites.

Financial institutions play a major role by supplying much needed capital to the tourism-based entrepreneurs at special concession rates.

As shown in the model an integrated process of developing tourism-based entrepreneurship can successfully overcome the difficulties of entrepreneurship generation by stability in business, increasing employment, household income, conservation incentive, tourism products and increased visitation to the region.

Final Phase

In the final stage certain sub-sections may be included, viz.:

1. Take-off of tourism industry.
2. Publicity drive at the national as well as international level.
3. Continuous feedback from the incubated entrepreneurs.
4. Gradual withdrawal of incubating facilities.

Tourism industry take-off is considered to be a subjective phenomenon. However, the incubating agency may fix certain target of industrial take-off based on the following criteria :

1. The annual increase in the flow of domestic as well as international tourists.
2. The annual increase in the flow of tourism revenue to the state treasury.
3. The annual increase of income to the incubated entrepreneurs.
4. The growth of entrepreneurs in the sector over the incubated ones.

There should be a continuous evaluation of the performance of the incubated enterprises and regular analysis of these in community forums. This has an added advantage of the growth of additional entrepreneurs in this sector.

The final step is to withdraw external support in gradual but regular intervals. This inevitability of withdrawal has the positive impact of increased competitiveness in the tourism industry for quality service.

Benefits

Tourism entrepreneurship development has two-way benefits. First, it gives tremendous economic impetus to a region in the form of certain of employment avenues and increased standard of living of the underdeveloped host community. Secondly, it is the wisest policy to conserve traditional cultural value with sufficient exposure to the world community and at the same time it provides security and advancement to the tourism products in a region.

These two approaches may withdraw the discontentment regarding tourism that it has every chance of destroying ecological balance of a region at the same time running the cultural trails of aboriginal communities. Tourism not only provides a fascinating variety in observation and experience but also helps the country in the following ways:

(1) The local population gets the benefit from every dollar that circulates many times, changing hands;
(2) It helps in breaking down the barriers, suspicions and prejudices that may exist between nations and thereby promotes international understanding;
(3) Socially and culturally, tourism brings people of different cultures, faiths, languages and life-styles very much closer, providing broader outlook in regard to wonders and variety of life and living;
(4) One of the biggest problems in India, at present, is the problem of unemployment. In this respect, tourism possesses a tremendous employment potential. Millions can gain employment in hotels, restaurants, motels, tour and travel agencies, tourist guidance agencies, entertainment enterprises, ancillary industries such as arts, crafts, etc. Hence, tourism can

boost the national economic activity and thereby promote cultural, social and educational values;

(5) Indian hospitality has rich traditions through centuries, wherein 'Vedas' guided the actions of people and taught them the principle of 'Atithi Devo Bhava' (treat guest as God);

(6) In some remote corners of the world, there are some people who still do not have a proper image of India. They consider India as a land of snake-charmers, elephants, poor people and beggars. This incorrect impression can be corrected very much by promoting tourism.

A part from the benefits that can be obtained from the visits of foreign tourists to India, tourism too is very much helpful in forging unity and goodwill amongst the people of various regions and different linguistic groups of the country. Domestic tourism can very well strengthen national integration. The more the people of different regions meet, the more they will know each other and develop feelings of adjustment and tolerance.

The Marketing Perspective

There is probably more talk about marketing today than at any previous time around the world. It is the term everyone wants to use everywhere to show what they are, how they are and what they intend to do. But the dilemma still remains that marketing, in the true sense of the word, is all too seldom applied in the business world and still less in the travel and tourism industry, its understanding and mutual appreciation. In fact, there is nothing that the world needs today more than mutual understanding.

But the focus on the development of tourism and the mutual understanding depend on how best the tourism products have been marketed or how best the strategies have been adopted. The marketing planning helps to a greater extent to tell about the rich heritage of the country. There are some tourism organizations, both in the public and private sectors which have wholeheartedly adopted the marketing philosophy and can be counted amongst the most effective tourism marketing organizations. But these remain the exception rather than the rule and good marketing practices are still rare amongst the smaller tourism-related organizations.

The tourism industry itself is very young and only now it is beginning to come to grips with the modern business practices. This has also played a part in inhibiting the development of modern marketing techniques.

The term 'Marketing' has been defined from many angles with their respective vantage points of view. Some see it from promotional and some from developmental viewpoint. But all end with showing some novelty in what they do and how they do it. Marketing is almost anticipating the demand, recognizing it, stimulating it and finally, satisfying it. It is like understanding that what can be sold, to whom, when, where and in what quantity and quality. Another definition states, "Marketing is the management function which organizes and directs all those business activities involved in assessing customer needs and converting customer purchasing power into effective demand for specific product or service, and in moving that product or service to the final consumer or user, so as to achieve the profit target or other objective set by the organization". Thus, the whole definition has three important implications, namely, (i) it is a management function within the organization, (ii) it underlies and provides a framework for all those activities which the organization wants to undertake, and (iii) it emphasizes the focus on customer needs and urges.

Thus, marketing is about finding out what the customer wants first and then plan accordingly to satisfy that want. For this, a variety of ways, modes and methods are devised to fit the urge of the individuals in the society.

Marketing Strategies in Tourism

The early post-World War-II years saw the birth of modern tourism as an industry. The spectacular growth of package holidays was generated by the ideas of entrepreneurs who saw opportunities to create holiday utilization. Because of its successes or the failures, a new thinking on these lines started. Certainly, good marketing will always need an element of entrepreneurial flair. The same trend was seen in the Indian scenario also. Historical and religious places allover India received a great deal of attention, publicity and marketing boost for their importance. The importance of the rich heritage of these places was marketing to the people through media, so as to let people know all about what they wanted to know about these. The well-known historical places include Delhi, Agra, Jaipur, Mysore, Goa, Mumbai and Gaya of Bihar are the important regions of rich historical heritage, which have preserved the status and prestige of Indian customs, traditions, and art. It was only because of the marketing strategies adopted by the public and private sector tourism organizations that the people around the globe came to know about these places and then they saw them.

The State Government, needless to say, publicized through various sources, namely, radio, brochures, pamphlets, cards and letters, the very importance of the rich heritage of historical places in these regions. People came to know about the forts and the temples only through well-planned tourism development schemes that had been adopted by the respective governments from time to time.

The Union Government has established the branches of the Indian Tourism Development Corporation (ITDC) at various places, including Maharashtra and Goa. The ITDC aims at the promotion and presentation of the tourism places. Thus, it has been understood that tourism, as an industry, has the potential to revitalize the developing economies with its proven multiplier effect.

Need for the Present Study

Tourism is a multifaceted activity. It touches nearly all the sectors of State's and national life. Rapid and continuous development has been the keynote of national and international tourism. The commercialization of this sector has, therefore, become an important index to look and work at.

Tourism has certain traits which need to be studied before an appropriate direction and destiny is found. Of which, the 'marketing' of the rich heritage of the country stands to be the most important. Every expenditure made by a tourist contributes to the prosperity and the development of the nation and study region as well.

Thus, in response to a call for the overall development of the nation's economy, social development, economic benefits, cultural exchange, educational development and the ideological exchange, a need has been felt to look back at the marketing system in Bihar regarding the development of tourism and suggest appropriate measures for future development and improvement. Thus, the present study is a humble attempt to study the marketing strategies for developing tourism in Bihar.

REFERENCES

Ahmed Salma (2008) : *Tourism—A Managerial Perspective.*

Badan, B.S. and Bhatt, H. (2007) : *Tourism and Economic Development,* Commonwelth Publishers, New Delhi-2.

Bansal S.P. and Gupta Sunil (2008) : *Impact of Tourism on Hilly Environment—Problems and Prospects.*

Barua Nayan and Choudhary A.J. (2001) : *Tourism in Assam: Paradigm of a Thriving Industry.*

Batra, G.S. (2001) : *Tourism Promotion in India: Strategic Issues.*

Bhatia, A.K. (2007) : *Tourism development : Principles and Practices,* 2nd Revised Edition, Sterling Publishers Private Limited, New Delhi-20.

Erasi K. (2008) : *Opportunities and Problems of Tourism Development in the City of Bangalore—A Study.*

http://www.indiaheritage.org/creative/creative_metal_work.htm

Iqbal B.A. (2008) : *Global Tourism: India in Global Perspective.*

Iqbal B.A. (2004) : *Advertisement and Adventure Tourism: A Case of North India.*

Report of the working group on Tourism (2007-12): *11th Five Year Plan,* Ministry of Tourism, Government of Bihar.

Sharma Pitamber (2008) : *Sustainable Tourism in the Hindu-Kush Himalayas: Issues and Approaches.*

Raut Bhauro : *Role of Transportation in the Promotion of Tourism.*

Singh, K.P. and Prasad, Alok : *Marketing of Tourism in Bihar.*

Patil, P.B. (2006) : *Tourism Development : Problem and Prospects*, Current Publications, Agra-10 (U.P.)

Verma, S.B.; Jiloka, S.K. and Thryambakam, P. (2006) : *Rural Tourism and Tribal Development*, Deep & Deep Publications Pvt. Ltd., New Delhi-27.

2

An Overview of the Study

Tourism allover world has become a powerful industry. After the World War-II, tourism has emerged as an industry in most countries, including India. In fact, India declared the year '1991' as "Visit India Tourism Year". The stress was on projecting new tourism destinations and activities, promoting shopping as a major attraction and stressing the cultural richness of the country. India is, no doubt, the most appropriate country as a year round destination.

Studies and papers written regarding tourism have focussed on various angles. Few authors have written on its role in national integration, thus binding all sections of people in the society. Some have concentrated on tourism's economic advantage for bringing about financial and economic gains. Few other authors have concentrated on the social aspects and cultural change, thus telling how social life can be changed by knowing the cultures of other countries. In fact, the role of tourism was first perceived in India way back in 1946, when a Committee under the Chairmanship of Sir John Sargent, Secretary, Department of Education, was appointed to advise the Government on the development of tourism. To this effect, a report too was submitted in 1947; as a result of which, small field offices were started and attention was further given to all other aspects of tourism development in almost all parts of India.

A study undertaken by Chamberlain (1982) dealt with knowing the growth of the international tourism. He observed that the most important contribution of tourism is of creating jobs. Commenting on similar lines, Montague (1984) emphasized that "tourism is a growing industry; it has the ability to create many more jobs".

The Indian Institute of Public Opinion has published various articles pertaining to the tourism. An issue of 'Monthly Commentary' (1988) carried an article titled "Focus on Tourism" and commenting that tourism is a crucial resource-generating activity and pushes up the pace of economic development. In another paper in the same issue, examples have been given cited of how tourism can help to achieve greater economic development. Referring to the trends in tourism in India, a record figure of Rs. 1,890 crores revenue was earned from the tourist visits in 1987-88 as against Rs. 1,800 crores in 1986-87. This obviously shows an inclination for the development of tourism, which is quite essential and urgent one. A paper on tourism and economic development in the same issue concludes that promoting tourism is an essential prerequisite of economic development, which has very many advantages.

A study undertaken in 1986 by the Indian Institute of Public Opinion cited the tourism status in India. The area identified were the need for trained manpower, transport needs, performance of travel agents, all showed unsatisfactory state. The overall conclusion drawn showed that apart from all other aspects in the development of tourism, marketing of tourism is quite essential. If at all tourism has to reach the larger population, then marketing needs have to be looked at very closely.

A paper entitled "Tourism" and published by the Indian Institute of Public Opinion in 1991 has highlighted the various aspects of tourism development in India. The paper says that while India has a many splendoured tourist attractions, their marketing and promotion lacked aggressiveness. The failure of India's performance in this area was compared with other Asian countries with growth rate statistics. The paper concludes that due to the lack of better marketing of this industry, India is lacking in its development. The key to the successes of Sri Lanka, Singapore, Thailand and Malaysia, as the paper says, is due to more stress laid on the marketing aspects of this industry.

Bhargava (1991), in his paper states that social and economic benefits of tourism are several and include sources of earning, increase in transportation, music clubs, national parks, tax revenues and the like. Apart from this, employment to a layer population is an additional advantage. Likewise, social benefits include the knowledge about other societies, cultures and other civilizations. A better and healthy human relationship between countries around the world is possible with the tourism. Apart from this, presentation of heritage and its conservation are also possible.

A study undertaken by Mahajan (1991) concentrated on various aspects of tourism in Goa. He has date with the relationship between tourism and the prevailing Western culture, infrastructural development, lucrative packages offered, the development of sports (whether winter or summer or even the water sports). Referring to the example of Goa State, the tourism involved a multiplicity of motives covering business, pleasure, sight-seeing, visiting friends and shopping. In fact, all this depends on time, space and money. Also knowing the culture of different societies is an important component of tourism. Moreover, Mahajan also stressed that if tourism has to become a successful business, a marketing strategy should be developed. It all depends on how marketing of the tourism products is developed. Finally, marketing of the tourism aspects is an added advantage at all places and at all times.

Another paper by Khanna (1991) stressed the development of tourism in 1990s. Heading the multi-crore Oberoi Hotels chain, Khanna was a pioneer in promoting and developing tourism in India. He has stressed more on professionalism. Along with well-developed marketing plans, the personnel responsible for implementing these plans need to be well-mannered and equipped with the knowledge of dealing with tourists. Motivation and commitment need to be inculcated in them. He very much feels that in order to boost tourism through marketing promotion, burdens like unnecessary procedure and controls, improvements of airports also need to be given much attention. Thus, he concludes that the need for professionalism, imagination and result-orientation—all depend on other aspects too.

Galiti (1993) has dealt with the prospects and problems of tourism. He observes that the lack of necessary political and administrative will, facilities of foreign exchange, exploitation by private hoteliers, tour guides with proper knowledge of cultural and historical heritage and hygienic restaurants are the scenario of tourism development in India. Thus, while concluding on how the tourism can be boosted in future, he strongly believes that all the bottlenecks should be removed. Along with this, a well-planned large-scale marketing strategy for the development of tourism is an added advantage for the industry. These aspects need to be very much taken care of.

An editorial appearing in the 'Monthly Commentary' published by the Indian Institute of Public Opinion in 1994 dealt with the funding of tourist projects and bottlenecks involved in it. Discrepancies like blockage of funds, delays, negligence of conditionalities and financial irregularities come in the way of tourism development. Apart from these, tourism till date has remained concentrated only in the urban parts of the country. Rural sector tourism has not yet caught serious attention in India. Thus, tourism, if at all has to become a real industry and to be sold to larger population, should have balanced regional planning and equal importance has to be given to all the sections, irrespective of region. This will also go well in boosting tourism with well-planned marketing strategy that has to be adopted.

In the foregoing discussion on the subject to tourism and its development as an industry, not a single paper dealt with exhaustively on the marketing aspect of the tourism, except for a paper entitled "Tourism Needs Aggressive Marketing Strategy" (1994) and relates to the importance of marketing of this industry. The paper further reported the foreign exchange earnings for three years from 1991 to 1993. At the beginning of 1991, a total Rs. 233.3 crores foreign exchange had been earned and at the end of the year, a total of Rs. 413.8 crores were earned, thus an overall increase of 2.3%. Looking into the earnings for 1992, a total of Rs. 327.2 crores and Rs. 423.2 crores were earned at the beginning and at the end of the year. The trend for 1993 also showed positive results with Rs. 367.3 crores at the beginning and an overall total of Rs. 543.6 crores by the end of the year. With all these statistics about the advantages and gains from the tourism industry, the paper concludes that when tourism is poised to become the single largest global industry by the turn of the century, India should adopt a systematic and well thought-out marketing strategy, if it is to partake of a fair chunk of the global tourism pie.

During the 10th Five Year Plan an attempt was made to position tourism as a major contributor of economic growth, and harness its direct and multiplier effects for employment and poverty eradication in an environmentally sustainable manner. Various schemes and activities were taken up during the 10th Plan period aimed at enhancing the employment potential within the tourism sector as well as at fostering economic integration through developing linkages with other sectors. Broadly, the attempt was to:

- Position tourism as a major engine of economic growth;
- Harness the direct and multiplier effects of tourism for employment generation, economic development and providing impetus to rural tourism;
- Focus on Domestic Tourism as a major driver of tourism growth;
- Position India as a global brand to take advantage of the burgeoning global travel and trade and the vast untapped potential of India as a destination;
- Acknowledge the critical role of private sector with government working as a pro-active facilitator and catalyst;
- Create and develop integrated tourism circuits based on India's unique civilization, heritage, and culture in partnership with State, private sector and other agencies;
- Ensure that the tourist to India gets physically invigorated, mentally rejuvenated, culturally enriched, spiritually elevated and "feel India from within".

The 10th Five Year Plan had a distinct shift from the approach adopted in the earlier plans. During the plan period, emphasis was laid on:

(i) Positioning and maintaining tourism development as a National priority activity;
(ii) Enhancing and maintaining the competitiveness of India as a tourist destination;
(iii) Improving India's existing tourism products and expending these to meet new market requirements;
(iv) Creation of world class infrastructure;
(v) Developing sustained and effective market plans and programmes;
(vi) Special thrust to rural and small segments tourism; and
(vii) Attention to civilisational issues and issues pertaining to civic administration, good governance and also to social and cultural values.

Keeping in view the l road priorities for development of tourism the 10th Plan 2002-07 as above, the broad fields of development taken up during the plan were:

- Integrated Development of Tourism Circuits;
- Product/infrastructure and destination development;
- Assistance for Large Revenue Generating Projects;
- Human Resource Development;
- Promotion and Publicity; and
- Others (Market Research/Computerization and IT/ Interest Subsidy).

(A) Integrated Development of Tourism Circuits

It was observed at the beginning of the 10th Plan that the Central Financial Assistance to the States had not been able to create a major impact in terms of creation of world-class tourism infrastructure. The experience showed that the resources available had been used to fund a large number of small isolated projects, spread throughout the length and breadth of the country, resulting in the resources being spread very thinly. The infrastructure schemes being Centrally Sponsored had to depend on the contribution of the State Governments and many times there had been delays in release of this contribution. Therefore, in order to provide quick and substantial impact, the revised scheme was taken up to identify key tourism circuits in the country on an annual basis, and develop them to international standards, with the objective of providing all infrastructure facilities required by the tourists within these circuits. Ministry of Tourism ensured convergence of resources and expertise through coordinated action with States/UTs and private sector. The master planning as well as the implementation and monitoring of works in the selected circuits, which included improvement in accessibility, improvement in environment including solid waste management and sewerage management around the destination, illumination of the destinations, lighting of the approaches, etc., was carried out directly by the Ministry of Tourism or through the State Tourism Departments.

(B) Product/Infrastructure and Destination Development

In the 9th Plan, destination development had tended to be somewhat *ad hoc,* with inadequate prioritization. During the 10th plan period, limited destinations in the States/UTs were identified on yearly basis for integrated intensive development.

While developing the destinations, the strategy followed, was to ensure that the developments take place in a regional planning framework that is not restricted to the immediate environs of the site but extends to the 'region of influence' of the attraction or cluster of attractions including the primary staging area and travel nodes. It was ensured that all development work was based on professionally prepared master plans, ideally using the best expertise and contained components that are conceived, to satisfy the preferences and requirement needs of a clearly identified target market. Efforts were made to see that the master planning approach included all stakeholders in the planning process—all levels of government and administration, various government agencies and departments, the local community, elected representatives, and members of the tourism industry or related industries.

Destinations were carefully selected in consultation with the State Governments, based on the tourism potential. The activities taken up under Product Development and strategies followed were as follows:

Priority was given to promote Rural Tourism as the primary tourism product to spread tourism and its socio-economic benefits to rural areas and its new geographic regions. Key geographic regions were identified for development and promotion of rural tourism. The implementation was done through a convergence committee headed by the District Collector. A sum of Rs. 50 lakh was made available for each project, and activities like improving the environment, hygiene, infrastructure etc. were assisted.

Heritage cities and towns were taken up for development to promote Heritage Tourism. Heritage cities like Agra, Jaipur, Madurai, Hyderabad, Gwalior etc. were taken up.

India with world's greatest bio-diversity with a variety of unique natural locales, is a perfect candidate for promotion of Eco-tourism. As such, the strategy followed for development of eco-tourism during the 10th Plan included identifying focal locations for eco-tourism like the Himalayas, North Eastern States, Western Ghats, Jharkhand, Andaman & Nicobar Islands, Lakshadweep; and providing financial assistance to the State Governments for development of these locations as eco-tourism sports.

India has some of the greatest varieties of fauna in the world that has not been exploited through its potential. Efforts were made to make wildlife sanctuaries and national parks as an integral part of the Indian tourism product. Assistance was provided to the State Governments to improve the facilities available in these parks. The Tiger and the Elephant were the 'brands' of Indian Wildlife Tourism.

India's greatest adventure tourism assets are in the form of Himalayas as well as in its mighty rivers. Mountain based adventure activities were promoted in the Himalayas, creating the Himalayas as the brand and the icon of Indian Adventure Tourism.

The holistic healing product were packaged and promoted, as going beyond Ayurveda and Yoga, etc. to showcase health Tourism products of India. The brand for this product was created and destination and sites for holistic healing which is governed by a well defined set of standards and regulations, were developed by the State Governments with assistance from the Ministry of Tourism.

Beach and Coastal Tourism forms the mainstay of international tourism and provides the volumes required for India's key markets, to create a suitable industry. A number of sites on the Coast of India were identified during the plan period for development of beach resorts.

India is a veritable shopper's paradise and the retail trade provides enormous forward and backward linkages throughout the economy. Recognizing shopping as an intrinsic part of the tourism experience and most valuable contributor to revenues, the strategy during the 10th plan was to encourage the development of dedicated shopping centres for traditional crafts, designed on the lines of ethnic village "haat" such as Dilli Haat and Shilpagram. Availability of information on where to procure specific crafts and produce reliable unbiased shopping guides were enhanced during the plan period.

A large number of pilgrimage centres exist in the country which require some investment for improvement and providing better amenities. These tourist and pilgrimage centres are mainly frequented by domestic tourists and in most cases the basic amenities are missing. A large number of such centres were taken up during the 10th Plan for development, and financial assistance was provided to States.

Tourist reception centres are basically meant for interpretation facilities, dissemination of information and provision of necessary communication facilities. Similarly, wayside amenities are meant to meet the requirement of the tourists travelling to tourist destinations by road and include facilities like lounge, cafeteria, toilets, parking etc. Financial assistance during the plan for structural improvements, construction of additional accommodation and other facilities and improvement of sanitary and electrical fittings, were given. Thrust was given to provide such facilities which are professionally designed and eco-friendly. It was also emphasized that the management of such facilities is out-sourced and operated on pay and use basis.

Refurbishment of Monuments/Heritage Building and Improvement of their Environs was intended to provide financial assistance to ASI and State/UT Governments for undertaking repair, refurbishment, beautification, landscaping, improvement of amenities, and illumination of monuments/heritage buildings falling in the jurisdiction of ASI or the State Governments. This ongoing scheme was continued in the 10th plan also and a number of monuments/sites were taken up during the plan period.

Illumination of monuments and SEL shows has helped in adding value to the tourist attractions. In the 10th plan, laser lighting and laser shows were included under the scheme. However, funds under this scheme were used only for major tourist attraction which fall within recognized tourism circuits or preferred destinations.

(C) Assistance for Large Revenue Generating Projects

A new schemes was introduced during the 10th Plan wherein support in the form of grant to act as a catalyst was provided to large revenue generating products through the State Tourism Development Corporations or the State Investment and Industrial Development Corporations and the State Financial Corporations. This assistance was, in turn, utilized by these Corporations as equity in projects to promote them or private sector projects. Projects like convention centres, luxury trains, cruise terminals etc. were taken up under this scheme.

(D) Human Resource Development

Tourism being an employment-oriented sector, it is estimated that the hotel and the catering sector provide more than 10%

of the total employment generated by the tourism industry. Being a labour-oriented industry, directly in contact with the country's tourists, skills required by personnel engaged in this sector are different from those required by personnel engaged in other sectors. At present there are 24 Institutes of Hotel Management, and 11 Food Craft Institutes. The IHMs conduct diploma courses, post-graduate diploma courses, craft and certificate courses. The FCLs conduct diploma courses in cookery, food and beverage services, housekeeping, etc. In order to harness the resources and provide a central thrust, the Ministry of Tourism has also established the National Council for Hotel Management and Catering Technology. The main objectives of the Council are to advise the Government on coordinated development of Hotel Management and Catering Edcuation; to prescribe educational and other qualifications for staff in the institutions; to give certification and accreditation, and to standardize the courses. Ministry of Tourism encouraged the Institutes of Hotel Management to explore appropriate means to generate their additional resources during the 10th Plan, so that these institutions gradually become self-supporting at least on revenue accounts. Assistance was given to them to enhance their infrastructure facilities.

The NCHM&CT, which has emerged as an apex formation in the country for hospitality management education, was assisted for construction of its new building at Noida. The Building is almost ready and it is expected that it will meet the requirements of Council.

The existing FCIs, IHMs and the institutes in the private sector cater to mainly the organized sector. The unorganized sector consisting of small hotels, *dhabas*, restaurants and other eatable joints spread all over the country hardly get an opportunity of training from skilled and professional trainers in the hospitality sector. As it is not possible and viable to set up FCIs in every district, a number of Capacity Building Programmes for the workers of un-organized sector were organized by FCIs and IHMs during the 10th Plan through outreach training programmes.

Indian Institute of Tourism and Travel Management (IITTM), established in 1983 as a registered society under the Minsitry of Tourism primarily for developing and promoting education, training and research in travel and tourism, which was just running a single P.G. Diploma Course, has started two new courses during the 10th Plan i.e., a Bachelor Degree in Tourism (a three-year course) and a Masters Degree in Business Administration (a two-year course) with specialization in tourism. During the year, the Institute has started construction of its Campus at Bhubaneshwar for its Eastern Regional Centre on the land provided by the State Government free of cost. The Institute also conduced a number of capacity building programmes for the workers in the unorganized sector like Railway Coolies, *Taxi walas, Dhaba* and Hotel Staff, unemployed youth, etc. The Institute also conducted a number of Guide Training Programmes during the plan period to upgrade the skills of existing guides as also to recruit new guides. During the 10th Plan, the Institute has become almost self-sufficient to meet its regular revenue expenditure.

Guide training courses are organized by the Ministry of Tourism and also by the State Governments. These courses include programmes for fresh tourist guides and refresher courses for those already active in guide services. The contents of these courses were restructured during the 10th Plan. Courses were also organized for Government officials who have an interface with the tourists in order to sensitize them.

(E) Marketing and Promotion

There is a vast untapped potential inherent in the tourism sector for generating more wealth, income and employment provided the Indian tourism product is promoted and marketed vigorously, both at home and abroad. One of the reasons why India is still lagging behind in this highly competitive market is the lack of adequate budgetary support for promotion and marketing as compared to some of the competing destinations, include those in India's neighbourhood. While the non-plan budget basically caters to salary of the establishment of the Tourist offices, including travelling expenses, office expenses, rent and taxes, the expenditure on promotion and marketing, which constitute the main area of operation, has to be met from the Plan budget. Within India, the Indian tourism product is promoted primarily by the Ministry of Tourism with the help of 5 regional offices and 16 sub-regional offices under them, with the involvement of the State Governments. Likewise, the Indian tourism product is promoted and marketed overseas through the Tourist Offices at 13 locations worldover, as also directly by the Ministry.

Domestic Promotion

During the 10th Plan period, a need was felt to launch a mass tourism awareness campaign highlighting the significant contribution of this sector in economic growth in general and creating employment in particular. This was required to bring tourism in the mainstream of our national development. The earlier policy of supplementing the effort of the State Tourism Departments/Corporations for promotion and marketing of their tourism products continued. The promotion effort had a multi-dimensional thrust. It covers imaged building, dissemination of information, and public relation efforts. The communication message was geared towards the travelling tourists, the tourist service providers, travel and consumer media. The efforts took into account new technology and means of communication like those based on Information Technology tools as well as conventional tools like brochures, advertisements, and telephone based information, face to face communication etc. The domestic campaign also envisaged highlighting the new tourism circuits created. The unique features of the domestic campaign were:

1. Creating high standard facilitation centres at all leading gateways, both railheads and airports.
2. Launching a tourism awareness campaign involving all service providers such as taxi drivers, guides etc.

3. Intensification of guides training.
4. Creating a unique brand for Indian tourism which is vibrant and based on sustainable development.
5. Using the digital technology to create the unique experiences of Indian tourism on the internet.
6. Using travel writers and photographers of regional languages to write about the other regions.

Fairs, Festivals and Craft Melas

The variety of fairs and festivals are a powerful tool for showcasing the Indian culture for the tourists. These events are keenly awaited and viewed with interest and curiosity by domestic and foreign tourists. Such events have been supported in the past and were also given support during the 10th Plan. However, as a matter of policy not more than two events from each State were supported in a year. The local administrators were encouraged to generate local resources to augment Government outlays. It is expected that such fairs and festivals would become self-sufficient in due course.

Hospitality

Under the Hospitality programme of the Ministry, travel writers, tour operators, media celebrities, TV film producers and opinion-makers were regularly invited and taken to different destinations. The overseas guests on arrival in India were looked after and escorted to various places of tourist interest. They, in turn helped disseminating information about India in their home markets.

Publicity

The Ministry has been adopting conventional publicity measures since the past plan periods. These include printing and distributions of brochures, folders, maps, information booklets etc. During the 10th Plan, this was continued with a qualitative improvement and with more focus on IT and with electronic media. The help of professional public relation agency was taken for the image building exercise.

Overseas Promotion

The Ministry of Tourism performs its main marketing function through a network of 13 Government of India Tourist Offices located overseas towards specific area demarcations under 5 distinct regions as given below:

New York—responsible for the entire North American and South American Continent.
Frankfurt—responsible for Continental Europe.
London—responsible for U.K. and Ireland.
Dubai—responsible for West Asia and South Africa.
Tokyo—responsible for East Asia.

The existing system is to develop marketing plans region-wise taking into account the existing market segments and consumer needs which vary between different regions. However, the operational elements of these different marketing plans can be classified as follows:

(a) Directing advertising,
(b) Public relations,
(c) Promotion.

Under direct advertising, the tourist offices release advertisement in leading travel magazine, newspaper etc. Sometimes, joint advertising and brochure support is also undertaken with tour operators etc. Under public relations, the offices in association with tour operators and airlines organize familiarization tours to India, for which expenditure is borne by the Ministry. Under promotion, the offices take part in special trade festivals like the ITB Berlin, WTM London, etc.

Although external publicity is a costly proposition, the fact remains that without aggressive promotion in the highly competitive tourist market overseas, India cannot achieve the targeted growth and increased share of global tourist arrivals and receipts. During the 10th Plan period, the strategies for promotion included:

(i) Dissemination of tourist information and attending to enquiries;
(ii) Creating awareness about Indian Tourism Product;
(iii) Maintaining close relation and co-ordination with Indian Missions, Travel and Trade Media, Airlines;
(iv) Liaison with local bodies, Chambers of Commerce and other professional bodies;
(v) Organizing Indian food festivals and participating in festivals/exhibitions;
(vi) IT based dissemination of information;
(vii) Appointing professional PR agencies;
(viii) Organizing festivals, Road Shows;
(ix) Special Promotion Campaigns;
(x) Marketing Partnerships;
(xi) Print and electronic media publicity;
(xii) Joint regional promotion;
(xiii) Hospitality;
(xiv) Gathering Marketing Intelligence;
(xv) Brand Building of India;
(xvi) Consumer-oriented advertising and net-based electronic media, FM Radio;
(xvii) Hospitality and Funding MO Passages; and
(xviii) Market Development Assistance.

(F) Others

Market Research and Perspective Plans

A comprehensive statistical research programme is an essential input for sustainable development of tourism. Lack of information about different aspects of tourism is one of the major reasons for the sector not getting its due place in the national development plans of several countries. Infrastructure development and marketing of tourism have to be based on research findings and analysis. Without quantitative information on the demand characteristics, profiles of tourists along with the statistics of availability of existing infrastructural facilities at various tourist destinations, it is not possible to plan effectively for tourism development and promotion. Compilation of statistics and commissioning of research studies are, therefore, very crucial, and so also is the preparation of perspective plans for States and master plans for regions.

The Ministry of Tourism is presently having a system under which foreign tourist arrival data are being collected from disembarkation cards. The data transcribed from these cards are computerized and tabulated. The estimates of foreign exchange earnings from tourism is estimated by the RBI as a part of balance of payments statistics based on a sample survey of foreign exchange transaction through authorized dealers. The statistics of domestic tourist visits are obtained from the State Government through a monthly return. The Ministry of Tourism also undertakes periodical surveys and studies of interest to Government.

During the 10th Five Year Plan, 20-year Perspective plans for all the States/UTs were prepared with the objective of development of tourism in an integrated way. These plans focussed on the development of important tourist areas falling in the respective State in a coherent manner by dovetailing the funds and resources at the command of the State and clearly identifying the requirement for infrastructure development.

The Ministry also undertook a number of research studies to provide inputs to policy-makers for planning and policy formulation. A few of the studies undertaken during the 10th Plan were:

(i) Impact of Civil Aviation Policies on Tourism;
(ii) Foreign Tourist Expenses on Handicrafts;
(iii) Domestic Tourism Survey;
(iv) International Passengers Survey;
(v) Cruise Tourism—Potential and Strategy;
(vi) Best Practices followed by States in the field of Tourism;
(vii) Kerala's Approach to Tourism Development; and
(viii) Manpower Requirements in Hotel Industry and Tour/Travel Sector.

An important study conducted by the Ministry during the 10th Plan was Development of Tourism Satellite Account for India giving the economic benefits of tourism in India like tourism's share to GDP and employment.

As part of its efforts to develop tourism infrastructure in the country in a systematic manner which is sustainable, a number of Detailed Project Reports (DPRs) were also prepared by the Ministry for the Destinations/circuits shortlisted during the 10th Plan.

Capital/Interest Subsidy for Hotels

Till the 8th Plan, there was a scheme for providing interest subsidy for hotels up to 3 star category in the non-metropolitan area. This scheme helped in meeting the accommodation demand of the middle income tourists to a large extent. However, administration of the scheme came in for criticism as the hotels had to approach the Ministry every time it had to claim the interest subsidy. As such, during the 10th Plan, the interest subsidy scheme was replaced by the capital subsidy scheme. However, this scheme of interest subsidy continued for the old projects sanctioned in the past. Under the revised scheme, the capital grants up to 10% of the total principal loan taken from designated financial institutions up to Rs. 25 lakh for 1-star hotels, Rs. 50 lakhs for 2-star hotels and Rs. 75 lakhs for 3-star and heritage basic category hotels, were given to encourage setting up of budget hotels in the country.

Information Technology

Information Technology was given a major thrust in the 10th Plan. Assistance was provided to the States to use IT in promotion and facilitation of tourism. IT was used as a major tool to promote Indian Tourism products in the country and abroad. The goals were to position India distinctively in the global tourism map using emerging technologies and new approaches in attention management to power India Tourism.

All these efforts made during the 10th Five Year Plan had a salutary effect on the India tourism. While the foreign tourist arrivals are expected to witness a growth of 78% during the period, growth in the foreign exchange earnings is expected to be of the order of 122%. India's share in world tourism which was 0.37% during 2001 end, is likely to increase to 0.53% during 2006. As per the estimates about 12.5 million additional jobs were created directly and indirectly in the tourism sector during the 10th Plan period. Tables 2.1 to 2.9 present the facts and figures.

Table 2.1 : Achievements during the 10th Five Year Plan 2002-2007
Foreign Tourist Arrivals to India (In Million)

Year	*Arrivals*	*% Change over previous year*
2002	2.38	(-)6.0
2003	2.73	(+)14.3
2004	3.46	(+)26.8
2005	3.92	(+)13.2
2006*	4.51	(+)15.0

Growth in 5 years i.e., 2006 over 2001: 78% (end of 9th Plan to end of 10th Plan)
* Predicted.

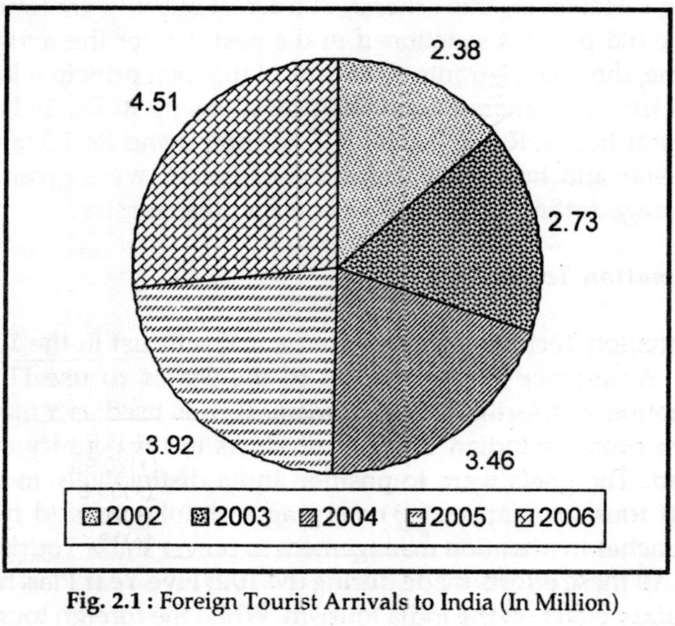

Fig. 2.1 : Foreign Tourist Arrivals to India (In Million)

Table 2.2 : India's share in world arrivals

Year	World Arrivals (In Million)	Arrivals India (In Million)	Share of India in world arrivals (%)
2002	702.8	2.38	0.34
2003	690.9	2.73	0.39
2004	766.0	3.46	0.45
2005	808.0	3.92	0.49
2006*	844.0	4.51	0.53

India's share in world arrivals increased to 0.53% in 2006 from the level of 0.37% in 2001

* Predicted.

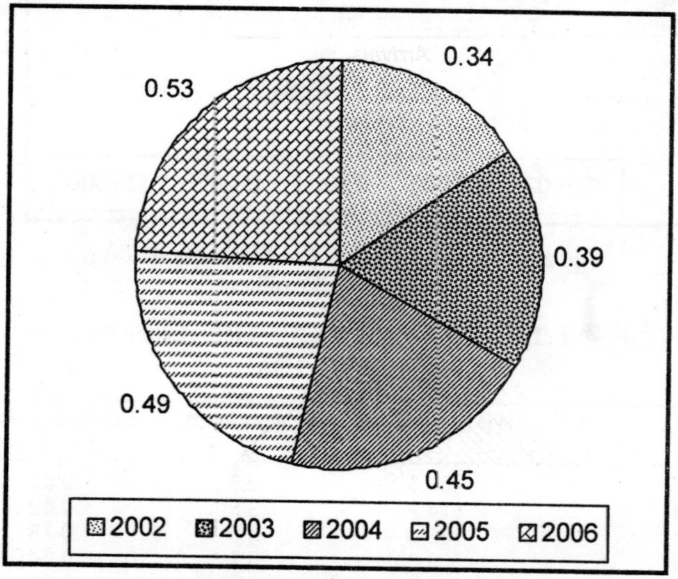

Fig. 2.2 : India's Share in World Arrivals

Table 2.3 : Foreign Exchange Earnings by India from Tourism

Year	Foreign Exchange Earnings (in US$ million)	% Change over previous year
2002	2923	(-)3.9
2003	3533	(+)20.99
2004	4769	(+)35.0
2005	5731	(+)20.2
2006*	6768	(+)18.1

Growth in 5 years i.e., 2006 over 2001: 122% (end of 9th Plan to end to 10th Plan)

* Predicted.

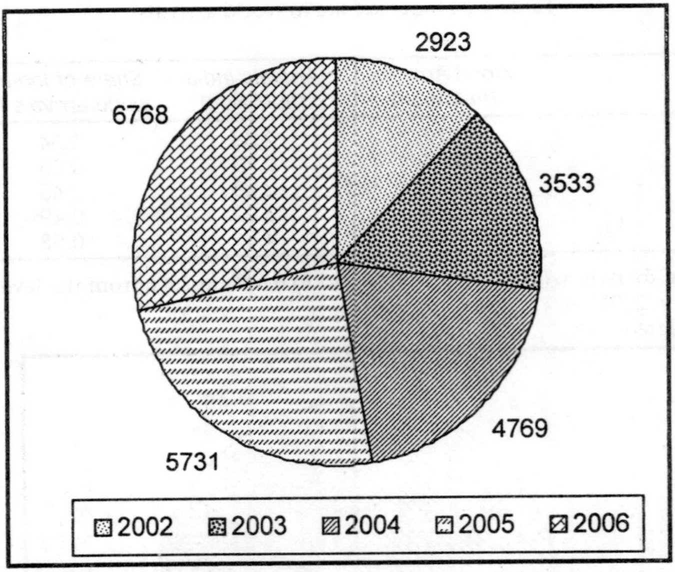

Fig. 2.3 : Foreign Exchange Earnings by India from Tourism (in US$ million)

Table 2.4 : India's Share in World Foreign Exchange Earnings (in Billion US$)

Year	*World Earnings*	*Earnings by India*	*Share of India in world earnings*
2002	482.3	2.9	0.62
2003	524.2	3.5	0.69
2004	633.0	4.8	0.76
2005	682.0	5.7	0.84
2006*	752.0	6.8	0.90

India's share in world arrivals increased to 0.90% in 2006 from the level of 0.66% in 2001 (end of 9th Plan to end of 10th Plan)
* Predicted.

Table 2.5 : India's Rank in Arrivals and Earnings

Year	*India's Rank*	
	In World Arrivals	*In World Earnings*
2002	54th	37th
2003	50th	36th
2004	47th	35th
2005	43rd	33rd

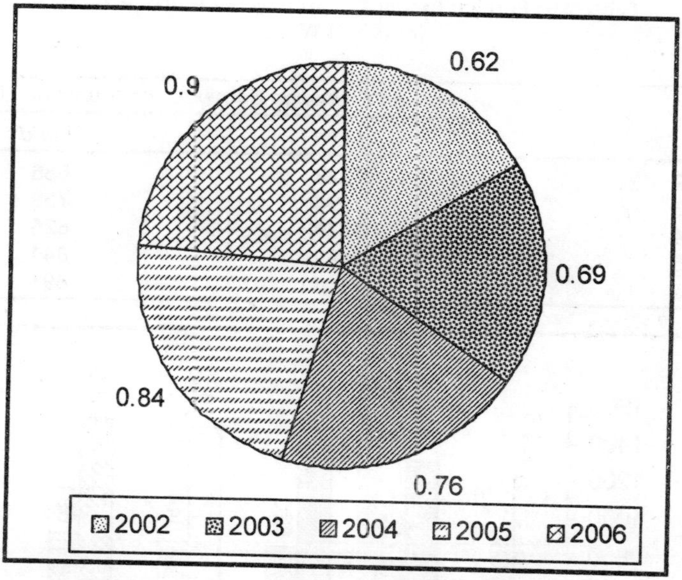

Fig. 2.4 : India's share in World Foreign Exchange Earnings (in Billion US$)

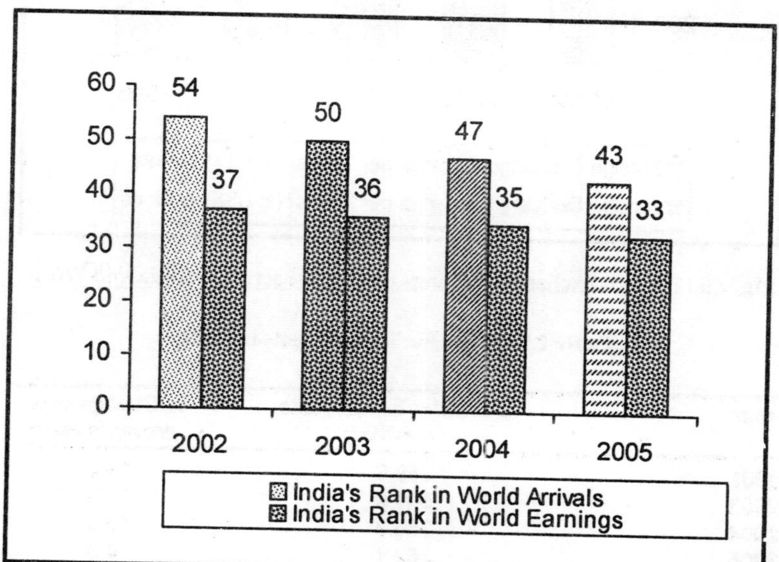

Fig. 2.5 : India's Rank in Arrivals and Earnings

Table 2.6 : Foreign Exchange Earnings per tourist arrival—India and World

Year	Foreign Exchange Earnings per Tourist (in US$)	
	India	World
2002	1228	686
2003	1294	759
2004	1378	826
2005	1462	844
2006	1501	891

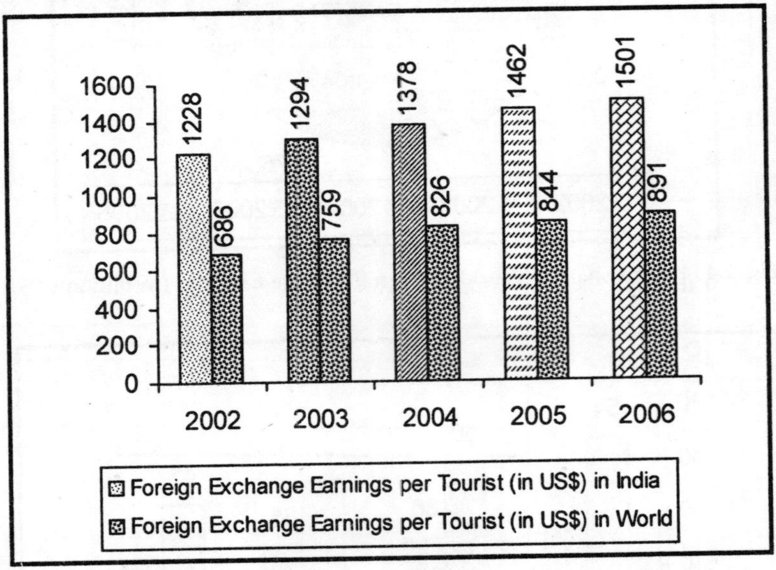

Fig. 2.6 : Foreign Exchange Earnings per tourist arrival—India and World

Table 2.7 : Domestic Tourist Visits in India

Year	Domestic Tourist Visits (in million)	% Change over previous year
2002	269.6	14.0
2003	309.0	14.6
2004	366.2	18.5
2005	382.1	4.3
2006	432.0	13.0

Growth in 5 years i.e., 2006 over 2001: 82.9% (end of 9th Plan to end to 10th Plan)

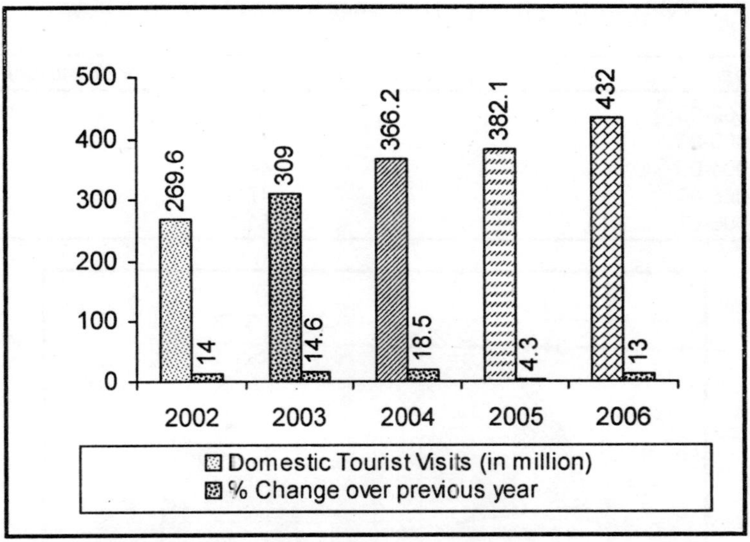

Fig. 2.7 : Domestic Tourist Visits in India

Table 2.8 : Share of Tourism Sector in India in GDP of the Nation

Year	*Total Share of Tourism in GDP*
2002-03	5.83%
2003-04	5.90%

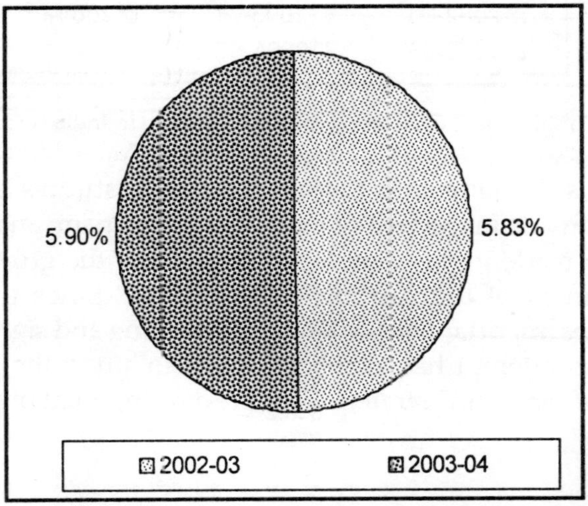

Fig. 2.8 : Share of Tourism Sector in India in GDP of the Nation

Table 2.9 : Employment Generation through Tourism in India

Year	*Total Employment in Tourism Sector (in million)*
2002-03	38.6
2003-04	41.8
2004-05	44.7
2005-06	47.8
2006-07	51.1

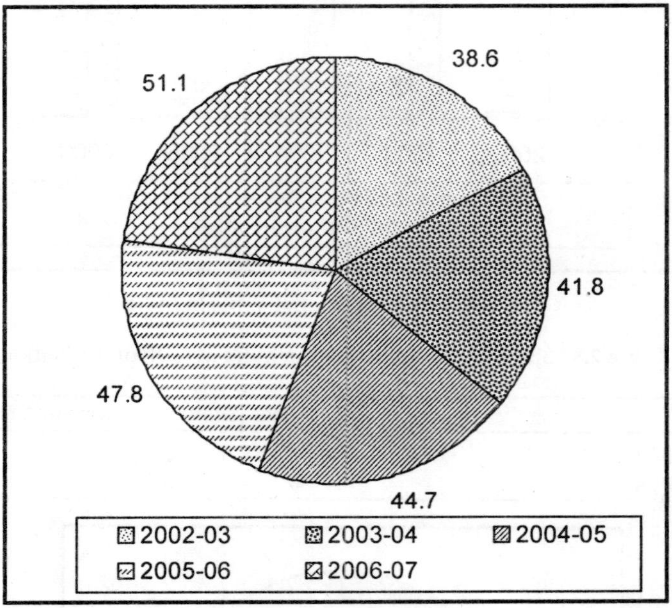

Fig. 2.9 : Employment Generation through Tourism in India (in Millions)

Thus, looking into the overall work, studies and the attempts made in the area of marketing of tourism, an attempt has been made in the present study to know the growth and development of tourism in the Bihar State. Since this area constitutes important ingredients for travelling and sightseeing places, an attempt has also been made to study the various aspects of marketing strategies for the development of tourism industry.

Hypotheses

Tourism has changed all walks of life. Irrespective of the age and sex factor, it is the industry that strengthens the economy of the country and fills up the exchange reserves of the nation. It is a way through which the country projects itself to the world.

Tourism brings together all ways of life and as people, we join hands with each other and know many things. Culture is shared between each other. Social life becomes known; economic aspects are understood: and more than all, we come to know the way the life is maintained by others, new things are learnt and old are polished. But this is possible only if you have better approaches to boost tourism. There are ways to do it. With better and scientific marketing strategies only, tourism industry can be developed. For this, we require timely marketing ways. Thus, the present study is undertaken in response to a call for developing marketing strategies to boost the tourism industry. The study restricts its area to the Bihar State only for knowing the methods used for tourism development. The study also suggests strategies for future development.

Objectives of the Study

The main objectives of the study are:

(1) To understand the conceptual framework of tourism as an emerging service industry with emphasis on its professionalization;
(2) To review the development of tourism industry in India with special reference to Bihar;
(3) To consider the conceptual framework of marketing strategies for service industry, in general, and the tourism industry, in particular;
(4) To understand the existing state of affairs of tourist services in the study area with a view to assess demand supply status for the tourist services;

(5) To chalk out essential elements of marketing strategies;
(6) To understand further the issues and challenges of marketing or tourist services;
(7) To assess and analyze the trends, and the seasonal fluctuations in the number of tourists arriving in Bihar;
(8) To arrive at conclusions and make suggestions on the basis of the findings of the study for the formulation and development of a tourist policy.

Scope of the Study

The present study was undertaken to highlight the places of interest and the facilities available for the promotion of tourism in Bihar. The study also concerned itself with the tourist services rendered by various organizations. It covered both the Government and non-Government sector service units in Bihar. Thus, the scope of the study is in two-fold:

(i) To know the present position of marketing strategies to develop tourism in this area; and
(ii) To know the problem areas and suggest the ways through which tourism can be developed.

Methods of the Study

The main purpose of the study was to know the marketing strategies adopted to boost the tourism in Bihar. It was therefore, decided to use explorative-cum-descriptive research design for the study. Multi-stage random sampling technique was used both for inbound foreign tourists and domestic tourists.

An exhaustive questionnaire was prepared and administered to a sample of 100 inbound foreign tourists. These tourists were approached in various hotels at five locations, namely Patna, Gaya, Bhagalpur, Muzaffarpur and Munger, in the tourist zone. This zone was devised by the researcher purely for the purpose of this study; and on the basis of location of different places of tourist interest. The foreign tourists were approached in their respective questionnaire. Foreign tourists broadly comprised (i) leisure tourists, and (ii) business tourists.

As domestic tourism, compared with inbound tourism, is quantitatively much larger and all domestic tourists visit more places, it was considered that a multi-stage random sample of 150 domestic meaningful. As the sample size here was large, a multi-stage random interest, namely, Patna, Gaya, Muzaffarpur, Bhagalpur and Munger.

As most of the domestic tourists do not seek accommodation in hotels, it was felt consistent to approach them at various tourist spots in each of these five places.

Sources of Data

The data was collected from two sources, namely, primary sources and secondary sources, primary data was collected by conducting personal interviews with the officers of the Tourism Department of the Government of Bihar and India Tourism Development Corporation.

Secondary data was obtained from various journals, periodicals, newspapers, Government hand-outs and publications, trade journals, research reports, annual reports of tourism development corporations and the reports of the Union Ministry of Tourism.

Structure of the Study

The present study is divided into Ten chapters. Chapter-I provides meaning and concept, nature and types, characteristics, benefits, the marketing perspective and utility of promoting tourism in India.

Chapter-II deals with the review of literature and research design. This chapter is based on the evaluation studies and paper written by various subject experts. The chapter also draws the importance of tourism development and their marketing promotion. The researcher concludes that while India has a many splendoured tourist attractions, their marketing and promotion lacked aggressiveness. The failure of India's performance in this area was compared with other Asian countries with growth rate statistics. Primary data and secondary data were used in this study.

Chapter-III is an attempt to highlight the contemporary issues. This chapter includes the main ideas on sustainable tourism, global tourism, impact of tourism on socio-economic development, various strategic issues and role of transportation related with tourism promotion.

Chapter-IV describes the profile of Bihar. Bihar lies mid-way between the humid West Bengal in the east and the sub-humid Uttar Pradesh in the west which provides it with a transitional position in respect of climate, economy and culture. It is bounded by the country Nepal in the north and by Jharkhand in the south. Nalanda was a centre of learning established by the 5th century BC in Bihar, India, one of the first great Medieval University (Asia) in recorded history. Its capital Patna, earlier known as Patliputra was an important centre of Indian civilization.

Chapter-V directs attention on tourism and tourist places in Bihar. The state has the capacity to attract tourists from across the globe with different interests like culture, holiday, study and adventure. The researcher also describes many important tourist places of Bihar.

Chapter-VI analyses the tourism and hospitality in Bihar. The researcher is of the opinion that tourism hospitality in Bihar has emerged as one of the key sectors driving the state's growth and is thriving, owing to a huge surge in both business and leisure travel by foreign and domestic tourists.

Chapter-VII highlights the competitive operating environment and culture in the form of fairs and festivals which attract the tourists in Bihar.

Chapter-VIII throws light on marketing of tourism in Bihar. In spite of mass poverty, social chaos, dirt, squalor and destitution, Bihar has a great potentiality to be one of the most important tourist destinations in the country. The potentiality is to be converted into tourist product by adopting proper marketing strategy.

Chapter-IX deals with the national tourism policy and Tourist policy of Bihar.

Chapter-X provides conclusions and suggestions for the study.

REFERENCES

Badan, B.S. and Bhatt, H. (2007) : *Tourism and Economic Development*, Commonwelth Publishers, New Delhi-2.

Banskota, K. and Sharma, B. (1994): "Carrying Capacity of Himalaya Resource for Mountain Tourism Development", Paper presented at the Regional Conference on Sustainable Development of Fragile Mountain Areas of Asia, 13-15 December, Kathmandu: *ICIMOD*, p. 12.

Bhargana, D., Bhadra, B. and S. Sharma (1995): Tourism for Local Community Development in Mountain Areas: A Synthesis Report, *ICIMOD Internal Document*, p. 56.

Bhatia, A.K. (2007) : *Tourism development : Principles and Practices*, 2nd Revised Edition, Sterling Publishers Private Limited, New Delhi-20.

Chamberlain and N.S. (1992) : "Mountain Perspective and Sustainability: A Framework for Development Strategies", In *Jodha et al.*, (eds.), *Sustainable Mountain Agriculture Perspectives and Issues*, Vol. 1, New Delhi, pp. 41-82.

Montague, B. and C. Von Furer (1984), *The Sherpas Transformed: Social Change in the Buddhist Society of Nepal*, New Delhi, Sterling, p. 21.

Patil, P.B. (2006) : *Tourism Development : Problem and Prospects*, Current Publications, Agra-10 (U.P.)

Report of the working group on Tourism (2007-12): *11th Five Year Plan*, Ministry of Tourism, Government of Bihar.

Sharma, P. (1990): "Tourism and Sustainable Development", In *Banskota, Sharma et al.*, Economic Policies for Sustainable Development in Nepal, Kathmandu: *ICIMOD*, p. 9.

Sharma, P.R., (1995), Culture and Tourism: Defining Roles and Relationships. MEI Discussion Paper Series 95/2, Kathmandu: *ICIMOD*, p. 149.

Singh K.P., Prasad Alok (2006): *Marketing of Tourism in Bihar*, CPC, New Delhi, p. 16.

Verma, S.B., Jiloka, S.K. and Thryambakam, P. (2006) : *Rural Tourism and Tribal Development*, Deep and Deep Publications Pvt. Ltd., New Delhi-27.

WCED (World Commission on Environment and Development (1987), *Our Common Future*, Oxford, New Delhi, p. 8.

3

Tourism in India

The development of tourism in India is a fascinating subject. What makes it fascinating is its history. Tourism thrives on history of the country. In fact, tourism cannot be isolated from history much less in a country like India whose cultural heritage has a wealth of attractions (Fig. 3.1).

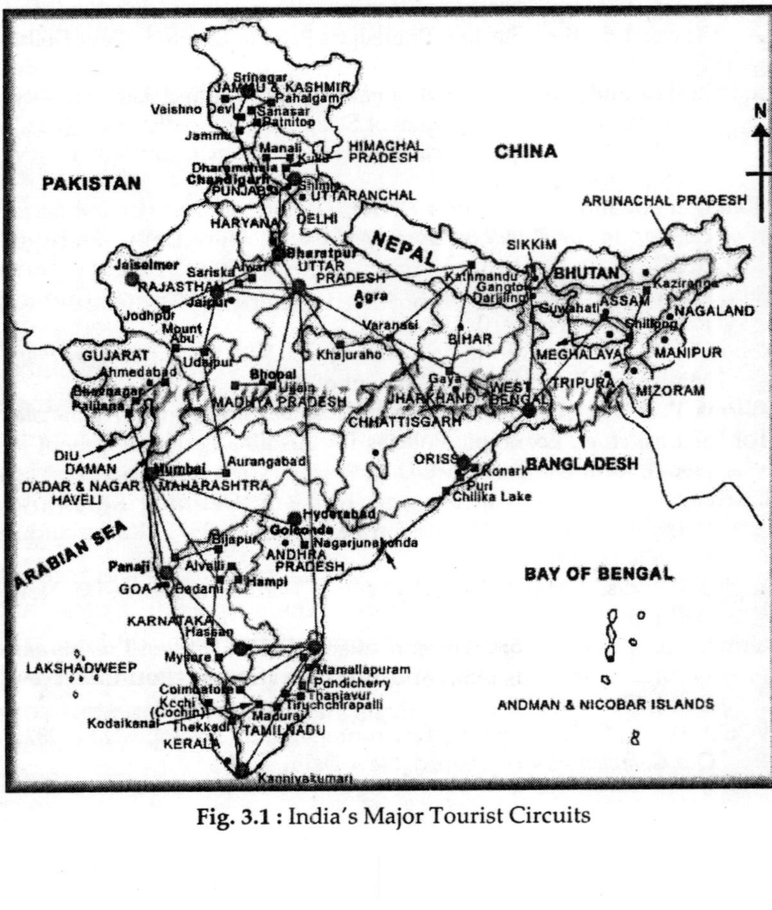

Fig. 3.1 : India's Major Tourist Circuits

India's glorious traditions and rich cultural heritage are closely linked with the development of tourism. Its magnificent monuments attract a large number of visitors from allover the world. The wealth of cultural traditions extending over thousands of years, the natural surrounding, the architectural masterpieces, the music, dance, painting, customs and languages—all these make India a tourist paradise. Few countries in the world provide such varied interests to a visitor.

In the words of Pt. Jawahar Lal Nehru, "India is a land of contrasts", where rural tranquility rubs shoulders with metropolitan bustle, austerity with pomp and show, and pageantry with simplicity. History has been equally generous in bequeathing a treasure of monuments. There is the immortal Taj, the Dravidian temple of South, especially those of Madurai, and the world-famous frescoes of Ajanta and Ellora. There is also no dearth of cities that create an impression on the tourist. In the words of Mark Twain, "India is the one country under the sun that is endowed with an imperishable interest for alien prince and alien present, for lettered and ignorant, wise and fool, rich and poor, bonded and free and on land that all men desire to have seen and having seen once by even a glimpse would not give that glimpse for the shows of all the globe combined". This sum up the relationship of history with tourism and how these two put together contribute towards the development of the country's economy.

Tourism industry in India has become one of the most efficient and dependable earners of precious foreign exchange for the country. Not only the Central but the State Governments too have begun to invest in tourism infrastructure and facilities to capitalize on this growing industry. As more and more people are acquiring surplus purchasing power, the demand for leisure activities is growing parallel with the development of the roads, rail and air networks. The surprising fact is that despite being in possession of some of the most diverse and compelling natural assets, ranging from rugged mountains and picturesque hills to marvellous beaches and forests, from historical splendors of forts and shrines to an amazing variety of wildlife, for many decades since Independence, these were not given more than cursory attention in the successive Development Plans of the country. It is only recently that the Government of India has woken up to the stark fact that tourism, if encouraged in a planned manner and in appropriate direction, can earn the country thousands of crores of Rupees in foreign exchanges as well as provide domestic tourism the necessary infrastructure to make it a truly desirable and attractive proposition. Fig. 3.1 shows the India's major tourist circuits.

Several years ago, a study of the still nascent tourist industry in the country revealed the investment in tourism has a multiplier effect of 3.2, that is, for every Rupee invested in building up tourism infrastructure, the revenue opportunities generated would be more than three times. In other words, an investment of Rs. 1,000 crores would lead to revenue generation of over Rs. 3, 200 crores. Even allowing for the recent spurt in the rate of inflation, the revenue-generating potential of this industry can be well understood. Thus, the Eighth Five Year Plan of the Government of India proposed an investment of Rs. 272 crores in the Central sector and of Rs. 502 crores in the State sector, totalling to Rs. 774 crores. It may be mentioned here that the multiplier effect would seem to be much more than 3.2, with an investment of Rs. 138.68 crores during the Seventh Plan, along with a sizable investment by the private sector, the earnings from tourism in the year 1991-92 were Rs. 3000+ crores. Of course, in the Private sector of tourism industry, particularly the hotel and travel industry, transportation and facilitation sector, the investments are of a much higher order. Nonetheless, the earnings too have substantially increased. Tourism has become a force to be reckoned with.

The remarkable and unpalatable fact is that during the four decades from 1951 to 1991, in spite of the increase in the number of foreign tourists from 17,000 to 1.7 million, India's share in the total world tourist arrivals has remained a negligible 0.28 to 0.42 per cent. However, it is anticipated that tourist traffic will grow at the rate of 12 to 15 per cent per annum during the next ten years and an estimated 2.75 million tourists will visit India during the period ending 2011. Table 3.1 and Fig. 3.2 gives trends in internal tourist arrivals in India in the decade of eighties.

Table 3.1 : Trends in Foreign Tourist Arrivals in India in the Eighties

Year	*Tourist Arrivals*	*Growth Rate in %*
1980	8,00,150	—
1981	8,53,148	6.6
1982	8,60,178	0.8
1983	8,84,731	2.9
1984	8,35,803	-0.5
1985	8,36,908	0.2
1986	10,80,050	29.1
1987	11,63,774	7.8
1988	12,39,992	6.5
1989	13,37,232	7.8

Source : Monthly commentary, New Delhi, June 1994.

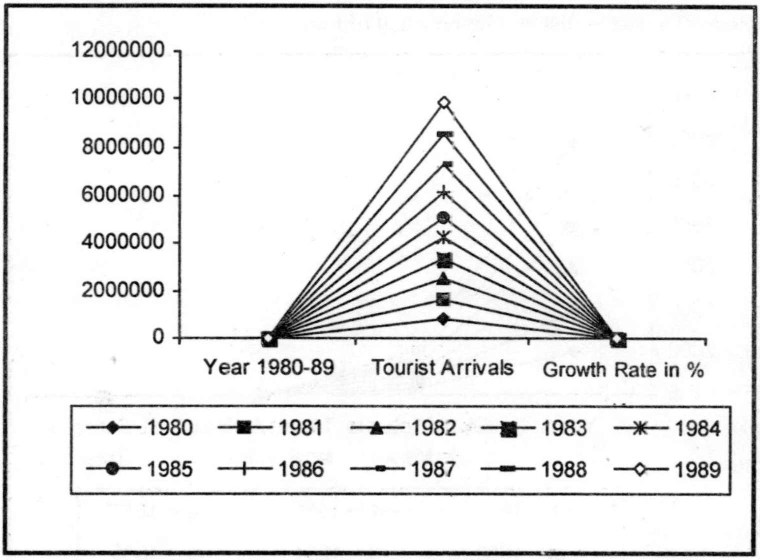

Fig. 3.2 : Trends in Foreign Tourist Arrivals in India in the Eighties

It is seen from the Table 3.1 and Fig. 3.2 that India registered a record increase in more than 67 per cent during the decade of eighties. But the trends have been of highly fluctuating and erratic nature. Now we would examine the place of India in the global tourist arrivals in the decade of eighties. Table 3.2 and Fig. 3.3 show the relative share of India in total international tourist arrivals between 1980 and 1989.

It is seen from Table 3.1 that during the decade of eighties India did improve its share, i.e. from a share of 0.28 per cent in 1980 to 0.42 per cent by the end of the decade of 80s, i.e. 1989.

Table 3.2 : Relative Share of India in Global Tourist Arrivals in the Eighties

Year	*Global Tourists (in Million)*	*Tourist Arrivals in India (in million)*	*% Share in Total*
1980	284.4	0.80	0.28
1985	326.5	0.84	0.39
1986	330.9	1.01	0.44
1987	356.8	1.16	0.42
1988	382.0	1.23	0.42
1989	451.6	1.33	0.42

Source : Tourist Statistics, Government of India, 1993.

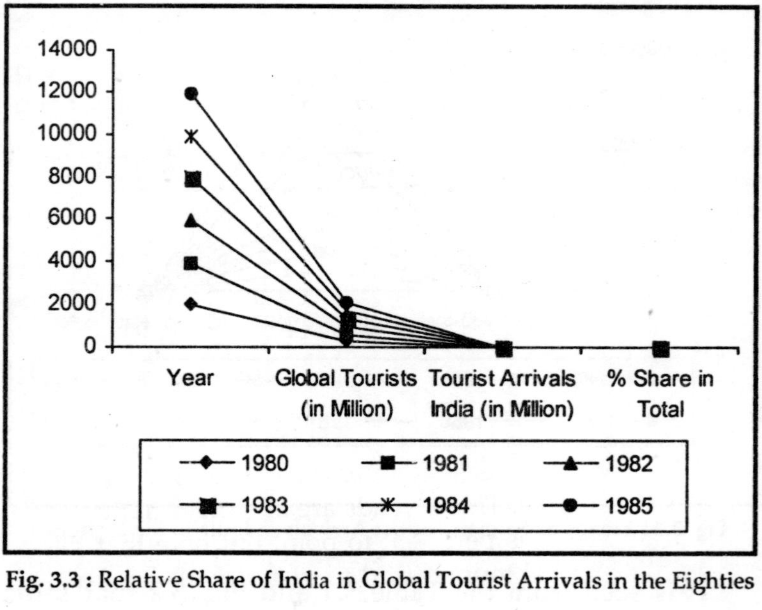

Fig. 3.3 : Relative Share of India in Global Tourist Arrivals in the Eighties

Trends in the Nineties

Since the beginning of the decade of nineties, the growth rate in foreign tourist arrivals in India has recorded an erratic trends. In the year 1990, there has been a negative growth rate, i.e. -0.5 per cent and thereafter there had been a tremendous increase in volume of foreign tourist arrivals in India and the rise as high as more than 26 per cent. Next year this figure went down to 11.3 per cent, i.e. in 1992. But the most alarming decline has been witnessed in the year 1993, i.e. a decline of nearly 6 per cent. Table 3.3 gives trends in foreign tourist arrivals in India between 1990 and 1993.

In the year 1990, the relative share of India in global tourist arrivals was 38 per cent, this figure has gone down to 0.36 per cent in 1993. This has been due to negative growth rate witnessed in 1993 by India when the decline took place by nearly 6 per cent (Table 3.3 and Fig. 3.4).

From the analysis it is clear that there had been an appreciable increase in the global tourist arrivals in the decade of nineties.

Table 3.3 : Trends in Foreign Tourist Arrivals in India in the Nineties

Year	*Volume of Tourist*	*Growth Rate in %*
1990	13,29,950	—
1991	16,77,508	26.1
1992	18,67,657	11.3
1993	17,64,830	-5.5
1999	18,48,720	8.6

Source : Tourist Statistics, Government of India, 2000.

The decade of nineties has witnessed a lesser growth rate as compared to eighties. These trends are of similar nature in regard to India. But it is pertinent to point out here that the share of India in global tourism and tourist arrivals has been of insignificant nature, i.e. nearly 0.36 per cent. This figure is

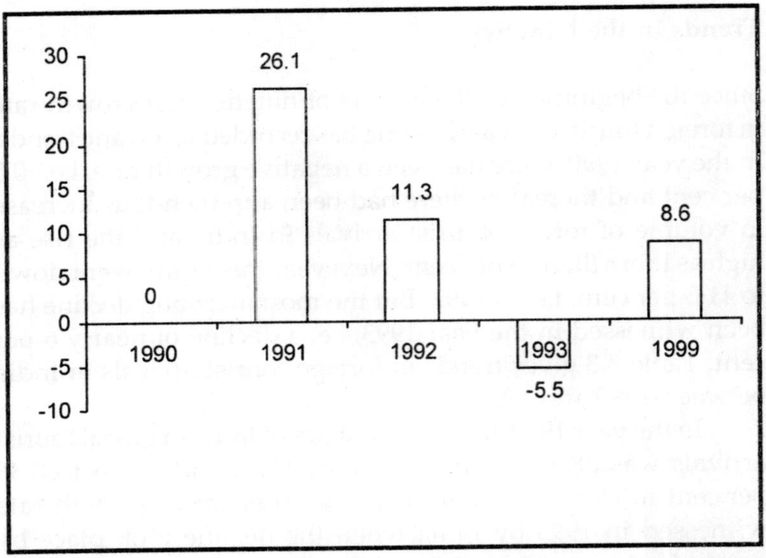

Fig. 3.4 : Trend in Foreign Tourist Arrivals in India in the Nineties

of disturbing nature as India has a great potential for growth and development of tourism. Hence, it is the need of the hour to adopt an aggressive strategy for attracting more foreign tourists in the country as it is one of the most vital means of earning foreign exchange which is badly needed by India for financing its developmental activities. There should be the guideposts for a long way in boosting India's image in global tourists so that more and more foreign arrivals could enter into India.

The Tenth Plan period was considered a watershed in the development of tourism in the country. For the first time, the vast potential of tourism as a foreign exchange earner and generator of employment opportunities was recognized. Several new policy initiatives were taken to develop the tourism sector on an accelerated growth path. Tourism was finally accorded the status of an industry. At present, 16 States and 3 Union Territories have declared tourism as an industry. In addition, four States have accorded this recognition to the hotel industry. Consequently, a number of incentives and concessions have been made available to the private sector tourism entrepreneurs for investment in infrastructural facilities. Particular attention is being paid to the private sector financing of luxury surface transport such as air-conditioned coaches and cars through easy loan schemes operated by banks and other financial institutions in the State.

Much of the credit for the development of the tourism industry in the country goes to the hotel and travel industries. Their concerted efforts to obtain industry status for the hospitality industry have been reflected in their resolutions at the annual meets of the Federation of Hotel and Restaurant Associations of India and the Travel Agents Association of India. The massive investments made by the courageous band of leaders of the industry such as ITDC, Oberoi Group, Sita World Travels, Travel Corporation of India, etc., and their innovative and result-oriented management techniques have benefited not only the industry but also the Government of India in terms of revenue as well as goodwill. Thanks to the private hoteliers and travel and tour operators, the foreign tourist to feel like a VIP at all times.

One wishes one could praise in unqualified terms the operations of the public sector in this regard, as the ITDC hotels continue to be network infrequently paralyzed by lightening strikes and labour problems. This point was emphasized at the annual convention of the Pacific Air Travel Association (PATA). Also, the absence of training institutions in the tourism sector are another hurdle in the way of the accelerated development of the industry. On the other hand, the States have begun to pitch in heavily in favour of the domestic tourism potential. The phenomenal success of Haryana State in highway tourism has been an eye-opener. As more and more holiday-maker of the upper middle class take to the roads in their marvellous little fuel efficient cars, the linkages between the growth of the tourism industry, the automobile industry and the motel/restaurant trade become visible. The age of leisure travel and holidays beyond congested city limits has been started on a sound footing. Now, it needs to be developed along the desirable viable line.

The Government of India is alive and active too in the situation. It set up the Tourism Development Corporation in 1989 to provide financial assistance for setting up, development and maintaining tourism-related activities and services which include hotels, restaurants, amusement parks, resorts and complexes for entertainment, education and sports. The marketing activities of private entrepreneurs and other agencies were given additional support through the scheme of 'Assistant for the Development of International Tourism' (ADIT). The Central Sector Tourism Plan encompasses activities in the area of manpower and institutional development.

It is envisaged that the Department of Tourism will carry out effective publicity and promotion and also provide infrastructural support and facilities for new forms of tourism like holidays and leisure tourism, wildlife, etc. The Department will, for the most part, play a promotional role in the development of tourism. The Eighth Plan envisages identification and development of 'Special Tourism Areas' with recognized high tourism potential. The on-going projects of Buddhist places of interest in Bihar and development of Ajanta-Ellora in Maharashtra have been taken up with external financial assistance. A number of new projects in the pipeline include Agra Heritage Project and Buddhist Places of Interest in Uttar Pradesh and Bihar and similar religious and pilgrimage tourism centres.

The ITDC has been working over past three decades in the area of tourism infrastructure development as well the overall development of the hospitality industry in the country. The Corporation runs 31 hotels and travel lodges, comprising a total of 3,762 rooms. Although the turnover of the ITDC is now over Rs. 125 crores, much remains to be done by it in the field of revamping its training-hotels and reordering the quality of the training imparted. Its Ashoka Group of accommodation network has yet to catch up with the kind of service that the private hotel chains offer. The Eighth Plan proposes sustained efforts to improve the profitability of ITDC's existing hotels. The measures include collaboration with well-known international hotel chains and travel agencies.

The fact remains that the scope for the development of tourism in the country is enormous and the Plan efforts represent only the tip of the iceberg. The private sector, due to obvious reasons, will continue to reap major benefits of the hospitality industry and, therefore, will continue to make large investments in the sector through well thought-out planning and projects. Travel agents and tour operators have only just begun to tap the huge potential in the adventure tourism sector. Climbing, trekking, river-rafting, hang-gliding and rapids-running are some of the more exciting lines of development. Given the ideals of political stability and economic liberalization, tourism too is all set to benefit in the decades to come.

Sustainable Tourism, Eco-Tourism, Wildlife Tourism and Adventure Tourism

India is a region of the world's greatest bio-diversity, with a variety of unique natural locales, and is therefore perfect for development as eco-tourism destination. What is needed is identifying focal locations for eco-tourism like the Himalayas, North-Eastern States, Western Ghats, Jharkhand, Andaman & Nicobar Islands, and Lakshadweep. There is a need to make eco-tourism a grassroot, community-based movement through awareness, education and training of the local community as guides and interpreters.

India also has some of the greatest variety of fauna in the world that has not been exploited to its full potential for tourism. Wildlife Sanctuaries and National Parks need be made an integral part of the India Tourism's product.

India also has greatest adventure tourism assets in the form of Himalayas, as well as in its mighty rivers. What is required is promoting mountain-based adventure activities in the Himalayas, creating the 'Himalayas' as the brand and icon of Indian adventure tourism, and promoting river rafting as a unique tourism product.

In view of immense potential for nature and adventure tourism in India, it should be promoted vigorously during the

11th Plan, particularly because the peak time for adventure tourism is during the so-called 'lean months' of cultural tourism, which can make India a round the year destination. Further, since adventure and wildlife tour operators operate in far-flung regions of the country, a more equitable distribution of the economic benefits of tourism is ensured beside integrating those remote areas into the national mainstream.

Tourism Under Five Year Plans

Tourism industry is a limitless industry with an immense potential for growth. It ranks next only to oil industry in terms of turnover the world-over. Tourism has tremendous positive impacts on the economic and social aspects of the host country. For reaping the economic and social benefits of tourism, every country is enjoying with each other to woo more international and domestic tourists. India is no exception, though her achievements are not astonishing. Nevertheless, tourism is a major industry in the country, as it contributed to about 4 per cent of our GDP, employed about 135 lakh persons (which amounts to 4.5 per cent of total employable labour force in the country) and earned foreign exchange value at about Rs. 3,500 crore per annum in 1991-92, Rs. 9,800 crore per annum in 2003-04. Constant efforts are called for to enhance India's tourism industry to put it on par with international standards. Our share in world tourism is 1 per cent only. For grabbing a respectable share in the world's tourism industry, several tourism inputs are needed to be harnessed. A planned approach to development of tourist attractions, accommodation and transport facilities is very essential.

Accordingly, under different Five Year Plans, the Government had been taking considerable efforts to develop tourism industry in the country.

First Plan

The First Five Year Plan covered the period 1951-56. At that time, tourism was not a conspicuous economic activity and was not given specific allocation. However, many promotional schemes for tourism were taken up. During this period, tourist promotion offices were established at nine places in India. Besides, overseas promotion offices were also established in the USA, Australia, England, France and Sri Lanka. During this period, foreign tourists arrival registered a compound growth of 8.6 per cent per annum and foreign earnings from tourism registered 10 per cent growth.

Second Plan

The Second Five Year Plan (1956-61) recognized tourism as a significant industry and made a modest, but specific, allocation of Rs. 3.36 crores was made for the development of tourism infrastructure. The Plan adopted a method of classification of tourism projects into three categories. Part-I schemes included development of infrastructure at places that were important from the viewpoint of attracting foreign tourists; Part-II schemes included development of places that were primarily of interest to domestic tourists; Part-III schemes were those that catered to the needs of localities. Part-I schemes were entirely Centre-financed, Part-II schemes were State-financed, while Part-III schemes were jointly financed. It was during the Second Plan period in 1958 that a separate Department of Tourism at the Centre was established. Promotional offices were also established—Frankfurt in Germany, Melbourne in Australia and Colombo in Sri Lanka.

Third Plan

The Third Five Year Plan (1961-66) made an allocation of Rs. 8.0 crores, again a small allocation, considering the vastness of the industry. During the Second Plan were completed new works at selected tourist centres such as Khajuraho, Bhubaneshwar, Konark, Mahabalipuram, Madurai, Trichy and many other places were taken up. Also during this period, ten per cent annual growth in earnings and two per cent growth in foreign tourist arrivals took place. However, the hostilities with China and the aftermath the followed resulted in lower growth in foreign tourist arrivals.

Annual Plan

Annual Plan were adopted for the years 1966-67, 1967-68 and 1968-69. During this period, a total of Rs. 7.0 crores were allotted to the tourism sector. More significant events also took place during this period. The Ministry of Tourism and Civil Aviation was established with two full-fledged Departments, namely the Department of Tourism & Department of Civil Aviation. Tourist arrivals registered a growth of six per cent per annum during this period.

Fourth Plan

The broad approach of the Fourth Plan was to expand and to improve tourists facilities with a view of promoting destinational traffic as distinct from transit traffic. Integrated development of selected areas and encouraging charter traffic were adopted. Emphasis was laid on the provision of accommodation, transport and recreational facilities. Efforts were concentrated in areas where there was an identified large flow of foreign tourists' traffic.

An outlay of Rs. 36 crores was proposed for tourism, including Rs. 25 crores for the Central programmes and Rs. 11 crores for the States. The provision in the Central sector including Rs. 14 crores for the department of Tourism and Rs. 11 crores for the ITDC. Provision of loans to the hotel industry in private sector, loans for the purchase of tourist vehicles by private operators and integrated development of selected centres were the thrust areas. The programmes of the ITDC included construction of hotesls, motels and cottages, renovation and expansion of tourist bungalows and setting up of transport units and duty-free shops.

In the State sector, programmes for development of budget hotels, rest-houses, development of tourist centres and their publicity were included. Foreign tourist arrivals registered about 15 per cent compound annual growth during the period.

Fifth Plan

The Fifth Plan made a provision of Rs. 2,362 crores for the Department of Tourism and Rs. 1,712 crores for the ITDC. The programme of the Department included loans to the hotel industry in the Private sector, integrated development of tourist resorts at Kovalam (Goa), Gulmarg and Kulu-Manali and construction of a number of youth hostels, tourist bungalows and forest lodges. The programmes under the ITDC included expansion of hotels and construction of travellers' lodges, motels and cottages. In the State sector, an outlay of Rs. 32.21 crores was made, making the total outlay of Rs. 73.95 crores. The outlay in the Fifth Plan was more than double the amount provided for in the Fourth Plan.

Sixth Plan

During the Fifth Plan, the major objectives of the investment in the tourism sector were to optimize the use of the existing capacity and to maximize the return on investments. In the development of tourism, 'selected travel circuit' approach was followed. Close coordination in regard to provision of facilities in the Central, State and Private sectors in the same areas and locations was to be maintained to obtain optimum results from the available resources. This approach would give flexibility in offering a mixed tourism package, help to recognize traffic and promote repeat visits to increase the overall volume of traffic. The broad division of responsibility between the Central and State Governments continued to be on the basis that larger schemes meant for foreign tourists were to be cared for by the Central Government and the schemes meant for domestic tourists were to be developed by the State Government concerned.

An outlay of Rs. 187.46 crores was provided in the Plan for the period 1980-85, which included Rs. 115.46 crores for the State sector, Rs. 72 crores for the Central sector. Of the Central sector share, Rs. 30 crores were provided to the Department of Tourism and the balance to the ITDC. In the programmes of the Department of Tourism, emphasis on beach and hill resort development, wildlife and cultural tourism, training and overseas promotion was given much importance. The private sector too was involved. Room capacity of the ITDC hotels was improved significantly.

It was also planned to request respective ministries to augment tourism infrastructural facilities that were under their respective purview. Investment of the tune of Rs. 5,100 crores in the Indian Railways, Rs. 2,252 crores in the airways and Rs. 4,625 crores in the roadways was decided upon, which would help the tourism industry.

Seventh-Tenth Plan

For the Seventh-Tenth Plan period, the aim was to achieve an annual growth rate of seven per cent in the foreign tourist arrivals. It would be possible to achieve this largest, given the desired improvement in the infrastructural facilities and a certain degree of relaxation in the policies and procedures regarding the admittance of foreign tourist into the country.

The main objectives for the tourism sector in the Seventh-Tenth Plan were: (i) faster development of tourism; (ii) according the status of an industry to tourism; (iii) redefining the role of public and private sectors to ensure that the private sector investment is encouraged in developing the tourism and the public sector investment is focussed mainly on the development of support infrastructure; (iv) exploiting tourism potential to support local handicrafts and other creative arts and to promote national integration.

The main thrust areas for the development of tourism in the Seventh-Tenth Plan were as follows:

(i) Development of selected tourism circuit/centres which are popular with the tourists, instead of spreading limited resources thin over a large number of circuits/centres;

(ii) Diversification of tourism from the traditional sight-seeing tours centred primarily on the places of cultural tourism interest, towards the more rapidly growing holiday tourism market within the framework of the country's milieu with a conscious attention to the aesthetic, environmental and socio-cultural implications of tourism projects;

(iii) Development of non-traditional areas such as (a) trekking, (b) winter sports, (c) wildlife tourism, and (d) beach resort tourism, to exploit the tourism resources of Himalayas, the sandy beaches, abundant sunshine and wildlife to attract more tourists and lengthen their period of stay in the country;

(iv) Restoration and balanced development of national heritage. For exploiting the advantages of India's unique place and as a cultural tourism destination and for utilizing tourism as a major force supporting the conservation of the national heritage;

(v) Exploration of new tourist generating markets, particularly in the Middle-eastern, South-eastern and East Asian countries, who have a broad spectrum of cultural affinity with India, providing a scope for larger ethnic tourism;

(vi) Launching of a National Image Building and Marketing Plan in key markets by pooling resources of the various public and private agencies instead of independent and disjointed efforts undertaken by diverse organizations to project a better image of the country which would yield abundant fallout for tourism growth and also be of advantage in trade and commerce.

(vii) Provision of inexpensive but clean accommodation at different places of tourist interests;

(viii) Streamlining of facilitation procedure for passengers at the airports, so that formalities and the time taken to complete them is minimal.

An outlay of Rs. 626.16 crores was provided in the Tenth Plan, which included Rs. 338.68 crores in the Central sector and Rs. 287.48 crores in the State sector. In addition, quite large investments were expected to be made by the Private sector.

Although the strategy in the Tenth Plan would be to diversify foreign tourism to other primary sources of interest, due attention would be given to meet the requirement of cultural tourism. High priority was given to the development of requisite facilities at more important centres such as Mathura, Agra, Varanasi, Rajgir, Brajkhoonsi, etc.

Sustained efforts were made for the development of Buddhist Pilgrimage Tourism, for which a great potential existed. The programmes in the Seventh Plan included integrated development of major Buddhist Pilgrimage Centres and provision of suitable accommodation, pavilion, mediation parks, etc. The Tenth Plan included augmentation of accommodation in order to promote the wildlife tourism and adventure tourism.

Strategy for Tourism Development in the 11th Five Year Plan of Government of India

During the 10th Five Year Plan, a doubled pronged strategy of upgrading the tourism infrastructure and vigorous marketing under the banner of 'Incredible India' campaign was followed to position India as a global brand. The following four-point journey was sought to be achieved to a large extent among the target tourists and in source markets:

- From non-awareness to awareness,
- From awareness to interest,
- From interest to desire, and
- From desire to final action i.e. booking a holiday.

The efforts made during the 10th Plan are now resulting into India registering a growth of 78% in foreign tourist arrivals and a growth of 122% in foreign exchange earnings in 5 year's time. Share of India in world arrivals, which was just 0.37% in 2001, is likely to be 0.53% in 2006. It has been estimated that about 12.5 million additional jobs have been created in the tourism sector during the 10th Five Year Plan.

The Working Group on Tourism for the 11th Five Year Plan 2007-12, set up by the Planning Commission, felt that keeping in view all variables in the environment, the product opportunities, the market scenario, the Indian planning and national objectives, following quantifiable goals may be set for the 11th Plan for India tourism.

International Tourism

Visitation

Achieve international visitor level of 10 million in 2011, at the end of 11th Plan.

Source markets

Diversify principal source markets to include countries such as South Africa, Israel, Spain, China, Japan, South Korea, Australia, Brazil, etc. which offer high growth potential and from where present level of inbound tourist is below par.

Concentrate on countries like South Africa, Mauritius, Kenya, Malaysia, Fiji, etc. with a large Indian Diasporas for greater visitations for those countries. Similarly target the PIOs and NRIs elsewhere to create greater resonance in them to visit the country of their origin and discover their roots. Target the 'Baby Boomers' group in Europe and North America by creating in them the desire to discover one of the oldest civilizations of the world and to enjoy the plurality of cultural enjoyments which this country has to offer.

Revenues

Maintain and increase per capita spending of international visitors.

Attract higher quality tourists, increasing per head spending, resulting in higher revenues. Concentrate on Cruise tourism, MICE sector which are considered to be higher revenue generating sectors of tourism.

Seasonality

Reduce the Seasonality in international tourist arrivals by targeting markets such as Australia, Spain, etc. It should be ensured that the drop in arrivals during 'lean season' is not more than 15% of the annual average.

Average Length of Stay

Maintain and initiate measures to ensure that the duration of stay is sustained, if not extended.

Purpose of Visit

Retain focus on Leisure Travellers. Promote business related travel, including MICE market by promoting Convention Centres of international standards in major cities or at major tourist centres.

Expenditure

Prepare strategies to increase per capita expenditure on shopping and other non-accommodation, non-transportation heads, to match international benchmark of 30%.

Domestic Tourism

Visitation

Achieve a level of 760 million for domestic tourist visits by the year 2011, the end of 11th Plan at an annual average growth of 12%. Complement international travel with domestic travel in order that the seasonality is eliminated. Promote greater dispersal of domestic visitations in order to spread the benefits of tourism to all areas.

Other Goals

Accommodation units

Increase approved quality accommodation units from the current level of about 100,000 rooms to at least 200,000 rooms by 2011, to meet the increased requirement of tourism. Set up hotels on the surplus land with Airport Authority of India near international Airports as the international practices. Promote development of budget hotels at the surplus Railway Land at specified Railway Stations. Create land banks in the States and encourage Single Window facility for the investors in tourism projects.

In order to achieve all these objectives, the Working Group felt that it was necessary that the momentum generated in tourism sector during the 10th Plan period is sustained, so that the full potential of the sector, as a major engine of economic growth, is realized, and the benefits of associated development reach all segments of the society. The recommendation of the Group was to adopt and apply sustainable practices and principles, and identify and resolve the constraints. The Working Group also felt it necessary that beside development of world class infrastructure and launching aggressive marketing campaigns, access and connectivity to India need be improved; new forms of tourism like rural tourism, cultural tourism, adventure tourism, cruise tourism, MICE tourism and medical tourism are taken up with renewed zeal and efforts; India is made a full year destination rather than a Oct.-March destination by diminishing the seasonality factor and promoting the Himalayas and the beaches during summers and the coastal regions during the monsoons; and India's competitiveness as a preferred destination is enhanced with rationalization of taxes, liberalization of visa regime, improvement of airports, removing barriers to travels, enhancing tourist safety and security, improving signages, etc. To achieve all these, the following six key strategic objectives need to be kept in view :

i. Positioning and maintaining tourism development as a national priority activity

- Provide effective linkages and close coordination between various Departments and Ministries of Government;
- Plan and implement a professionally managed integrated communications strategy to increase awareness about tourism and its social and economic impact on the society.

ii. Enhancing and maintaining the competitiveness of India as a tourist destination

- Take effective steps for easier and faster availability of visas;
- Increasing air connectivity and seat capacity from major overseas markets;
- Improving facilities and quality of services at international and major domestic airports;
- Rationalization of taxes;
- Removing restrictions like RAP/PAP/ILP.

iiii. Improving India's existing tourism products further and expanding these to meet new market requirements

- Develop sustainable beach, coastal and cruise tourism;
- Package and market India's wide variety of traditional cuisines;
- Encourage adventure and rural tourism;
- Develop and promote round-the-year tourism;
- Pursue the Medical Tourism vigorously;
- Take advantage of MICE segment;

iv. Creation of world class infrastructure

- Identify travel circuits for development as international standard destinations;

- Construction and improvement of highways for good connectivity with tourist destinations;
- Introduction of special tourist trains, establishment of budget hotels on surplus land available with Railways and Airport Authority of India.

v. Developing strategies for sustained and effective marketing plans and programmes

- Maintain and develop the India tourism brand position established with the 'Incredible India' campaign;
- Evolve and maintain a system of market research activities in India's major source markets to continuously receive, analyze and respond to information on pricing, security issues, health, safety and quality of tourism services and products etc.;
- Make use of the various technological tools, including the internet, for advertising for greater and wider impact. Further, encourage e-commerce portals to extend effective marketing support to small and medium enterprises and also offer competitive packages.

vi. Developing Human Resources and Capacity Building of Service Providers

The Working Group on Tourism, therefore, felt that in view of the multi-faceted aspects of tourism, sub-groups may be constituted consisting of experts in different fields to deliberate on identified key segments in a focussed manner, and come up with recommendations for accelerating the growth rate in the tourism sector.

REFERENCES

Badan, B.S. and Bhatt Harish (2007): *Tourism and Economic Development*, Commonwealth Publishers, New Delhi, p. 19.

Bhardwaj, B. (1994): India's Declining Share in Tourism; *The Hindustan Times*, 29 August, New Delhi, p. 7.

Bhardwaj, B. (1994): How to Promote Tourism; *The Hindustan Times*, 22 December, New Delhi, p. 8.

Bhardwaj, B., (1995): Planning for Tourism; *The Hindustan Times*, 27 March, New Delhi.

Bhatia, A.K. (2007) : *Tourism Development : Principles and Practices*, 2nd Revised Edition, Sterling Publishers Private Limited, New Delhi-20.

http://www.indiaheritage.org/creative/creative_metal_work.htm

Patil, P.B. (2006): *Tourism Development*, Current Publications, Agra, pp. 29-33.

Patil, P.B. (2006) : *Tourism Development : Problem and Prospects*, Current Publications, Agra-10 (U.P.)

Report of the Working Group on Tourism (2007-12): *11th Five Year Plan*, Ministry of Tourism, Government of Bihar.

Selvan, M. (Feb., 1993): *Tourism Under Plans;* Monthly Commentary; (Blue Supplement), New Delhi, p. 1.

Singh Asha, Gupta, M.S. and Shandilya (2010) : *Banking and Financial Sector Reforms in India*, Serials Publications, New Delhi-2.

Tourism in India (June, 1994): Monthly Commentary (Blue Supplement), New Delhi, p. 1.

Tourism, (June, 1994): Need for Aggressive Marketing Strategy; Monthly Commentary, New Delhi, p. 3.

Verma, S.B., Jiloka, S.K. and Thryambakam P. (2006) : *Rural Tourism and Tribal Development*, Deep & Deep Publications Pvt. Ltd., New Delhi-27.

4

Profile of Bihar

Introduction

Bihar is known as major state in eastern India. Bihar is the 12th largest state in terms of geographical size 99,200 km^2 and 3rd largest by population. Close to 85 per cent of the population lives in the rural countryside. Almost 58 per cent of Biharis are below the age of 25, which is the highest in India. Bihar lies mid-way between the humid West Bengal in the east and the subhumid Uttar Pradesh in the west which provides it with a

Fig. 4.1 : Tourist Map of Bihar

transitional position in respect of climate, economy and culture. It is bounded by the country Nepal in the north and by Jharkhand in the south. The Bihar plain is divided into two unequal halves by the river Ganga which flows through the middle for west to east. Bihar has notified forest area of 67,645.14 km^2, which is 7.1 per cent of the geographical area.

Nalanda was a centre of learning established by the 5th century BC in Bihar, India, one of the first great Medieval University (Asia) in recorded history. The 2nd century Buddhist Philosopher Nagarjuna was based there. Hindi and Urdu are the official languages of the state, although the majority of the people speak one of the Bihar languages (once considered to be dialects of Hindi)—Bhojpuri, Magadhi, Maithili or Angika. Ancient Bihar, known as Magadha, was a center of power, learning and culture in ancient and classical India. From Magadha arose India's first greatest empire, the Maurya empire as well as one of the world's greatest pacifist religions, Buddhism. Magadha empires, notably under the Maurya and Gupta dynasties, unified large parts of South Asia under a central rule. Its capital Patna, earlier known as Patliputra, was an important centre of Indian civilization.

Today Bihar lags behind the other Indian states in human and economic development terms, whilst ethnic Biharies living in other states of India are victims of racist hate, crimes and prejudice. Economists and social scientists claim that this is a direct result of the skewed policies of the Central Government like freight equalization policy, its apathy towards Bihar, lack of Bihari sub-nationalism (resulting in no spokesperson for the state), and the Permanent Settlement of 1793 by the British East India Company. The current state government has however made significant strides in improving governance. The improved governance has led to an economic revival in the state through increased investment in infrastructure, better health care facilities, greater emphasis on education, and a reduction in crime and corruption. Indian and global business and economic leaders feel that Bihar now has good opportunity for sustainable economic development and as such have shown interest in investing in the state.

Etymology of the Name

The name Bihar is derived from the Sanskrit word Vihâr (Devanagari) which means "abode". The word Vihâr is itself derived from the word Brahmavihâr meaning "Brahma abidings", or "Sublime attitudes". The region roughly encompassing the present state was dotted with Buddhist Vihara, which were the abodes of Buddhist monks in the ancient and medieval period.

History

Bihar was called "Magadha"in ancient times. From Magadha arose two traditions—Jainism and Buddhism. The greatest Indian empire, the Maurya empire, originated from Magadha, with its capital at Patliputra (modern Patna) in 325 BC. The Mauryan Emperor, Ashoka, who was born in Patliputra (Patna) is believed to be one of the greatest rulers in the history of India and the world. After seeing all the carnage that war causes he was placed on the path of Lord Buddha by his spiritual guide Manjushri. According to ideologist A.L. Basham, the author of the book *The Wonder that was India,* "The age in which true history appeared in India was one of great intellectual and spiritual ferment. Mystics and sophists of all kinds roamed through the Ganga valley, all advocating some form of mental discipline and asceticism as a means to salvation; but the age of the Buddha, when many of the best minds were abandoning their homes and professions for a life of asceticism, was also a time of advance in commerce and politics. It produced not only philosophers and ascetics, but also merchant princes and men of actions."

Bihar remained an important place of power, culture and education during the next one thousand years. The Gupta Empire, which again originated from Magadha in 240 CE, is referred to as the Golden Age of India in science, mathematics, astronomy, religion and Indian philosophy. The peace and prosperity created under leadership of Guptas enabled the pursuit of alongside with the Han Dynasty, Tang Dynasty and

Roman Empire as a model of a classical civilization. The capital of Gupta empire was Pataliputra, present day Patna. The Vikramshila and Nalanda University, writers believe the period between the 400 CE and 1000 CE saw gains by Hinduism at the expense of Buddhism. Although the Hindu kings gave much grants to the Buddhist monks for building Brahmaviharas. A national Geographic edition reads, "The essential tenets of Buddhism and Hinduism arose from similar ideas best described in the Upanishads, a set of Hindu treatises set down in India largely between the eighth and fourth centuries B.C."

The Buddhism of Magadha was finally swept away by the Muslim invasion under Muhammad Bin Bakhtiar Khilji, during which many of the viaharas and the famed universities of Nalanda and Vikramshila were destroyed, and thousands of Buddhist monks were massacred in 12th century CE.

The region saw a brief period of glory for six years (1540-1546 CE) during the rule of Sher Shah Suri, who built the longest road of the Indian subcontinent, the Grand Trunk Road. The economic reforms carried out by Sher Shah, like the introduction of Rupee and Custom Duties, is still used in the Republic of India. He revived the city of Patna, where he built up his headquarters.

During 1557-1576, Akbar, the Mughal emperor, annexed Bihar and Bengal to his empire. With the decline of the Mughals, Bihar passed under the control of the Nawabs of Bengal. Thus, the medieval period was mostly one of anonymous provincial existence.

The 10th and the last Guru of Sikhism, Guru Govind Singh was born in Patna. After the Battle of Buxar (1764), the British East India Company obtained the *diwani* rights (rights to administer, and collect revenue or tax) for Bihar, Bengal and Orissa. From this point, Bihar remained a part of the Bengal Presidency of the British Raj until 1912, when the province of Bihar and Orissa was carved out as a separate province. In 1935, certain portions of Bihar were recognized into the separate province of Orissa.

Babu Kunwar Singh of Jagdishpur and his army, as well as countless other persons from Bihar, contributed to the India's First War of Independence (1857), also called the Sepoy Mutiny by some historians. Resurgence in the history of Bihar that Mahatma Gandhi launched his pioneering civil-disobedience movement, Champaran Satyagraha. Bhumihar Brahmins in Champaran had earlier revolted against indigo cultivation in 1914 (at Pipra) and 1916 (Turkaulia) and Pandit Raj Kumar Shukla took Mahatma Gandhi to Champaran and the Champaran Satyagraha began. Raj Kumar Shukla drew the attention of Mahatma Gandhi to the exploitation of the peasants by European indigo planters. Champaran Satyagraha received the spontaneous support from many Biharis, including Sri Krishna Sinha, the first Chief Minister of Bihar, Rajendra Prasad, who became the first President of India and Anugrah Narayan Sinha who ultimately became the first Deputy Chief Minister-cum-Finance Minister of Bihar.

In North and Central Bihar, peasants' movement was an important side effect of the freedom movement. The Kisan Sabha movement started in Bihar under the leadership of Swami Sahajanand Saraswati who had formed in 1929 the Bihar Provincial Kisan Sabha (BPKS) in order to mobilize peasant grievances against the *zamindari* attacks on their occupancy rights. Gradually, the peasant movement intensified and spread across the rest of India. All these radical developments on the peasant front culminated in the formation of the All India Kisan Sabha (AIKS) at the Lucknow Session of the Indian National Congress in April 1936 with Swami Sahajanand Saraswati elected as its first President. This movement aimed at overthrowing the feudal (zamindari) system instituted by Britishers. It was being led by Swami Sahajanand Saraswati and his followers Pandit Yamuna Karjee, Rahul Sankrityayan, Pandit Karyanand Sharma, Baba Nagarjun and others. Pandit Yamuna Karjee along with Rahul Sankrityayan and a few others started publishing a Hindi weekly *Hunkar* from Bihar, in 1940. *Hunkar* later became the mouthpiece of the peasant movement and the agrarian movement in Bihar and was instrumental in spreading the movement.

Bihar's contribution in the Indian freedom struggle has been immense with outstanding leaders like Swami Sahajanand Saraswati, Dr Rajendra Prasad, Sri Krishna Sinha, Dr Anugrah Narayan Sinha, Brajkishore Prasad, Mulana Muzharul Haque, Jayaprakash Narayan, Satyendra Narayan Sinha, Bsawon Singh, Rameshwar Prasad Sinha, Yogendra Shukla, Baikuntha Shukla. They worked for India's freedom relentlessly and helped in the upliftment of the underprivileged masses. Khudiram Bose, Upendra Narayan Jha "Azad", Prafulla Chaki and Baikuntha Shukla were active in revolutionary movement in Bihar.

The state of Jharkhand was carved out of Bihar in the year 2000. 2005 Bihar assembly elections ended the 15 years of continuous RJD rule in the state, giving way to NDA led by Nitish Kumar. Bihari migrant workers have faced violence and prejudice in many parts of India, like Maharashtra, Punjab and Assam.

Geography

Bihar is mainly a vast stretch of very fertile flat land. It is drained by the Ganges river, including northern tributaries Gandak and Koshi originating in the Nepal Himalayas and the Bagmati originating in the Kathmandu Valley that regularly flood parts of the Bihar plains. The total area covered by the state of Bihar is 94,163 km^2. The state is located between 21°-58'-10" N ~ 27°-31'-15" N latitude and between 82°-19'-50" E ~ 88°-17'-40" E longitude. Its average elevation above sea level is 173 feet (53m). The Bihar plain is divided into two unequal halves by the River Ganga which flows through the middle from west to east. Other Ganges Tributaries are the Son, Budhi Gandak, Chandan, Orhani and Falgu. The Himalayas begin at foothills a short distance inside Nepal but influence Bihar's landforms, climate, hydrology and culture. Central parts of Bihar have some small hills, for example the Rajgir hills. The Himalayan Mountains are to the north of Bihar. To the south is the Chota Nagpur plateau, which was part of Bihar until 2000 but now is part of a separate state called Jharkhand. Bihar has notified forest area of 6,76,414 km^2, which is 7.1 per cent of its geographical area.

Climate

Bihar is mildly cold in the winter (the lowest temperatures being around 5 to 10 degrees Celsius; 40 to 50 degrees Fahrenheit). Winter months are December and January. It is hot in the summer (with average highs around 35-40° Celsius; 95-105 Fahrenheit). April to mid-June are the hot months. The monsoon months of June, July, August, and September see good rainfall. October and November and February and March have pleasant weather.

Bihar has notified forest area of 6,764.14 km^2, which is 7.1 per cent of its geographical area. The sub-Himalayan foothill of Someshwar and Dun ranges in Champaran district another belt of moist deciduous forests. These also consist of scrub, grass and reeds. Here the rainfall is above 1,600 mm and thus promotes luxuriant Sal forests in the favoured areas. The hot and dry summer gives the deciduous forests. The most important trees are Shorea robusta (Sal), Shisham, Cedrela toona, Khair, and Semal. Thus type of forests also occurs in Saharasa District and Purnia district. Shorea robusta (Sal), Dispyros melanoxylon (Kendu), Boswellia serrata (Salai), Terminalia tomentose (Asan), Terminalia bellayoica (Bahera), Terminalia arjuna (Arjun), Pterocarpus marsupium (Paisar), Madhuca indica (Mahua) are the common flora across the forest of Bihar.

The Ganges river dolphin, or "susu" occur in the Ganga and Brahmaputra, South Asia's largest river system. It can now be considered amongst the most endangered mammals of the region.

The Ganges River dolphin ranges from 2.3 to 2.6 meters in length. The tail fluke is on average 46 cm in width. Females are larger than males. The colour of this dolphin varies from lead-coloured to black. The undersides are lighter in colour, the rostrum is 18 to 21 cm in length and the forehead is steep and rises abruptly from the base of the snout. The dorsal fin is rudimentary and ridge-like, and the ends of the pectoral fins are squared instead of tapered. The neck is visibly constricted and the blowhole is a longitudinal slit. There are 28 to 29 teeth on either side of the jaw. The eye and optic nerve of the Ganges river dolphin are degenerate. The eye lacks a lens and is therefore incapable of forming images on the retina. However, it functions in light-detection. It is believed that the lack of a true visual apparatus in the river dolphin is related to its habitat; the water in which it lives is so muddied that vision in essentially useless.

Valmiki National Park, West Champaran district, covering about 800 km^2 of forest, is the 18th tiger Reserve of India and is ranked fourth in terms of density of tiger population. It has diverse landscapes, sheltering rich wildlife habitats and floral and faunal composition, with the prime protected carnivores.

Demography of Bihar

Bihar is the third most populated state of India with total population of 82,998,509 (43,243,795 male and 39,754,714 female—Table 4.1 and Fig. 4.2). Nearly 90 per cent of Bihar's

Table 4.1 : Population Growth

Census Population	*Total Population*	*Male Population*	*Female Population*	*% ±*
1951	29,085,000			–
1961	34,841,000			19.8%
1971	42,126,000			20.9%
1981	52,303,000			24.2%
1991	64,531,000			23.4%
2001	82,999,000	43,243,795	39,754,714	28.6%
2011P*	106,200,000	55,330,270	50,869,800	
2021P*	135,800,000	70,751,800	65,048,200	
2031P*	173,800,000	90,549,800	83,250,200	

Source : Census of India, 2001.
* Population Projection

population lives in rural area. Almost 58 per cent of Biharis are below 25 years of age, which is highest in India. Hinduism is practiced by 83.2% of the population and forms the majority religion in the state. Islam is practiced by 16.5% of the population, and other religions less than 0.5%. Since ancient times Bihar has attracted migrants and settlers including Aryans, Bengalis, Turks from Central Asia, Persian, Afghans and Punjabi Hindu Refugees during the Partition of India in 1947. Bihar has a total literacy rate of 47% (59.7% for males and 33.1% for females).

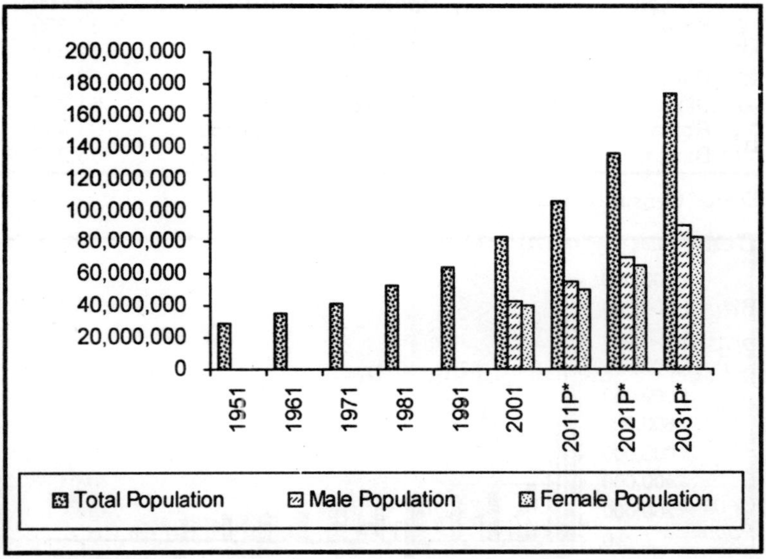

Fig. 4.2 : Population Growth

* Population Projection

Table 4.2 and Fig. 4.3 shows the population of major districts in Bihar which is very important for Tourism point of view.

The constitutional head of the Government of Bihar is the Governor, who is appointed by the President of India. The real executive power rests with the Chief Minister and the cabinet. The political party or the coalition of political parties having a majority in the Legislative Assembly forms the Government.

Table 4.2 : Population of Major Districts in Bihar

Sl. No.	*Districts*	*Total Population*	*Male Population*	*Female Population*
1	Patna	1,697,976	922,971	755,005
2	Gaya	385,432	204,483	180,949
3	Bhagalpur	340,767	182,806	157,961
4	Muzaffarpur	305,525	164,000	141,525
5	Darbhanga	267,348	142,377	124,971
6	Nalanda	232,071	122,019	110,052
7	Bhojpur	203,380	109,867	95,513
8	Munger	188,050	101,264	88,786
9	Saran	179,190	95,494	83,696
10	Katihar	175,199	93,617	81,582
11	Purnia	171,687	92,826	78,851
12	Bihar Sarif	131,176	69,419	61,757
13	Rohtas	131,172	69,682	61,490
14	Banka	35,416	19,242	16,213

Source: Census of India, 2001.

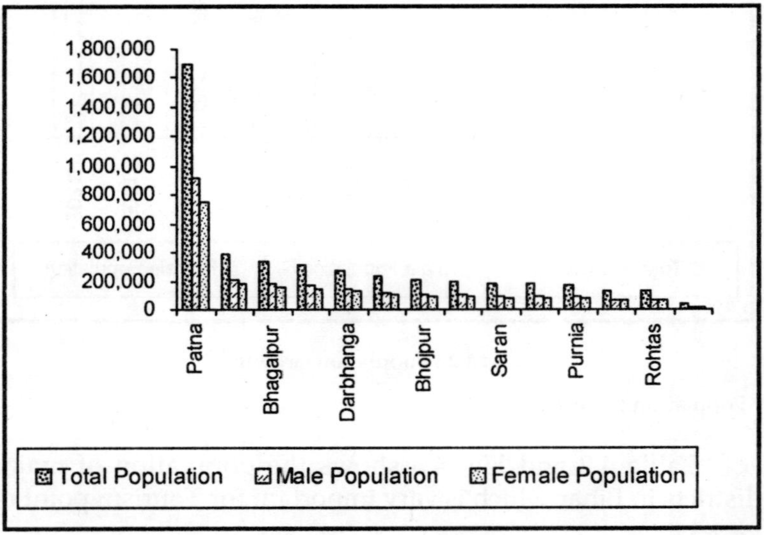

Fig. 4.3: Population of Major Districts in Bihar

The current incumbent, Chief Minister Nitish Kumar, succeeded Rabri Devi, wife of the Former Chief Minister Lalu Prasad Yadav (Former Cabinet Minister for Railways) in 2005.

The head of the bureaucracy of the State is called the Chief Secretary. Under him is a hierarchy of officials drawn from the Indian Administrative Service, Indian Police Service, and different wings of the State Civil Services. The judiciary is headed by the Chief Justice. Bihar has a High Court which has been functioning since 1916. All the branches of the government are located in the state capital, Patna.

The state is divided into 9 divisions and 38 districts, for administrative purposes. The various districts included in the divisions—Patna, Tirhut, Saran, Darbhanga, Kosi, Purnia, Bhagalpur, Munger and Magadh (Table 4.3).

Table 4.3 : Major Cities/Districts in Bihar

Division	*Headquarters*	*Districts*
Bhagalpur	Bhagalpur	Banka, Bhagalpur.
Darbhanga	Darbhanga	Begusarai, Darbhanga, Madhubani, Samastipur.
Kosi	Saharsa	Madhepura, Saharsa, Supaul.
Magadh	Gaya	Arwal, Aurangabad, Gaya, Jehanabad, Nawada.
Munger	Munger	Jamui, Khagaria, Munger, Lakhisarai, Sheikhpura
Patna	Patna	Bhojpur, Buxar, Kaimur, Patna, Rohtas, Nalanda.
Purnia	Purnia	Araria, Katihar, Kishanganj, Purnia.
Saran	Chapra	Gopalganj, Saran, Siwan.
Tirhut	Muzaffarpur	East Champaran, Muzaffarpur, Sheohar, Sitamarhi, Vaishali, West Champaran.

Bihar was an important part of India's struggle for independence. Gandhi became the mass leader only after the Champaran Satyagraha that he launched on the repeated request of a local leader, Raj Kumar Shukla, he was supported by great illumanaries like Rajendra Prasad, Anugrah Narayan Sinha and Brajkishore Prasad. After independence also, when India was falling into an autocratic rule during the regime of Indira Gandhi, the main thrust to the movement to hold elections came from Bihar under the leadership of Jaya Prakash Narayan. This has two consequences:

The identity of Bihar (from the word Bihar meaning monasteries) representing a glorious past was lost. Its voice often used to get lost in the din of regional clamor of other states, specially the linguistic states like Uttar Pradesh, Madhya Pradesh etc.

Bihar gained an anti-establishment image. The establishment oriented press often projected the state as indisciplined and anarchist.

Since the regional identity was slowly getting sidelined, its place was taken up by caste based politics, power initially being in the hands of the Brahmins, Bhumihar Brahmins and Rajputs. After independence the power was shared by the two great Gandhians—Dr Sri Krishna Sinha who later became the first Chief Minister of Bihar and Dr Anugrah Narayan Sinha who decidedly was next to him in the cabinet and served as the first Deputy Chief Minister-cum-Finance Minister of Bihar. In late 60s death of late Mr. Lalit Narayan Mishra (who was killed by a hand grenade attack for which central leadership is blamed most of the time) pronounced the end of indigenous work oriented mass leaders. For two decades Congress ruled the state with the help of puppet Chief Minister's hand in glove with the Central Government (Mrs. Indira Gandhi) ignoring the welfare of the people of the state. It was the time when a prominent leader like Satyendra Narayan Sinha took sides with the Janata Party and deserted Congress from where his political roots originated, following the ideological differences with the Congress. Idealism did assert itself in the politics from time to time, viz., 1977 when a wave defeated the entrenched Congress Party and then again in 1989 when Janata Dal came to power on an anti-corruption wave. In between, the socialist movement tried to break the stranglehold of the *status quo* under the leadership of Mahamaya Prasad Sinha and Karpoori Thakur. Unfortunately, this could not flourish, partly due to the impractical idealism of these leaders and partly due to the machinations of the central leaders of the Congress Party who felt threatened by a large politically aware state. The Communist Movement in Bihar was led by veteran communist leaders like Pandit Karyanand Sharma, Indradeep Sinha, Chandrashekhar Singh and others.

Janata Dal came to power in the state in 1990 on the back of its victory at the national stage in 1989. Lalu Prasad Yadav became Chief Minister after winning the race of legislative party leadership by a slender margin against Ram Sundar Das, a former Chief Minister from the Janata Party and close to eminent Janata Party leaders like Chandrashekhar and S.N. Sinha. Later, Lalu Prasad Yadav gained popularity with the masses through a series of populate and populist measures. The principled socialists, Nitish Kumar included, gradually left him and Lalu Prasad Yadav was the uncrowned king by 1995 as both Chief Minister as well as the President of his party, Rashtriya Janata Dal. He was a charismatic leader who had people's support and Bihar had got such a person as the Chief Minister after a long time. But he couldn't bring the derailed wagon of development of the state on to the track. When corruption charges got serious, he quit the post of Chief Minister but anointed his wife as the Chief Minister and ruled through proxy. In this period, the administration deteriorated fast.

By 2004, 14 years after Lalu's victory, the *Economist* magazine said that "Bihar had become a byword for the worst of India, of widespread and inescapable poverty, of corrupt politicians indistinguishable from mafia dons they patronize, caste-ridden social order that has retained the worst feudal cruelties." In 2005, the World Bank believed that issues faced by the state was "economous" because of "persistent poverty, complex social stratification, unsatisfactory infrastructure and weak government."

In 2005, as disaffection reached a crescendo among the masses, middle classes included, the RJD was voted out of power and Lalu Prasad Yadav lost an election to a coalition headed by his previous ally and now rival Nitish Kumar. Nitish Kumar has regained Bihar's true identity, which is the place from where people who changed the world come like Gautam Buddha or Asoka or Sher Shah Suri or the Sikh Gurus. People love him and he is desperate to put Bihar in the mainstream development path. Despite the separation of financially richer Jharkhand, Bihar has actually seen more positive growth in recent years.

Currently, there are two main political formations: the NDA which comprises Janata Dal and Bharatiya Janata Party and the Rashtriya Janata Dal led coalition which also has the Indian National Congress. There are myriad other political formations. Ram Vilas Paswan led Lok Janshakti Party is a constituent of the UPA at the centre, but does not see eye to eye with Lalu Prasad Yadav's RJD in Bihar. Bihar People's Party is a small political formation in north Bihar. The Communist Party of India had a strong presence in Bihar at one time, but has got weakened now. CPM and Forward Bloc have minor presence. Ultra left parties like CPML, Party Unity etc. have presence in pockets and are at war with the state.

Economy

The economy of Bihar is largely service oriented, but it also has a significant agricultural base. The state also has a small industrial sector. As of 2008, agriculture accounts for 35%, industry 9% and service 55% of the economy of the state Manufacturing has performed very poorly in the state between 2002-2007, with an average growth rate of 0.38% compared to India's 7.8%. Bihar has the lowest GDP per capita in India but there are pockets of higher than the average per capita income. Between 1999 and 2008, GDP grew by 5.1% a year, which was below the Indian average of 7.3%. More recently, Bihar's state GDP recorded a growth of 18% between 2006-2007, and stood at 9,42,510 Crores Rupees ($21 billion nominal GDP- Table 4.4 and Fig. 4.4). This makes Bihar the fastest growing major state. In actual terms, Bihar state GDP is ranked 14th out of 28 states. Corruption is an important hurdle for the government to overcome according to "Transparency International India", who highlighted Bihar as the Union's most corrupt state in a 2005 report. Despite many recent economic gains, significant challenges remain to do business in the state and the government has also stated that combating corruption is now the biggest challenge facing the administration. Life expectancy in Bihar (61 years) is almost on par with the national life expectancy of 62.7 years.

Table 4.4 : Gross State Domestic Product

Year	*Gross State Domestic Product (millions in Indian Rupees)*
1980	73,530
1985	142,950
1990	264,290
1995	244,830
2000	469,430
2008	568,450

Source : Bihar Economic Survey, 2008-09.

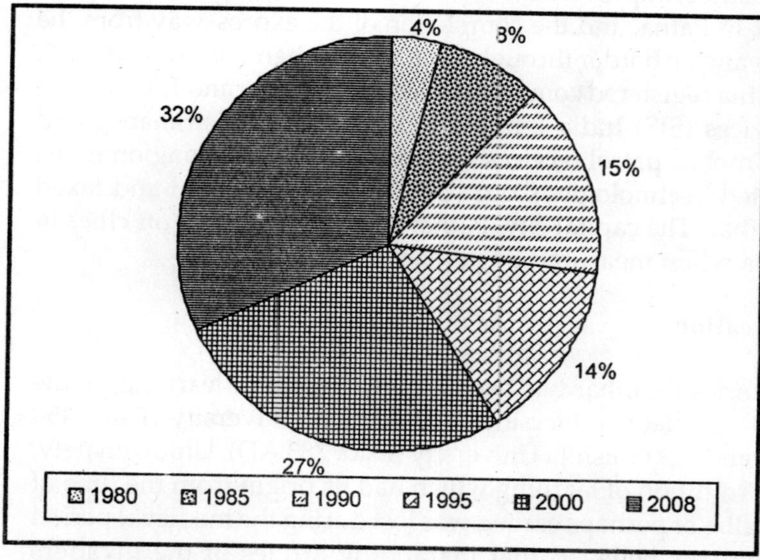

Fig. 4.4 : Gross State Domestic Product (millions in Indian Rupees)

Bihar has significant levels of production for the products of mango, guava, litchi, pineapple, brinjal, cauliflower, bhindi, and cabbage in India. Despite the state's leading role in food production, investment in irrigation and other agriculture facilities has been inadequate in the past. Historically, the sugar and vegetable oil industries were flourishing sectors of Bihar. Until the mid-fifties, 25% of India's sugar output was from Bihar, Dalmianagar was a large agro-industrial town. There have been attempts to industrialize the sate between 1950 and

1980: an oil refinery in Barauni, a motor scooter plant at Fatuha, and a power plant at Muzaffarpur. However, these were forced to shut down due to Central Government policy which neutralized the strategic advantages of Bihar. Hajipur, near Patna, remains a major industrial town in the state, linked to the capital city through the Ganga Bridge and good road infrastructure.

The Finance Ministry has given top priority to create investment opportunities for big industrial houses like Reliance. Further development have taken place in the growth of small industries, improvements in IT infrastructure, the new software park in Patna, and the completion of the expressway from the Purvanchal border through Bihar to Jharkhand. In August 2008, a Patna registered company called the Security and Intelligence Services (SIS) India Limited took over the Australian guard and mobile patrol services business of American conglomerate, United Technologies Corp (UTC). SIS is registered and taxed in Bihar. The capital city, Patna, is one of the better off cities in India when measured by per capita income.

Education

Historically, Bihar has been a major centre of learning, home to the ancient universities of Nalanda University (Estd. 450 CE) and Vikramshila University (Estd. 783 AD). Unfortunately, that tradition of learning which had its origin from the time of Buddha or perhaps earlier, was lost during the medieval period when it is believed that marauding armies of the invaders destroyed these centers of learning.

Bihar saw a revival of its education system during the later part of the British rule when they established Patna University (Estd. 1917) which is 7th oldest University of the Indian sub-continent. Some other centers of high learning established by British rule are Patna College (Estd. 1839), Bihar School of Engineering (Estd. 1900, now National Institute of Technology, Patna), Prince of Wales Medical College (Estd. 1925, now Patna Medical College and Hospital), Science College, Patna (Estd. 1928) and many more.

After independence Bihar lost the pace in terms of establishing center of education. Modern Bihar has a grossly inadequate educational infrastructure creating a huge mismatch between demand and supply. This problem further gets compounded by the growing aspirations of the people and an increase in population. The craving for higher education among the general population of Bihar has led to a massive migration of the student community from the state. This has prompted many students to seek educational opportunities in other states, such as New Delhi and Karnataka, even for graduation level college education.

Bihar has the lowest literacy rate in India, with women's literacy being only 33.57% (Table 4.5 and Fig. 4.5). At the time of independence women's literacy in Bihar was 4.22%. It is a pleasant surprise to find that in spite of the meagre investment on education in Bihar, specially compared to other Indian states, the students have done very well. Famed national institutes of learning such as IITs, IIMs, NITs and AIIMS have always have had a good representation from Bihar which is usually higher than their proportion of the population, though none of these institutions are physically located in Bihar. Other institutions of higher learning, and coveted positions in the government also show a greater share than the percentage of their population. A recent survey by Pratham rated the absorption of their teaching by the Bihar children better than those in other states.

Bihar established several new educational institutes between 2006-2008. BIT Mesra started its Patna extension centre in September 2006. On 8 August, 2008 IIT of India was

Table 4.5 : Literacy Rate from 1951-2001 (in %)

Year	*Total*	*Males*	*Females*
1951	13.49	22.68	4.22
1961	21.95	35.85	8.11
1971	23.17	35.86	9.86
1981	32.32	47.11	16.61
1991	37.49	51.37	21.99
2001	47.53	60.32	33.57

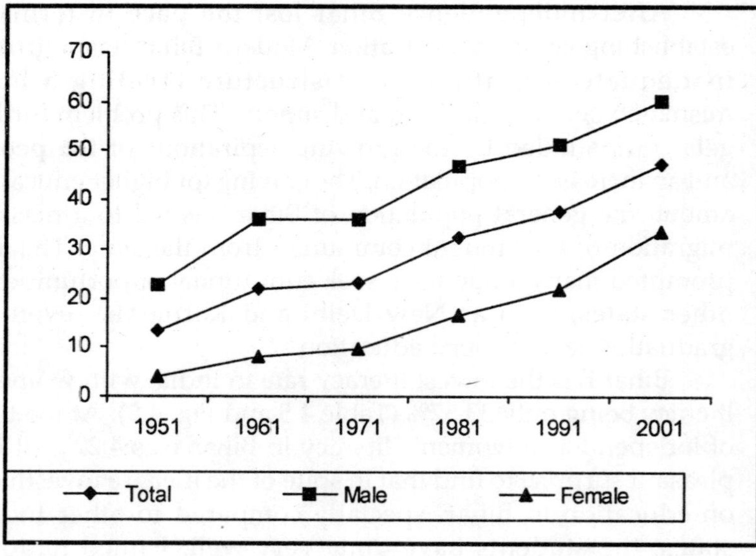

Fig. 4.5 : Literacy rate from 1951-2001 (in %)

inaugurated in Patna with 109 students from allover India. National Institute of Pharmaceutical Education and Research (NIPER) is being set up in Hajipur. On 4 August, 2008, National Institute of Fashion Technology, Patna was established as 9th NIFT of India. Chanakya National Law University a law university and Chandragupta Institute of Management of management institute was established in later half of 2008.

Bihar e-Governance Services and Technologies (BeST) along with the Government of Bihar has initiated a unique programme to establish a Centre of excellence called Bihar Knowledge Centre, a finishing school to equip students with the latest skills and customized short-term training programmes at an affordable cost. The centre aims to attract every youth of the state to hone up their technical, professional and soft skills and prepare them for the present industry requirement/job market.

Culture

Arts and Crafts

Madhubani paintings is a style of Indian painting, practiced in the Mithila region of Bihar. Tradition states that this style of painting originated at the time of the *Ramayana*, when King Janak commissioned artists to do paintings at the time of marriage of his daughter, Sita, to Lord Ram. The paintings was traditionally done of freshly plastered mud wall of huts, but now it is also done on cloth, hand-made paper and canvas. Madhubani painting mostly depict nature and Hindu religious motifs, and the themes generally revolve around Hindu deities like Krishna, Ram, Shiva, Durga, Lakshmi, and Saraswati, Natural objects like the sun, the moon, and religious plants like *tulsi* are also widely painted, along with scenes from the royal court and social events like weddings. Generally no space is left empty. Traditionally, painting was one of the skills that was passed down by women. The painting was usually done on walls during festivals, religious events, and other milestones of the life-cycle such as birth, *Upanayanam* (sacred thread ceremony), and marriage.

Manjusha Kala or Angika Art is an art form of Anga region of Bihar.

Patna School of Painting or Patna Qallam, sometimes also called Company painting, offshoot of the well-known Mughal Miniature School of Painting flourished in Bihar during early 18th to mid-20th century. The practitioners of this art form were descendants of Hindu artisans of Mughal painting who facing persecution from the Mughal Emperor, Aurangzeb found refuge, via Murshidabad, in Patna during late 18th century. They shared the characteristics of the Mughal painters, but unlike them (whose subjects included only royalty and court scenes), the Patna painters also started painting bazar scenes. The paintings were executed in watercolours on paper and on mica. Favourite subjects were scenes of Indian daily life, local rulers, and sets of festivals and ceremonies. Most successful were the studies of natural life, but the style was generally of a hybrid and undistinguished quality. It is this school of painting that formed the nucleus for the formation of the Patna Art School under the leadership of Shri Radha Mohan. College of Arts and Crafts, Patna, is an important center of Fine Arts in Bihar.

The artisans of Bihar have been very skillful in creating articles using local materials. Baskets, cups and saucers made from bamboo-strips or cane reed are painted in vivid colours are commonly found in Bihari homes. A special container woven out of sikki grass in the north, the "pauti", is a sentimental gift that accompanies a bride when she leaves her home after her wedding. The weavers of Bihar have been practicing their trade for curtains. They are produced buy artisans in central Bihar, particularly in the Patna and Bihar Sharif areas. These colourful sheets, with motifs of Buddhist artifacts, pictures of birds, animals, and/or flowers, gently wafting in the air through doors and windows, blown by a cool summer breeze, used to be one of the most soothing sights as one approaches a home or an office. Bhagalpur is well known for its seri-culture, manufacture of silk yarn and weaving them into lovely products. It is known as the tussah or tusser silk.

Performing arts

Bihar has contributed to the Indian (Hindustani) classical music and has produced musicians like Bharat Ratna Ustad Bismillah Khan and dhrupad singers like the Malliks (Darbhanga Gharana) and the Mishras (Bettiah Gharana). Bihar has a very old tradition of beautiful talk songs, sung during important family occasions, such as marriage, birth ceremonies, festivals, etc. and the most famous folk singer has been Padma Shri Sharda Sinha. They are sung mainly in group settings without the help of many musical instruments like Dholak, Bansuri and occasionally Tabla and Harmonium are used. Bihar also has a tradition of lively Holi songs known as "Phagua", filled with fun rhythms. During the 19th century, when the condition of Bihar worsened under the British misrule, many Biharis had to migrate as indentured labourers to West Indian islands, Fiji, and Mauritius. During this time many sad plays and songs called biraha became very popular, in the Bhojpur area. Dramas on that theme are very popular in the theaters of Patna.

Dance forms of Bihar are another expression of rich traditions and ethnic identity. There are several folk dance forms that can keep one enthralled, such as *dhobi nach, jhumar nach, manjhi, gond nach, jitiya nach, more morni, dom-domin, bhuiababa, rah baba, kathghorwa nach, jat-jatin, launda nach, bamar nach, jharni, jhijhia, natua nach, bidapad nach* and *sohrai nach.*

Theatre is another form in which the Bihari culture expresses itself. Some forms of theater with rich traditions are Bidesia, Reshma-Chuharmal, Bihula-Bisahari, Bahura-Gorin, Raja Salhesh, Sama Chakeva, and Dom Kach. These theater forms originate in the Anga region of Bihar.

Language and literature

Hindi and Urdu are the official languages of the state, while the majority of the people speak one of the Bihari languages—Bhojpuri, Magadhi, Maithili or Angika. Bihari languages were once mistakenly thought to be dialects of Hindi, but these have been more recently shown to be descendant of the language of the erstwhile Magadha kingdom—Magadhi Prakrit, along with Bengali, Assamese, and Oriya.

The number of speakers of Bihari languages are difficult to indicate because of unreliable sources. In urban region most educated speakers of the language name Hindi as their language because this is what they use in formal contexts and believe it to be the appropriate response because of unawareness. The uneducated and the rural population of the region return Hindi as the generic name for their language.

Despite large number of speakers of Bihari languages, they have not been constitutionally recog-nized in India. Hindi is the language used for educational and official matters in Bihar. These languages were legally absorbed under subordinate label of HINDI in the 1961 Census. Such state and national politics are creating condition for language endangerment. The first success for spreading Hindi occurred in Bihar in 1881, when Hindi displaced Urdu as the sole official language of the province. In this struggle between competing Hindi and Urdu, the potential claims of the three large mother tongues in the region—Magahi, Bhojpuria and Maithili were ignored. After independence Hindi was again given the sole official status through the Bihar Official Language Act, 1950. Urdu became the second official language in the undivided State of Bihar on 16 August, 1989.

The relationship of Maithili community with Bhojpuri and Magahi communities—the immediate neighbours have been neither very pleasant nor very hostile. Maithili has been the only one among them which has been tying to constantly deny superimposition of Hindi over her identity. The other two have given up their claims and have resigned to accept the status of dialects of Hindi.

Bihar has produced a number of writers of Hindi, including Raja Radhika Raman Singh, Shiva Pujan Sahay, Divakar Prasad Vidyarthy, Ramdhari Singh 'Dinkar', Ram Briksh Benipuri, Phanishwar Nath 'Renu', Pandit Nalin Vilochan Sharma, Gopal Singh 'Nepali', Baba Nagarjun, Mridula Sinha, and Pankaj Rag. Mahapandit Rahul Sankrityayan, the great writer and Buddhist scholar, was born in U.P. but spent his life in the land of Lord Buddha, i.e., Bihar. Hrishikesh Sulabh is the prominent write of the new generation. He is short story writer, playwright and theatre critic. Arun Kamal and Aalok Dhanwa are the well-known poets. Different regional languages also have produced some prominent poets and authors. Sharat Chandra Chattopadhyay, who is among the greatest writers in Bangla, resided for some time in Bihar. Of late, the latest Indian writer in English, Upamanyu Chatterjee also hails from Patna in Bihar. Devaki Nandan Khatri, who rose to fame at the beginning of the 20th century on account of his novel such as *Chandrakanta* and *Chandrakanta Santati,* was born in Muzaffarpur, Bihar. Vidyapati Thakur is the most renowned poet of Maithili (c. 14-15th century).

The world famous literary and cultural movement 'Bhookhi Peedhi' or Hungry generation was launched from

PLATE - I

Ruins of Ancient Nalanda University

Gautama Buddha undertaking extreme ascetic pratices before his enlightenment on the bank of river Falgu in Bodh Gaya

PLATE - II

Kalidasa's Sanskrit play AbhijñānaSākununtala is one of the Legacy of the Gupta empire.

PLATE - III

Emperor Ashoka the Great was born in Patna, Bihar

Guru Govind Singh

Shershah Suri

Babu Kunwar Singh

PLATE - IV

Topographic map of Bihar

Gangetic Dolphins are known as Susu locally

PLATE - V

Nitish Kumar, The Chief Minister of Bihar

Lalu Prasad Yadav

Ramdhari Singh Dinkar

Dr Rajendra Prasad,
1st President of India

Baba Nagarjun

PLATE - VI

Valmiki National Park, West Champaran

JP called for Sampurna Kranti at a historic rally of students at Patna's Gandhi Maidan on the 5th of June, 1975.

PLATE - VII

A Village Market

Litchi Production in Bihar

Patna Women's College

Madhubani Painting

PLATE - VIII

Manjusa Painting

A painting of the city of Patna, on the River Ganges, Patna School of Painting

Bharat Ratna Ustad Bismillah Khan, from Dumraon, Bihar

Magahi folk singers

Bihar's capital in November 1961 by two firebrand brothers Samir Roy Choudhury and Malay Roy Choudhary. The movement had impacted most of the Indian languages of the time.

Cuisine

The cuisine of Bihar for the Hindu upper and middle classes is predominantly vegetarian, although some of the Hindu classes are non-vegetarian. The Muslims in Bihar however do generally eat meat as well as vegetables. The staple food is *bhat* (boiled rice), *dal, roti, tarkari* and *achar*. It is prepared from rice, lentils, wheat flour, vegetables, and pickle. The traditional cooking medium is mustard oil. *Khichdi,* a brother of rice and lentils seasoned with spices and served with several accompanying items, constitutes the mid-day meal for most Hindu Biharis on Saturdays. The favourite dish among Biharis is *litti-chokha. Litti* is made up of *sattu* and *chokha* is made of mashed potatoes, tomatoes, and brinjals.

Chitba and *Pitthow* which are prepared basically from rice, are special foods of the Anga region. *Tilba* and *Chewda* of *Katarni* rice are also special preparations of Anga. *Kadhi bari* is a popular favourite and consists of fried soft dumplings made of *besan* (gram flour) that are cooked in a spicy gravy of yoghurt and *besan.* This dish goes very well with plain rice.

Bihar offers a large variety of sweet delicacies which, unlike those from Bengal, are mostly dry. These include *Anarasa, Belgrami, Chena Murki, Motichoor ke Ladoo, Kala Jamun, Kesaria Peda, Khaja, Khurma, Khubi ki Lai, Laktho, Parwal ki Mithai, Pua* and *Mal Pua, Thekua, Murabba* and *Tilkut.* Many of these originate in towns in the vicinity of Patna. Several other traditional salted snacks and savouries population in Bihar are *Chiwra, Dhuska, Litti, Makhana* and *Sattu.*

There is a distinctive Bihari flavour to the non-vegetarian cuisine as well, although some of the names of the dishes may be the same as those found in other parts of North India. Roll is a typical Bihari non-vegetarian dish. These are popular and go by the generic name Roll Bihari in and around Lexington Avenue (South) in New York City.

Islamic culture and food, with Bihari flavour are also part of Bihar's unique confluence of cultures. Famous food items include *Biharee Kabab, Shami Kabab, Nargisi Kufte, Shabdeg, Yakhnee Biryanee, Mutton Biryani, Shaljum Gosht, Baqer Khani, Kuleecha, Naan Rootee, Sawee ka Zarda, Qemamee Sawee, Gaja ka Halwa, Ande ka Zafrani Halwa* etc.

Religion

Hindu take bath in the hotsprings at Lakshmi Narayan Mandir, Rajgir. In ancient times, hot springs used to be the site of the Tapodarama, a Buddhist monastery at the time of Gautama Buddha. It is said that King Bimbisara also used to take his bath here sometimes. Gautama Buddha attained enlightenment

Table 4.6 : Religion in Bihar

Religion	*Per cent*
Hinduism	83.2%
Islam	16.5%
Other	0.3%

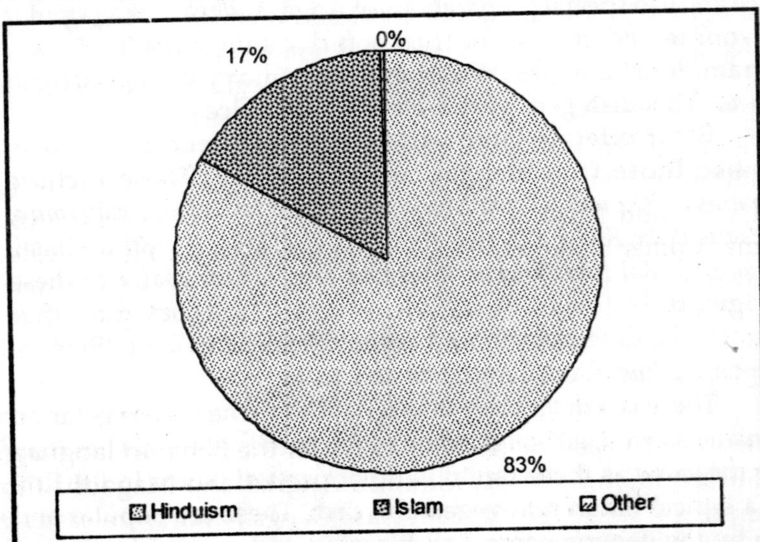

Fig. 4.6: Religion in Bihar (Per cent)

at Bodh Gaya, a town located in the modern day district of Gaya in Bihar. Vardhamana Mahavira, the 24th and the last Tirthankara of Jainism, was born in Vaishali around sixth century B.C.

A typical Hindu Bihari household would begin the day with the blowing of a conch shell at the dawn. The *adhan* the low-pitched chanting of a Buddhist monk or the tolling of a church bell reminds people to pay their salutations to God.

In rural Bihar, religion is the main component of popular culture. Shrines are located everywhere—even at the foot of trees, roadsides, etc., religious symbols or images of deities can be found in the most obscure or the most public places. From the dashboard of a dilapidated taxi to the plush office of a top executive, holy symbols or idols have their place.

Hindus are a majority in the state (Table 4.6 and Fig. 4.6). Most of the festivals are Hindu festivals. There are many variations of the festival theme. While some are celebrated all-over the state, others are observed only in certain areas. But Bihar being so diverse, different regions and religions have something to celebrate at sometime or the other during the year. Many festivals take place round the year. Many of these are officially recognized by the days on which they take place being proclaimed as Government holidays.

One of the battle cry of the Bihar Regiment, consisting of 17 battalions, is "Jai Bajrang Bali" (Victory to Lord Hanuman). Dariya Sahib, was a saint (who was born in Shahabad in the 1700s) influenced by Kabirdas and Dharamdas, brought the Hindu and Muslim communities closer. Dariya Sahib, like many other Bhakti saints, is known as Dariyadas. He was listed by Brahm Sankar Misra as one of India's greatest saints. Many of his followers believe that he is the reincarnation of Kabir.

Cinema

Bihar has a robust cinema industry for the Bhojpuri language. There are some small Maithili, Angika and Magadhi film industry. First Bhojpuri Film was "Ganga Jamuna" released in 1961. "Lagi nahin chute ram" was the all-time superhit Bhojpuri film which was released against "Mugal-E-Azam" but was a superhit in all the eastern and northern sector. Bollywood's "Nadiya Ke Paar" is among the most famous Bhojpuri language movies. The first Maithili movie was "Kanyadan" released in 1965, of which a significant portion was made in the Maithili language. "Bhaiyaa" a Magadhi film was released in 1961. Bhojpuri's history begins in 1962 with the well received film "Ganga Maiyya Tohe Piyari Chadhaibo" (Mother Ganges, I will offer you a yellow sari), which was directed by Kundan Kumar. Throughout the following decades, films were produced only in fits and starts. Films such as "Bidesiya" (Foreigner, 1963, Directed by S.N. Tripathi) and "Ganga" (Ganges, 1965, Directed by Kundan Kumar) were profitable and popular, but in general Bhojpuri films were not commonly produced in the 1960s and 1970s.

In the 1980s, enough Bhojpuri films were produced to tentatively make up an industry. Films such as "Mai" (Mom, 1989, directed by Rajkumar Sharma) and "Hamar Bhauji" (My Brother's Wife, 1983, directed by Kalpataru) continued to have at least sporadic success at the box office. However, this trend faded out by the end of the decade, and by 1990, the nascent industry seemed to be completely finished.

The industry took off again in 2001 with the super hit "Saiyyan Hamar" (My Sweetheart, directed by Mohan Prasad), which shot the hero of that film, Ravi Kissan, to superstardom. This success was quickly followed by several other remarkable successful films, including "Panditji Batai Na Biyah Kab Hoi" (Priest, tell me when I will marry, 2005, directed by Mohan Prasad) and "Sasura Bada Paisa Wala" (My father-in-law, the rich guy, 2005). In a measure of the Bhojpuri films industry's rise, both of these did mainstream Bollywood hits at the time, and both films, made on extremely tight budgets, earned back more than ten times their production costs. "Sasura Bada Paisa Wala" also introduced Manoj Tiwari, formerly as well loved folk singer, to the wider audiences of Bhojpuri cinema. Nowadays, he and Ravi Kissan are still the leading actors of Bhojpuri films, and their fees has increased with their fame. The extremely rapid success of their films has led to dramatic increases in Bhojpuri cinema's visibility, and the industry now supports an awards show and a trade magazine, "Bhojpuri City", which chronicles the production and release of what are now over one hundred films per year. Many of the major stars of mainstream Bollywood cinema, including Amitabh Bachchan, have also recently worked in Bhojpuri films.

Thus, Bihar has a glorious historic, geographic, politic, economic and education and culture.

REFERENCES

Ahmad Qeyamuddin, (1988): *Patna Through the Ages, Glimpses of History, Society and Economy*, Commonwealth Publishers, p. 15.

Alan Trevithick (1949): *The Revival of Buddhist Pilgrimage at Bodh Gaya, Anagarika Dharmapala and the Mahabodhi Temple*, p. 36.

Askari S.H., (1990): *Medieval Bihar Sultanate and Mughal Period*, Khuda Bakhsh Oriental Public Library, Patna, p. 16.

Badan, B.S. and Bhatt, H. (2007) : Tourism and Economic Development, Commonwelth Publishers, New Delhi-2.

Bhatia, A.K. (2007) : *Tourism Development : Principles and Practices*, 2nd Revised Edition, Sterling Publishers Private Limited, New Delhi-20.

Brass Paul R., (1990): *The politics of India since Independence*, Cambridge University Press, p. 7.

Crindle John W. Mc., (1927): *Ancient India as Described by Ptolemy*, Munshiram Manoharlal, New Delhi, pp. 11-13.

Das Arvind N., (1992): *The State of Bihar: An economic history without footnotes*, Amsterdam: VU University Press, Muzaffarpur, p. 10.

Dwivedi Acharya Hazari Prasad, (1975): *Rachnawali*, Rajkamal Prakashan, Delhi, p.11.

http://www.tourism.gov.in/survey/BIHAR%20TOURISM%20 ANNUAL%20STATISTICS%20%20REPORT%20Final.pdf Statics Tourism in Bihar on Indian Government's tourism website

http://drdapatna.bih.nic.in/patna_at_glance.html

http://www.indiaheritage.org/creative/creative_metal_work.htm

Omalley L.S.S., (2005): *History of Magadh*, Veena Publication, New Delhi, p. 31.

Patra C. (1996) : *Life in Ancient India as Depicted in the Digha Nikaya*, Punthi Pustak, New Delhi, p. 12.

Pathak Prabhu Nath, (1988): *Society and Culture in Early Bihar (C.A.D. 200-600)*, Commonwealth Publishers, New Delhi, p. 6.

Patil, P.B. (2006) : *Tourism Development : Problem and Prospects,* Current Publications, Agra-10 (U.P.)

Singh Asha, Gupta, M.S. and Shandilya (2010) : *Banking and Financial Sector Reforms in India,* Serials Publications, New Delhi-2.

Verma B.S., (1962); *Socio-religious Economic and Literary Condition of Bihar,* Munshiram Manoharlal, New Delhi, pp. 21-25.

Verma, S.B.; Jiloka, S.K. and Thryambakam, P. (2006) : *Rural Tourism and Tribal Development,* Deep & Deep Publications Pvt. Ltd., New Delhi-27.

Waddell Austine L., (1903): *Report on the Excavations at Pataliputra (Patna)—The Palibothra of the Greeks,* Asian Publicational Services, Calcutta, pp. 5-7.

Yang, Anand A. (1999): *Markets, Society, and the Colonial State in Bihar,* University of California Press, p. 18.

Yadav Ramendra Kumar, (2004): *Bihar : Myth and Reality,* Hope India, New Delhi, p. 29.

5

Tourism and Tourist Places in Bihar

Tourism

Tourism holds the potential to emerge as the leading industry in the state. From a historical perspective, Bihar holds strategic advantages in terms of monuments and remains of international importance. The state has the capacity to attract tourists from across the globe with different interests like culture, holiday, study and adventure. The tourist map of Bihar contains Buddhist Monasteries, Jain temples, Sikh Gurudwaras and Sufi shrines reflecting the state's historical association with Lord Buddha, Lord Mahavira, Guru Govind Singh, and the great Sufi saints. Bihar is also associated with the great Chinese tourists Fahien and Huen Tsang. The state offers tourists a variety of historical sites like Rajgir and Patliputra (the ancient capital of Magadh Empire), Vaishali (the first republic of the world), Bodh Gaya, Nalanda (the renowned seat of learning and intellect) and Patna Sahib (the birth place of the last guru of the Sikhs).

Bihar is a state having a very rich cultural heritage. The government is taking several measures to protect this valuable heritage. Some of the recent measures taken by the Department of Art, Culture and Youth are the following:

- On the eve of 2550th Anniversary of Lord Buddha (Mahaparinirvana), many cultural programmes were organized throughout the places associated with Lord Buddha.
- A cultural troop visited Mauritius and shows were organized. A new scheme, 'Trace Your Roots', for

persons of Bihari origin living in Mauritius has been announced.

- Cultural programmes were organized in Naxal-affected regions.
- Sports awards were given to top 144 sportspersons of international and national repute.
- Construction of the Multipurpose Cultural Complex at Kankarbagh, Patna was started.

However, the fact remains that, despite the huge potential, the tourism industry in the state is still in its infancy. In spite of that, there is a steady increase in the number of Indian and foreign tourists to Bihar, the total of which increased from 61.06 lakh in 2003 to 107.65 lakh in 2006 (Table 5.1).

Table 5.1 : Number of Tourists in Bihar

Year	*No. of Tourists*		
	Indian	*Foreign*	*Total*
2003	60,44,710	60,820	61,05,530
2005	86,67,220	63,321	87,30,541
2006	1,06,70,268	94,446	1,07,64,714

Source: Department of Tourism, Government of Bihar

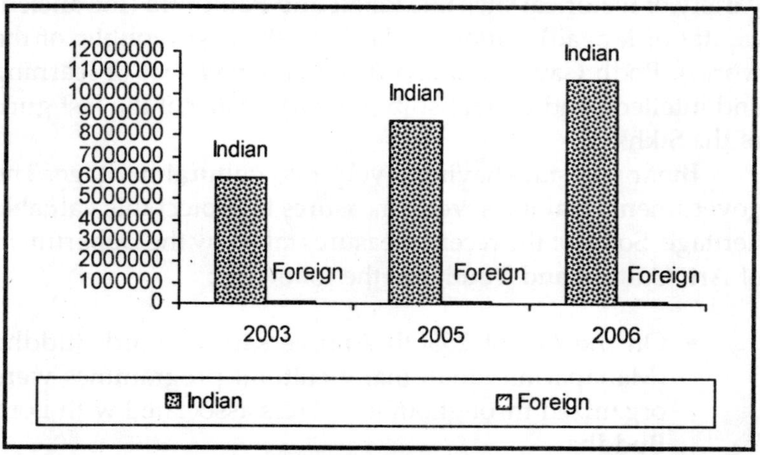

Fig. 5.1 : Number of Tourists in Bihar

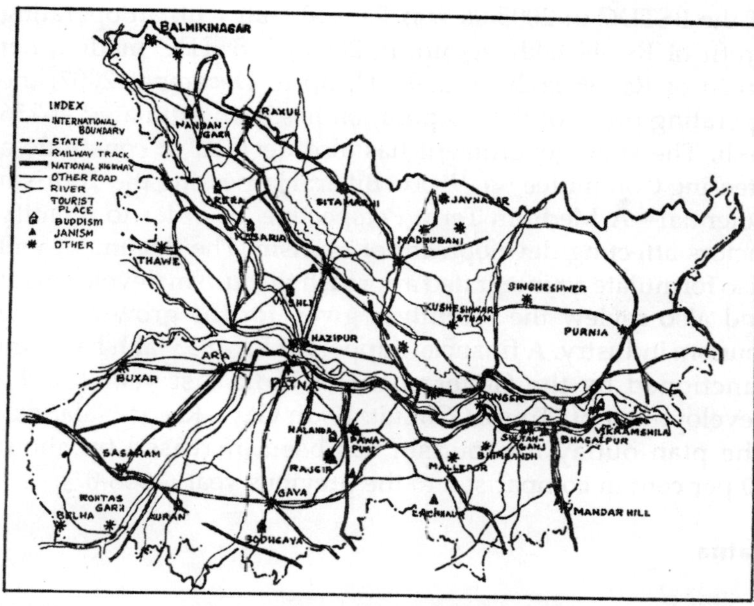

Fig. 5.2 : Major Tourist Places in Bihar

The distribution of tourists in Bihar in 2006-08 by their destinations is given in Table 5.1 and Fig. 5.1. This reflects the preference of the tourists and the places to be developed further to attract more of them in future.

Major Tourist Places

Bihar is a land affluent in natural beauty, whispering forests, sparkling lakes, forts and places, holy rivers, holy shrines and natural hot springs emerging from a backdrop of eternal snow. Fig. 5.2 shows the major tourist places in Bihar.

Recognising the potential of the sector and the need to revitalize tourism, the Government of Bihar has declared the tourism sector at par with other industries and a draft policy on tourism is in the pipeline. It aims at rejuvenation of the Bihar State Tourism Development Corporation (BSTDC) which will operate tourist bungalows and hotels at strategic locations. It will also provide transport and communication facilities to market tourism as a commercial enterprise. The total income of the BSTDC in 2005-06 was Rs. 418 lakh with an operating profit of Rs. 44 lakh. Again, in 2006-07, BSTDC made a net profit of Rs. 66 lakh. In 2007-08, up to December 2007; the operating profit of the Corporation has been estimated at 156 lakh. The state government has also decided to constitute a Steering Committee on 'Vision Bihar: Harnessing the Tourism Potential—A Medium Term Perspective' in order to identify factors affecting development of tourism. The document will also formulate an integrated approach to tourism development and also review the incentives given for the growth of the tourism industry. A financial support of Rs. 1833 lakh has been sanctioned by the Government of India last year for the development of 'Tourist Circuit: Bodh Gaya-Rajgir-Nalanda'. The plan outlay for tourism has been increased by about 50 per cent in comparison to the previous year (2006-07).

Patna

Indian history one comes across the name of the pre-eminent city of Pataliputra located at the site where Patna is today. This

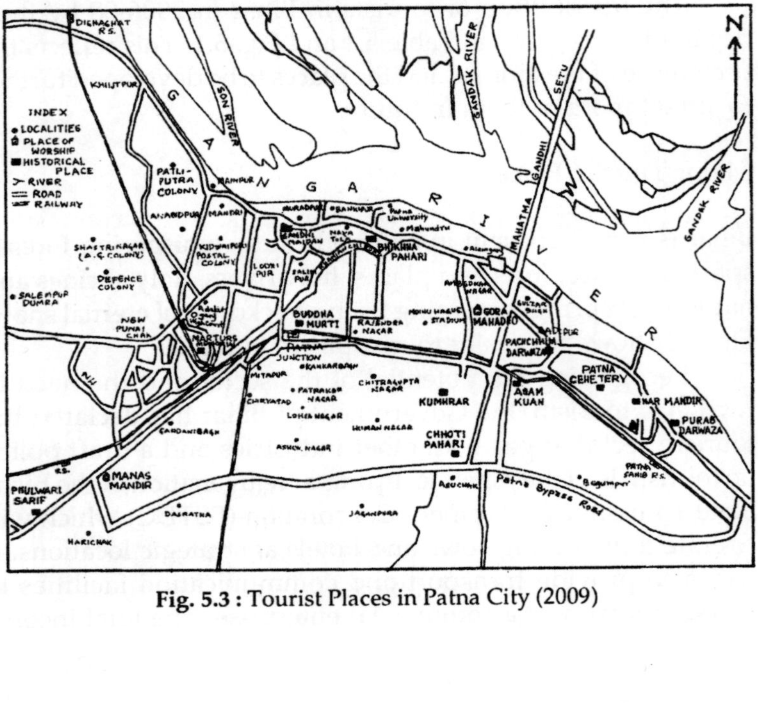

Fig. 5.3 : Tourist Places in Patna City (2009)

city saw the rise and fall of India's first major kingdoms. Its period of glory spanned a thousand years from the 6th century B.C. to 5th century. A.D.

Ajatshatru, second in the line of Magadh King, built a small fort at Pataligram in the vicinity of the river Ganga. This later became the famous metropolis of Pataliputra and was ruled by Chandragupta Maurya (a contemporary of Alexander) and his son Ashok, acclaimed for the spread of Buddhism. Other emperors who ruled from Patna were the Guptas and Sung. Sher Shah Suri (16th Century) and Azim-Ush-Shan (18th Century), grand-son of Mughal emperor Aurangzeb, who renamed it Azimabad, also ruled from here.

Vestiges of the ancient Pataliputra can still be seen spread over here and there within the city boundaries.

Golghar

This huge and impressive beehive-shaped structure was constructed in July 1786 by Captain John Garstin following a terrible famine in 1770, to serve as a state granary. A flight of steps winds round this 29 m high building leading to the top from where one gets a fine view of the river Ganga and Patna City.

Patna Museum

It contains metal and stone sculptures of the Maurya and Gupta periods, terracotta figurines, and archaeological finds from sites in Bihar. Among its prized exhibits is a 16 m long fossilized tree.

Khuda Bakhsh Oriental Public Library

Set up at the turn of the century, the library has a distinguished collection of rare Arabic and Persian manuscripts, Rajput and Mughal paintings and oddities like an inch-wide Quran. It also contains the only books rescued from the plunder of the University of Cordoba in Spain. It is one of the National libraries of India.

Harmandir Jee

This shrine consecrates the birthplace of the tenth religious preceptor of the Sikh faith, Guru Govind Singh. Originally built by Maharaja Ranjit Singh, a ruler of Punjab, Harmandirji is one of the holiest Sikh shrines. Standing in the Chowk area of Old Patna, this dome-shaped structure contains Sikh scriptures and the personal belongings of the guru.

Agamkuan

The antiquarian significance of this well was pointed out in Waddell's report which says that this was "so called hell of Ashok with its fiery cauldrous..... Here was the site of the royal slaughter house or out-kitchen". The well is at resent held sacred by the local Hindus who make offerings of money and flowers into in and pray for protection against small pox. The temple of Sitala Mata, the goddess of small-pox stands nearby.

Pathar-Ki-Masjid

Situated on the bank of river Ganga, this mosque is known variously as Saif Khan's mosque, Chimni Ghat mosques or Sangi Masjid. It was built by Parwez Shah, son of the Mughal emperor Jahangir, during his tenure as governor of Bihar.

Kamaldah

In the area called Kamaldah, near the Gulzarbagh railway station, is a high mound of brick ruins on which stand two Jain temples. There are mausoleum of Jain Saint Sthoolbhadra and the temple of Sudarshan Swami. On one of them is an inscription dated V.S. 1848 (A.D. 1792).

Chhoti Patan Devi

This is situated inside the old city in the Chowk area near the eastern gate and close to Harmandir Jee. The image inside as said, was installed by Raja Man Singh, the General of Akbar.

Bari Patan Devi

This temple is situated in Maharajganj area of the city just outside of what was once its western gate. It is sacred to the goddess Durga, the guardian deity of Patna.

Kumhrar

Kumhrar, site of the ancient city of Patliputra, lies 5 km. from Patna Railway Station on the Kankarbagh Road. Excavations here have revealed relics of four continuous periods from 600 BC to 600 AD. The fifth period begins from 1600 AD. An important find is the 80-pillared huge hall of the Mauryan dynasty.

Padri-ki-haveli

A church of Dutch Style. Mother Teressa had done here apprenticeship in nursing.

Sanjay Gandhi Biological Park

This biological park is an attractive picnic spot in the heart of the Patna town. Various species of animals and medicinal plants/trees etc. add much charm to the park.

Maner

Maner Sharif is located 25 km. away from West of Patna on NH-31, sacred to the memory of the 13th century Sufi Saint Manceri. Bari Dargah, his cenotaph and the tomb of his disciple Shah Daulat are visited by streams of Muslim pilgrims. Area around the shrine is a picnic spot also.

Nalanda

Nalanda is like stepping back into a delightful and near forgotten era. Here lies ruins of the world renowned University of Nalanda. The structural remains at Nalanda belong to

5th-12th centuries. This vast residential university provided scholarly pursuits to about 10 thousand students under thousand teachers from different part of Asia.

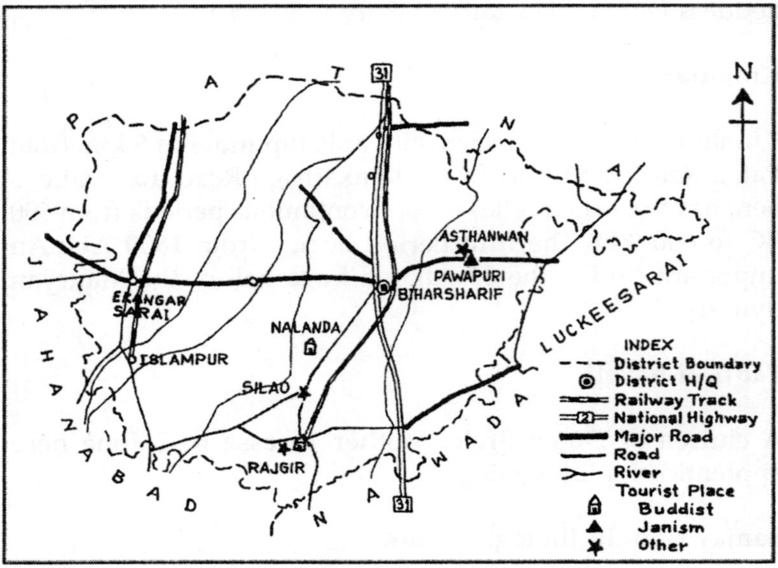

Fig. 5.4 : Tourist Places in Nalanda (2009)

Excavated remains reveal stupa, a large stair, lecture halls, dormitories, meditation centres, wells etc.

The famous Chinese traveller Hieun Tsiang spent years at Nalanda and has left a vivid description of the university. Nagarjuna—Mahayana Philosopher, Dinnaga—founder of the school of logic and, Dharmpal—the Brahmin scholar taught here. King Harshwardhan gifted 25 mtr. high copper image of the Buddha and Kumargupta of the Gupta dynasty endowed a college of fine arts here.

The Archaeological Museum at Nalanda contains a number of statues and other remains of the university's exceptional significance. The Nav Nalanda Mahavir, 2 kms from the ancient ruins, is a modern institute. It houses many rare Buddhist manuscripts.

Ruins of the University Complex

The total area of excavation is about 14 hectares. The ruin contains a number of Buddhist stupas and chaityas, monasteries, hostels, cells or rooms on four sides with a central courtyard, lecture halls and amphitheaters.

Archaeological Museum

Opposite the entrance to the ruins of the university and houses, it has a small but beautiful collection of Buddhist and Hindu bronzes and a number of undamaged statues of the Lord Buddha that were found in the area. Two enormous terracotta Jars of the first century stand intact behind the museum in a shaded enclosure. The collection includes copper plates and stone inscriptions, coins, pottery and samples of burnt rise (12th century AD) found among the ruins here. Open during 10.00 to 17.00 hours. Closed on Friday.

Nav Nalanda Mahavihar

In keeping with the ancient tradition of Nalanda, the Government of Bihar has established a Pali Postgraduate Research Institute known as Nav Nalanda Mahavihar.

Hiuen Tsiang Memorial Hall

Constructed in memory of the 5th century Chinese traveller.

Bargain

There is a Sun temple and lake.

Silao

A small village situated between Nalanda and Rajgir on the road side is famous for 'Khaja', a very popular sweet.

Rajgir

Known in ancient times as Rajagrih, meaning 'Home of Royalty', which it was in 6th century B.C., Rajgir is a hill girt town in the midst of lush green forests. This was the first recorded capital as per Indian history. Rajgir had in close association with the life and words of Lord Buddha. He not only spent many rainy seasons here but also delivered very important sermons and, it was the sacred Griddhakoot Hill where he proselytized emperor Bimbisar to Buddhism.

Within the Valley, the Jivak Amravan monastery has been excavated and is said to have been favourite retreat of Lord Buddha. It was here that the famous physician Jivak—treated Devdatt. Bimbisar had presented a monastery—Venuvan Vihara—to Lord Buddha for his residence at Rajgir.

The teachings of the Buddha hitherto unwritten were penned down at Rajgir after his death. Rajgir was also the venue of the first Buddhist Council.

Rajgir is a pleasant valley and is a very important pilgrim centre for the Hindus and Jains. It is a most popular winter health resort with number of hot water springs.

Griddhakoot Hill

It is associated with Lord Buddha.

Bimbisar Jail

King Bimbisar was imprisoned here by his son Ajatshatru.

Maniar Math

Considered to be an ancient Jain shrine.

Swarn Bhandar Caves

Rock-cut caves having figures of Jain Tirthankars.

Ranbhum Area

About a mile south-west of Sonbhandar caves is a spot locally called 'Akhara' or a battle-field where, the people believe, the famous duel between Jarasandh and Bhim was fought in the Mahabharat period.

Jarasandh Ki Baithak or Pippala Stone House

On the ascent to the top of the hill from the hot springs is seen a large stone structure. It is associated with the primeval King of Rajgir viz. Jarasandh who, it is said, had his *baithak* or open sit-out here.

The tradition, as quoted by Fa Hian, says that there was the Pippala Cave here where Buddha used to sit in deep meditation after his mid-day meal.

Saptaparni Cave

On the northern cave of Vaibhar hill, a little below the old Jain temple of Adinath, is a series of six caves contained in natural bend of rock.

Ajatshatru Stupa

To the east of the Venuvan close by the side of the road on its east are the ruins of a stone structure.

The fortification walls

The ancient town Rajagrih was protected by walls, called as inner-fortification walls. Traces of fortification wall are noticed on the top of the hills at Rajgir.

The Venuvan Vihar

Between the larger fortification of the old town and the hills along the east of the river Saraswati is an extensive area called

Venuvan or Bamboo garden of king Bimbisar, who made it as a gift to Lord Buddha. According to Buddhist tradition, it was the favourite resort of Buddha when he stayed at Rajgir.

Hot Water Springs

Opposite the Vaibhar hill is the Viput hill towards the east. Here, at the north-western foot of the Viput hill are other hot and cold water springs, like those at the Vaibhar hill.

Many more sites of archaeological importance are here in and around Rajgir besides those mentioned above.

Kurkihar

According to historians, true name of the place is said to be Kurak-vihar which Cunningham believed to be a contracted form of Kukkutapada-Vihara, since the Sanskrit word Kukkuta is the same as the Hindi Kukkar or Kurak. A large vihara of this name is mentioned by Hiuen Tsiang as existing near Pataliputra or Patna. Cunningham identified the ruins at Kurkihar with the Kukkul-pada-giri of the Chinese pilgrims, which according to Buddhist tradition was the scene of some of the miracles of Maha Kashyapa.

Kurkihar is a village about 4.8 kms north-east of Wazirganj on the Nawada-Gaya road. Antiquarian remains of this village were first brought to notice by Kittoe in 1847. He collected several Buddhist idols, many of the Tantrika periods, some of which are now preserved in the Indian Museum, Kolkata. In 1866, Peppe took photographs of some of the images at Kurkihar and published his brief notes thereon. Cunningham also visited this place twice in 1861-62 and 1879-80 respectively. Bengal List and the Gazetteer give a brief account of the ruins based on earlier references. Stein also paid an exploratory visit to Kurkihar mainly with a view to identify places visited by Hiuen Tsiang in the locality. Kurkihar suddently came to limelight in 1930 because of an important discovery of the hoard of 226 bronzes and five other objects. These objects are now in the Patna Museum. Main mound of Buddhist ruins to the south of the village, the Devisthana or Vagishwari Temple of the north-eastern part of the village and, Sugatghar mound to the north of the village are places of archaeological interest at Kurkihar.

Bodhgaya

Set on the bank of river Niranjan (Falgu) and silhouetted against a row of hills, it was here in 531 B.C. that Sakya Prince Siddhartha first saw 'Light' under the Bodhi Tree. The Prince became Buddha—the Enlightened One. Bodhgaya is the greatest pilgrim centre for Buddhists of the world. Many south-east Asian countries have established their monasteries here in their native architectural styles.

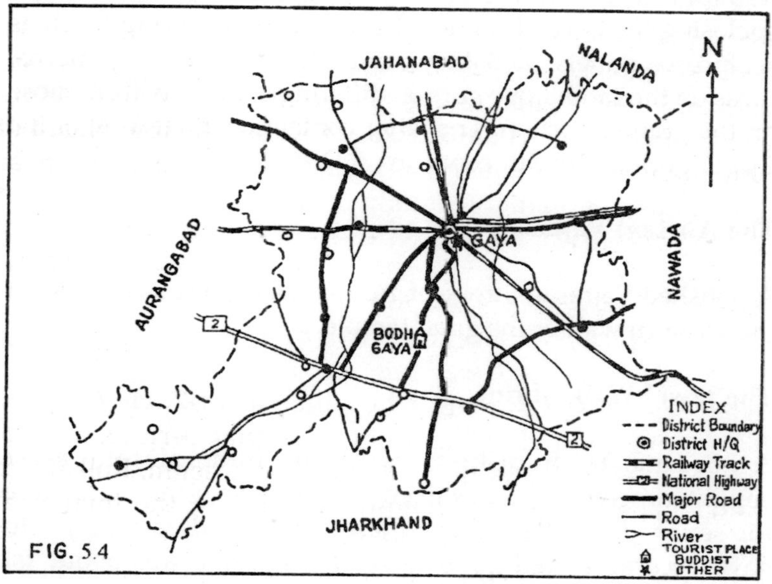

Fig. 5.5 : Tourist Places in Gaya (2009)

The Mahabodhi Temple

The main Shrine of Supreme Enlightenment, the Mahabodhi temple is unique amongst other north Indian temples. It is having a spire instead of the usual curvilinear contours. The four small towers at the four corners give balance to the structure. Inside the Shrine is a gilded image of the Buddha. The carved railings round the temple are the oldest remains at Bodhgaya.

The Bodhi Tree

The most sacred *pipal* tree under which Prince Siddhartha became Buddha—the Enlightened one. It is believed to be the fourth or fifth generation offsprings of the original. Its saplings are still in great demand in India and abroad.

The Stone Railing

Remains of a massive stone railing are at present found enclosing the Great Temple. The railing bear carvings such as sculptured panels, medallions and other ornamental patterns, those on the sand-stone portion differing materially from those on the granite portion. The latter contain characteristic of the Gupta period (4th-5th centuries A.D.).

The Ancient Vajrasan

A polished Vajrasan throne of grey sandstone is placed against the western wall of the great temple.

The Jewel Walk Shrine

According to Buddhist tradition, immediately after enlightenment, Buddha walked to and fro near the sacred tree for seven days. The spot, where he so walked, appear to have become sacred quite early and a shrine was about 1st century B.C.

Muchalinda Tank

Close to the south of the Great Temple is a sacred tank named after a Nagaraj—Muchalinda who, according to tradition, protected the Buddha while engrossed in Samadhi after his enlightenment.

Other Sites of attraction

The Hindu Monastery, temples and samadhis, Tara Devi Temple, Animesh Lochan Chaitya, Monasteries of Japan, China, Thailand, Korea, Burma, Tibet etc. etc.

Vaishali

Puranas as well as the *Ramayan*, both of these refer to Vaishali as a separate kingdom. Raja Vishal—son of Ikshvaku is considered to be founder of the Vaishali kingdom.

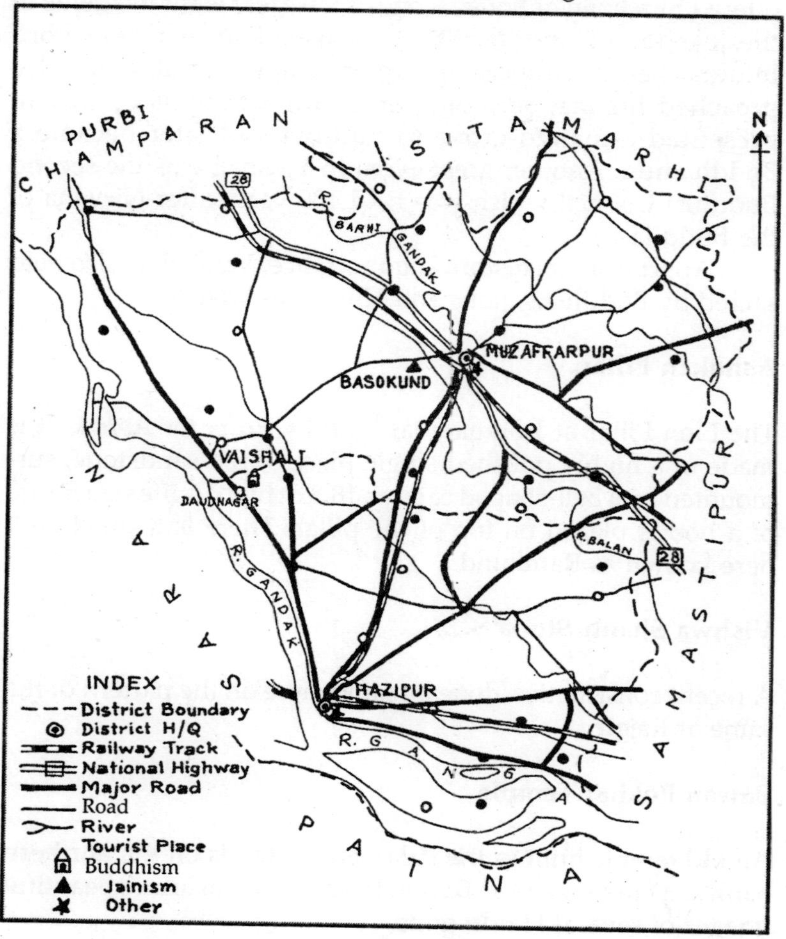

Fig. 5.6 : Tourist Places in Muzaffarpur-Vaishali (2009)

Apart from Hindu mythology, Vaishali also figures prominently both in Jain and Buddhist literature.

According to Jain literatures Vardhman Mahavir—The 24th Tirthankar of the Jains—was born in Kundapur of Kundgram—a suburb of Vaishali.

Vaishali was also seat of the 'Vajji Republic'—the world's fist republic with a duly elected assembly or representatives and efficient administration.

Lord Buddha, in his lifetime had visited Vaishali at least three times. According to Buddhist traditions, in one of these visits several monkey supposedly dug a tank for him and offered him bowl of honey—one of the great eight incidents in the legends of Buddha. It was Vaishali itself where Lord Buddha had announced his approaching Nirvana and also preached his last sermon. Amrapali, a famous courtesan presented a mango-grove to Buddha and later became a Buddha nun. Another great event in Vaishali was the second Buddhist Council which was held 100 years after Nirvana of the Buddha.

Apart from its historical importance, Vaishali is also held sacred by Buddhists, Jains and Hindus as well.

Ashokan Pillar

The Lion Pillar at Kolhua, was built by Emperor Ashok. It is made of a highly polished single piece of red sandstone, surmounted by a bell-shaped capital; 18.3 m high. A life size figure of a lion is placed on top of the pillar. There is a small tank here known as Ramkund.

Vishwa Shanti Stupa

A recent construction done by Japan here on the pattern of the same at Rajgir.

Bawan Pokhar Temple

An old temple built in the Pala period stands on the northern bank of a tank known as Bawan Pokhar and enshrines beautiful images of several Hindu gods.

Coronation Tank (Abhishek Pushkarani)

Its water was believed to be sacred in the old days and all of Vaishali's elected representatives were anointed here before their swearing in.

Chaumukhi Mahadev

A four-head lingam has been found in excavations.

Buddha Stupa-I

The exterior of this stupa which is now in a dilapidated condition has a plain surface. One-eighth of the sacred ashes of the lord Buddha were enshrined here in a stone casket.

Buddha Stupa-II

Excavation of this site in 1958 led to the discovery of another casket containing the ashes of the Lord Buddha.

Basokund (Birth Place of Lord Mahavir)

It is believed that the Jain Tirthankar, Lord Mahavir was born over 2550 years ago. Mahavir is said to have spent the first 22 years of his life here.

Raja Vishal Ka Garh

A huge mound with a circumference about one kilometre and walls nearly 2 m high with a 43 m wide moat around them, is said to be the ancient parliament house. Over seven thousand representatives of the federal assembly gathered here to legislate and discuss the problems of the day.

Aurangabad

Headquarters town of the district of the same name, is situated nearly 14 kms from Aurgangabad railway station.

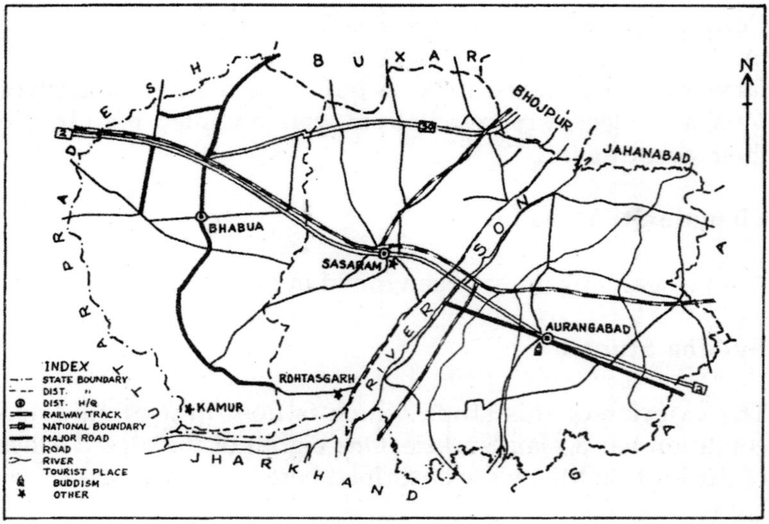

Fig. 5.7 : Tourist Places in Bhabua, Rohtas and Aurangabad (2009)

A group of hills near Madanpur between Aurangabad and Sherghati, on the Grand Trunk Road, traces of Buddhist Shrines are found among the rocks, Burhi, nearly 3 kms to the east, contains several sites in which 'Chaitya' and large 'Vihara' or Buddhist monastery one stood, and there are some hot mineral springs, to which the place probably owed its former importance, Generally nearly 4 kms to the south-east was also the site of a large town and of a 'Vihara' the name of which appear has a five statue of Buddha and some smaller Buddhism and Saivite figures.

Sasaram

Sasaram is one of the important ancient towns in Bihar. Legendary tradition, as in vogue in the locality, would associate Sasaram with the famous Haihaya king named Sahasrarjun. The followers of Sahasrarjun, it is said, settled down here and founded the town which was named after the king who was killed by Parasuram. The modern name being a corrupt form of the latter name Sahasrarjunapura or Sahasram.

Early in the sixteenth century Sasaram was a Muhammedan town, forming part of the Jaunpur Kingdom and under the control of Hasan Khan Sur, the Pathan Chief and father of the famous Sher Shah of Muslim history of India. The town lost its importance afterward, though it has continued to flourish as one of the few large towns in the district.

Ashokan Inscription and a rock-cut cave

Near the top of the Chandan Shaheed Hill is a small rock-cut-cave locally called as Chirag-dan. It has been presumed to be an Ashokan cave with usual Mauryan polish on its interior. Inside the cave, on a small rocky boulder, is an inscription on 8 lines of archaic Brahmi characters.

Tomb of Shershah

The great mausoleum of Sher Shah is situated in the western outskirts of the town in the centre of a large excavated tank or lake.

Rohtasgarh

The hill of Rohtas is situated along the western bank of the river Sone about 38 kms south of Sasaram.

There are number of historical events associated with this fort. Inscriptions, buildings, gates, Baradari, Rangmala, Sheesh Mahal, Phool Mahal, Temples, Mosques and Tombs etc. are the object of chief attraction inside the fort area.

Mosque at the foot of the Hill

A small ruined mosque contains an inscription referring to its construction during the reign of Jehangir in 1613 A.D.

Tara Chandi Hill

This hill is situated about 1 km south of the Chandan Shaheed hill. The hill is named after an image of the goddess Tara-Chandi carved on a ledge of its rock which is still worshipped.

Barabar (Jehanabad)

The Barabar and Nagarjuni hills are situated 24 kms north of Gaya and contain, in all, seven rock-cut caves of which four are in the Barabar hills. The four caves in Barabar hills have seven chambers and these are popularly known as Satgharwa. The hills have been identified with the Gorathagiri mentioned in the *Mahabharat* by Jackson who discovered two inscriptions mentioning the name Gorathagiri in the hill itself.

The Karan Chaupar Cave

The cave facing north is known as Karan Chaupar. Right above to the entrance is a damaged inscription of the 19th regnal year of Ashoka (i.e. 245 B.C.) outside the cave. To its west, on the rock are two rudely carved human figures and a linga.

The Sudama Cave

The second cave faces south, it being on the opposite side of the hill. An inscription on the eastern wall of the entrance recess refers to the excavation of the cave in the 12th regnal year of Ashoka (i.e., 252 B.C.).

The Lomas Rishi Cave

Two inscriptions of later Gupta period (7th-8th centuries A.D.) both referring to kings Sarddhulavarman and his son Anantvarman of Maudhari dynasty, and another inscription in Brahmi have been discovered there in this cave.

The Viswa Jhopri Cave

In its outer room, on the right hand wall is an inscription recording its excavation in 12th regnal year of Ashoka (i.e. 252 B.C.) for the Ajivikas and referring to the name of the hill as Khalatika.

Saiva Temple

On one of the highest peaks in the range of the hills, locally known as Surajanaka, is the Saiva Temple of Siddheshwar Nath standing on the original basement of an ancient temple.

Tank

At the southern foot of the hills, near the pathway to the caves is a tank called as Patal-Ganga held sacred by the Hindus.

Rock-cut Images

On the rock in a narrow passage leading to the Siddheshwara temple are some sculptures representing lingas, figures of Ganesh, etc.

Vikramshila

Remains of the ancient Vikramshila University have been excavated at Village Antichak in the Bhagalpur district.

Excavation at this site were done in 1960-61 and have disclosed different periods of habitation. The natural structure exposed and the antiquities discovered reiterate the site was probably the remains of the large monastery. A number of Buddha images of stones and terracottas have been discovered, some inscribed seals and stupas have also been found.

King Dharampala who founded the University had generously endowed it with his magnificent grants. The University building made provisions for the maintenance of 108 residential professors and also for a number of non-residential professors, pilgrims and other members of the staff. A big Vihara (monastery) was constructed in the University quarters, and it was protected with strong walls. In the centre there was big Buddhist temple, surrounded by 108 smaller temples. The affairs of the university were entrusted by King Dharampala to one very eminent and learned scholar who was also highly religious. The controlling authority which administered the affairs of the Vikramshila University also looked the Nalanda University.

Kesaria

Two miles to the south stands of lofty brick mound capped by a solid brick tower of considerable size, which itself is a remains of a Buddhist stupa. The mound itself is a ruined circumference at its base, while the stupa which is in ruins, a diameter of 68 ft. at its base and a total height of 5½ ft. Originally, it was crowned by pinnacle which must have stood 80 or 90 ft. above the ground. General Cunningham was of opinion that it dates back to AD 200 to 700 and that it was built upon the ruins of a much older and larger stupa. This ancient monument is known to the people as the Deora of Raja Ben, who is said to have been one of the five supreme emperors of India and is therefore admired as Raja Ben Chakrabarty. It can hardly be doubted that the tradition of Raja Ben preserves the story recorded by Hiuen Tsiang, according to whose account this stupa was referred to a Chakaravarty Raja by the Buddhist of the 7th century.

This stupa is in fact, one of the many memorable stupas which are concerned with the remarkable events in the life of Buddha.

Lauria Nandangarh

A village in the Bettiah subdivision about 24 kms north-west of Bettiah, which contains some of the most interesting remains in the district viz. the Lion Pillar of Ashoka and some ancient sepulchral monds.

The Piilar's shaft is formed of a single block of stone stands less than half a km to the east of the village is a polished sand stone Ashokan Pillar 32 ft. and 9 ft. ½ inches in height, with a diameter at base of 35.5 inches and of 26.2 inches at top. The capital which is 6 ft. 10 inches in height, is bell shaped, with a circular abacus supporting the statue of a lion. The column has a light and elegant appearance, and is altogether more pleasing monument than the shorter and stauter pillar of Bakhra. The lion has been injured in the mouth, and the column has itself been slightly dislodged by the stock.

The pillar is much thinner and much lighter than those of Bakhra and Areraj. The weight of the polished portion of its shaft is only 18 tons, or rather less than half than that of the Bakhra pillar and somewhat more than half of the Areraj pillar. The Pillar is inscribed with the edicts of Ashoka in the same clear and beautifully-cut character on those of the Areraj pillar.

Munger

Munger Fort

The most important of the monuments at Munger is the ancient fort, built on a rocky eminence projecting into the river Ganga that protects it from west and partly from the north, the other sides being defended by a deep moat. The rampart was provided with four gateways, one on each side, and with circular or octagonal bastions, at regular intervals, carrying the usual battlements. Of the gates only the northern gate, called Lal Darwaza, is somewhat preserved, with some carved stones built into it, which originally belonged to some Hindu or Buddhist structure.

Bihar Yoga Bharti

It is located within the Ganga Darshan Complex in Munger on a powerful energy center, about 172 kms. from Patna. It is on the top of a hill overlooking the river Ganga and is pinpointed to become a spiritual oasis in the technological desert of the 21st century.

Swami Shivananda first had the vision of a Yoga University then he established the Yoga Vedanta Forest Academy, in Rishikesh. Paramahamsa Satyanand who established the Ganga Darshan Complex in Munger carried his inspiration forward. And now, Paramahamsa Niranjanananda, with the blessings of his predecessors has fully founded and established the Bihar Yoga Bharti in order to preserve and regenerate the total scope of Yogic science, with the objective of combining academic and scientific methodology with spiritual vision.

This institution is being conducted along the lines of the great spirit of University of Nalanda and Vikaramshila and is the first institute of its kind in the world that eventually imparts comprehensive Yogic education with provision for M.A., M. Sc., M. Phil., Ph.D., D.Sc., and D.Litt. Along with Yogic education the student imbibes dedication, compassion and the spirit of selfless service.

Against this background of the description of various tourist destinations in Bihar, the research has undertaken a survey with the following two, among others, as the objectives:

(i) To understand the existing status to tourist services in Bihar, with a view to assess demand and supply status for the tourist services;

(ii) To understand further the issues and challenges of marketing of tourist services in Bihar.

The sample respondents, comprising both foreign and domestic tourists, were selected by using multistage random sampling technique. The final sample comprised 100 foreign and 150 domestic tourist interviewed at 5 locations of tourist interest in Bihar. Primary data from these respondents was collected by administering them a detailed questionnaire. The findings of the survey could be summarized as under:

I. **Sex Ratio and Age-groups**—Among the sample foreign tourists, the sex ratio was 3 males to 2 females, while among the domestic tourists, the sex ratio was 13 males to 7 females. This *prima facie* indicates that because of the cultural differences, foreign women are more outbound and inquisitive than the Indian women, who are more homebound and shun the hustle and bustle of unknown places.

The largest age-group among both the foreign and domestic tourists was 31-45 years of age, followed by

16-30 years. Evidently, youth, whether foreign or domestic, had a greater fascination for travel. Among the foreign tourists, 26% were above 46 years of age, but among the domestic tourists, this percentage was significantly higher at 33%.

II. **Education, Occupation and Family Income**—Among the foreign tourists, 88% were graduates and postgraduates, 10% were undergraduates and only 2% were with formal school education. On the other hand, among the domestic tourists, 46% were graduates and postgraduates, 32% were undergraduates and 22% were with formal school education. Evidently, education level has no association with travel instinct, but it is also true that with higher education, one is in a better position to appreciate the cultural heritage and beauty of the place being visited.

Among the foreign tourists, 35% were professionals, 24% were self-employed, 17% were teachers/ professors, 16% were employees in business and industry, 5% were students and 3% were housewives. Among the domestic tourists, 28% were professionals, 16% were self-employed, 26% were employees in business and industry, 10% were teachers/professors, 12% were housewives and 8% were students. It is clear that both in India and abroad, persons with greater freedom with time and money (professionals and self-employed) took better advantage of their resources by mixing business with pleasure.

It was pointless to ask foreign tourists about their monthly family income; because each would have quoted a figure in a different currency and which, in any case, would not have been comparable with the Indian situation.

Among the domestic tourists, it was found that 48% had a monthly family income above Rs. 15,000, 32% had it between Rs. 10,000 and 15,000, 11% between Rs. 5,000 and 10,000 and only 9% below Rs. 5,000. Although the instinct to travel for business, recreation and pilgrimage purposes and need not necessarily be associated with one's family or personal income, it is obvious that higher the income, better is one's economic situation to take up travel.

III. **Earlier Travels and Preferred Places of Stay**—Majority of the foreign tourists responded that during the preceding three years, they had undertaken at least one excursion overseas. Some of them had already come to Bihar on earlier occasions and visited places like Patna, Gaya and Muzaffarpur.

IV. **Means of Travel**—Invariably, the foreign tourists had arrived in Bihar travelling in Economy class. Within India, they opted to travel by rail (air-conditioned chaircar, air-conditioned first or second class and even ordinary second class, whatever was available because of time pressures) as well as private or state road transport corporation's luxury tourist buses.

V. **Quantum of Money Spent**—The foreign tourists responded that, excluding airfares, they would spend between US$ 5,000 to 10,000 in India on hotel bills, travel, food and beverages, photographic supplies, etc., before they leave for the home country. They carried their money in international traveller's cheques or credit cards. The notable fact was that a foreign tourist was neither a spendthrift nor extravagant; he just spent this money wisely.

VI. **Preferred Ways of Spending the Time**—The domestic and foreign tourists, slightly more than half were interested in visiting celebrated temples, around one-fifth wished to spend the day and early evening at a scenic spot on Falgu Nadi at Bodhgaya, Rajgir, Nalanda, Bihar Yoga Bharti, Munger, Mandar Hill, Vikramshila, Ajgaibi Nath Mandir, Bateshwar Asthan etc.

VII. **Interests En route**—On arriving in Bihar and while proceeding towards the already chosen tourist destinations, about one-third foreign tourists would have liked to visit Gaya, Nalanda Rajgir and Bihar Yog Bharti.

PLATE IX

Golghar, Patna

Patna Museum

PLATE X

Khuda Bakhsh Oriental Public Library, Patna

Harmandir Jee, Patna

PLATE XI

Agamkuan, Patna

Pathar-Ki-Masjid, Patna

PLATE XII

Bari Patan Devi, Patna

Mauryan Hall Pillar, Kumhrar, Patna

PLATE XIII

Sanjay Gandhi Biological Park

Bari Dargah, Maner Sharif

Chhoti Dargah, Maner Sharif

Excavated Ruin of Nalanda Maha Vihar

PLATE XIV

Hsuen Tseng Statue

Rajgir Peace Stupa of Budha

Ruins of the University Complex, Nalanda

PLATE XV

Archaeological Museum

Rajgir Ruin

PLATE XVI

Griddhakoot Hill, Rajgir

Maniyar Math, Rajgir

PLATE XVII

Swarn Bhandar Caves, Rajgir

Jarasandh ki Baithak or Pippala Stone House, Rajgir

PLATE XVIII

Jain Temple, Rajgir

The Venuvan Vihar, Rajgir

PLATE XIX

Hot Water Springs, Rajgir

The Mahabodhi Temple, Bodh Gaya

Bodhi Tree, Bodh Gaya

Kurkihar, Patna

Monastery Vaisha i

Ruins of Vaishali

PLATE XX

Ashokan Pillar, Vaishali

Stone Statue at Aurangabad

Vishwa Shanti Stupa, Vaishali

PLATE XXIII

Vikramshila University

Kesaria Bodh Temple, East Champaran

PLATE XXIV

Munger Fort

Bihar Yoga Bharti, Munger

VIII. Miscellaneous Opinions—About 80% foreign tourists and 40% domestic tourists expressed the need of good and reliable communication facilities like fax, e-mail and Internet at the hotels; 80% foreign tourists and 70% domestic tourists expressed that hotels may provide handouts about the various tourist sights in the vicinity; 70% foreign tourists and 90% domestic tourists felt that the hotel should have a shopping complex, a gymnasium/recreation centre; in addition, 55% domestic tourists felt that hotels should have a swimming pool. About 10% tourists in both categories also felt the need of a newspapers/periodicals reading room-cum-bookstore in the hotel lobby. Further, 90% foreign tourists and 40% domestic tourists expressed that the State-wise information about the hotels, their tariffs and the distance from the airport/railway station/bus-stand be made available on a single web site, so that itineraries could be planned well beforehand and reservations made.

IX. Specific Opinions of Foreign Tourists—While in Bihar, 60% foreign tourists preferred Bihari food, 30% Continental food and only 10% Chinese food; a large majority of 60% tourists wanted only lodging facilities, while 40% wanted both lodging and boarding facilities.

Majority of the foreign tourists felt that the Bihari hoteliers/hotel chains catering to foreign tourists should advertise on CNN or BBC channels of satellite television. These hoteliers/hotels chains may also get themselves listed with Indian Embassies and Consulates abroad. Also, the tourism authorities of Bihar should establish a well advertised web site exclusively devoted to tourism in Bihar.

REFERENCES

Anand, M.M. (1976): *Tourism and Hotel Industry in India*, Prentice Hall of India Ltd., New Delhi.

Badan, B.S. and Bhatt, H. (2007) : *Tourism and Economic Development*, Commonwelth Publishers, New Delhi-2.

Bhatia, A.K. (2007) : *Tourism Development : Principles and Practices*, 2nd Revised Edition, Sterling Publishers Private Limited, New Delhi-20.

http://drdapatna.bih.nic.in/patna_at_glance.html

http://www.tourism.gov.in/survey/BIHAR%20TOURISM%20ANNUAL%20STATISTICS%20%20REPORT%20Final.pdf Statics Tourism in Bihar on Indian Government's tourism website

http://www.indiaheritage.org/creative/creative_metal_work.htm

Mishra Shreegovind, (1970): *History of Bihar—1740-1772*, Munshiram Manoharlal, New Delhi.

Patil, P.B. (2006) : *Tourism Development : Problem and Prospects*, Current Publications, Agra-10 (U.P.)

Saraswati Swami Sahajanand, (2003): *Cultural Heritage of India*, Rachnawali Prakashan Sansthan, Delhi.

Sinha, Indradeep (1969): *Sathi ke Kisanon ka Aitihasic Sangharsha* (Historic Struggle of Sathi Peasants), in Hindi, Patna.

Verma, S.B., Jiloka, S.K. and Thryambakam, P. (2006) : *Rural Tourism and Tribal Development*, Deep & Deep Publications Pvt. Ltd., New Delhi-27.

Yadav Ramendra Kumar, (2004): *Bihar: Myth and Reality*, Hope India, New Delhi.

6

Tourism and Hospitality in Bihar

Introduction

India offers myriad exciting experiences to tourists. They boasts of the world's highest mountains, miles of coastline with excellent beaches, tropical forests and wildlife, lagoon backwaters, ancient monuments and World Heritage sites, forts and palaces, and of course, the Taj Mahal. Bihar tourism and hospitality industry has also emerged as one of the key sectors driving the State's growth and is thriving, owing to a huge surge in both business and leisure travel by foreign and domestic tourists.

According to the latest Tourism Satellite Accounting (TSA) research, released by the World Travel and Tourism Council (WTTC) and its strategic partner Accenture, India's travel and tourism industry was estimated to generate approximately US$ 100 billion in 2008. This figure is expecte to go up to almost US$ 275.5 billion by 2018, growing at an average of 9.4 per cent over the next ten years. Moreover, according to the TSA research, travel and tourism is expected to contribute 6.1 per cent to India's national Gross Domestic Product (GDP) and provide almost 40 million jobs by 2018. Significantly, a Country Brand Index (CBI) 2008 survey, conducted by Future Brand—a leading global brand consultancy—in collaboration with public relations firm Weber Shandwick's Global Travel and Lifestyle Practice, has ranked India second in the value-for-money index.

The rapid growth of India's tourism industry has been instrumental in making South Asia the preferred tourist destination as noted by the UN World Tourism Organisation (UNWTO).

In fact, according to the World Travel and Trade Council, demand in tourism in India will continue to grow at a rapid pace. It estimates the demand to grow at an average of 8.8 per cent between 2004 and 2013, making India the world's third fastest-growing tourist market. The boom in the Indian tourist industry has percolated to the rural areas as well. India continues to attract tourist owing to its spending historical architecture and rich culture along with beautiful beaches and rural tourism. The statistics on Annual tourist composition in Bihar is given in Fig. 6.1.

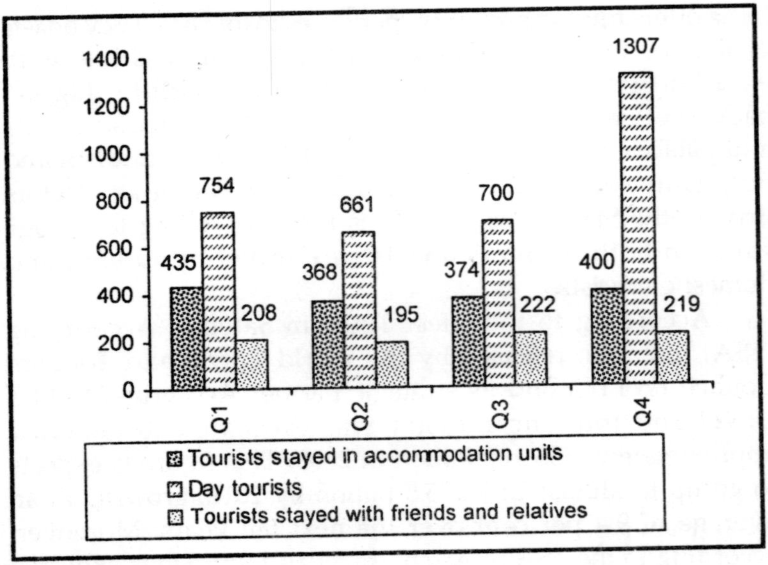

Fig. 6.1 : Annual Tourist Composition

Table 6.1 shows that almost 67% of the tourists in Bihar were married. Majority of the tourists were less than 35 years of age. Foreign tourists were marginally older than domestic ones; 19% of them were more than 44 years of age.

Table 6.2 shows the age and gender of tourists in Bihar. There is no significant difference in the age profile of male and female tourists.

Table 6.1 : Marital Status and Age of Tourists (%)

Marital Status	*Domestic Tourists*	*Foreign Tourists*	*Overall*
Single	33	35	33
Married	66	64	67
Age Groups (Years)	*Domestic Tourists*	*Foreign Tourists*	*Overall*
0-14	0.4	0.4	0.4
15-24	32.7	19.5	31.5
25-34	37.2	38.1	37.3
35-44	20.7	23.1	21.0
45-54	6.3	9.7	6.6
55-64	2.0	6.0	2.4
>65	0.6	3.1	0.9

Table 6.2 : Age and Gender of Domestic and Foreign Tourists

Age Groups	*Domestic Tourists*		*Foreign Tourists*		*Overall*	
(Years)	*Male*	*Female*	*Male*	*Female*	*Male*	*Female*
0-14	64	36	100	-	68	32
15-24	87	13	80	20	87	13
25-34	89	11	82	18	88	12
35-44	91	9	87	13	91	9
45-54	86	14	79	21	85	15
55-64	73	27	58	48	70	30
>65	77	23	61	39	72	28
Overall	**88**	**12**	**80**	**20**	**87**	**13**

Note: There is no significant difference in the age profile of male and female tourists.

Foreign Tourist Arrivals

Estimates of Foreign Tourists Arrivals (FTAs) and Foreign Exchange Earnings (FEE) (on the basis of data received from major airports) are important indicators of the tourism sector.

FTA figures for 2008 were 5.37 million against 5.08 million in 2007, showing a 6-8 per cent rise over 2007, indicating that despite the global financial meltdown and the recent terrorist attacks, the number of tourists coming to India have gone up.

In fact, the Indian growth rate of 5.6 per cent for international tourist arrivals exceeded the United Nations World Tourism Organisation's (UNWTO) forecast of a growth rate of 2-3 per cent for international tourist arrivals in the world for 2008.

According to figures released by the Tourism Ministry, FEE from this sector posted a rise of 8 per cent at US$ 11.5 billion in 2008 as against US$ 10.70 billion registered in 2007. Table 6.1 and 6.2 show the marital status and age of tourists in Bihar.

Promoting Tourism

Amidst fears of global meltdown likely to impact the tourism sector in India, the government is trying to woo tourists.

The Bihar government has launched the Bihar Rajya Home Stay Scheme 2008. Under the scheme, tourists are given the opportunity to see the rural areas of Bihar, enjoying their stay in comfortable home-stay accommodations. Every Stay Unit owner shall get the unit registered with the state department of tourism and the owner of the Home Stay Unit would charge the rates approved by the department.

Tourist Traffic in Bihar

A total of 58,44,196 tourists (including day tourist) visited the 24 destinations, in the period January-December 2005. The peak in tourist traffic came in the fourth quarter, which accounted for 33% of all tourists. This rise can be attributed to the Sonepur cattle fair, which was attended by approximately 5,80,000 day tourists in the months of November-December. There was a significant increase in the tourists traffic in September because of higher numbers visiting Gaya for Vishnu Puja and religious rites (Pind-dan). The months of January and December witnessed higher numbers of foreign tourists. Tourist traffic remained weak at both Buddhist and non-Buddhist destinations in the summer months. Foreign tourists accounted for almost 7% of the traffic at Buddhist destinations and less than 1% at non-Buddhist destinations (Table 6.3).

Table 6.3 : Domestic Tourist Traffic (2005)

	Domestic Tourists Staying Overnight in Accommodation Units													
Destinations	*Months*												*Total*	*Contri.*
	Jan	*Feb*	*Mar*	*Apr*	*May*	*Jun*	*Jul*	*Aug*	*Sep*	*Oct*	*Nov*	*Dec*		*%*
Patna/Sonepur Maner/Hajipur/ Sasaram	62113	42460	60692	68821	57843	62130	64418	62458	61872	52117	51618	61277	706919	46.72
Muzaffarpur	14383	17420	16184	11799	12414	9147	10378	9267	10095	9085	10363	9921	140456	9.28
Gaya	13559	9192	10359	15506	10446	10614	10814	13304	19190	12358	12244	12401	149987	9.91
Bhagalpur/ Sultanganj	11302	19956	7383	5190	5542	5080	8114	7550	7576	10023	8095	12481	108292	7.16
Sitamarhi	5560	5229	4316	3707	3503	2734	2715	2788	3466	3503	4113	3846	45480	3.01
Darbhanga	3639	5413	5190	8155	5928	5279	5704	5434	6699	6849	7179	8074	73543	4.86
Pawapuri	3700	1200	2474	572	61	310	844	1743	2965	180	1300	3740	19089	1.26
Raxaul	2296	1452	1704	2334	2218	2317	2293	2228	2322	2180	2022	2315	25681	1.70
Munger	2231	2810	1860	808	1326	1392	1495	1298	1374	1632	2424	2071	20721	1.37
Madhubani	2048	1336	1645	1724	1941	812	1516	1481	1387	1755	1402	1766	18813	1.24
Madhepura/ Singheshwara	1587	7175	2513	1627	1968	1911	1817	1240	827	1109	1312	1805	24891	1.65
Saharsa	1086	1033	1381	676	1591	1618	1545	1479	1380	1319	1332	1658	16098	1.06
Overall in non-Buddhist destinations	123504	114676	115701	120919	104781	103344	111653	110270	119153	101210	103404	121355	1349970	89.22
Bodhgaya	6545	16977	3390	3271	3057	4759	3300	2926	3978	4349	5229	5583	63364	4.19
Rajgir	8113	10295	7081	7543	6194	6734	4298	4731	5661	10508	7771	10853	89782	5.93
Nalanda	2000	277	277	360	109	147	127	505	906	551	1549	1313	8121	0.54
Areraj	320	55	70	40	0	2	20	0	0	0	90	70	667	0.04
Vaishali	181	16	108	8	244	64	3	5	22	28	6	7	692	0.05
Kesaria	30	7	0	4	0	10	17	105	95	2	144	104	518	0.03
Overall in Buddhist destinations	17189	27627	10926	11226	9604	11716	7765	8272	10662	15438	14789	17930	163144	10.78
Overall in Bihar	140693	142303	126627	132145	114385	115060	119418	118542	129815	116648	118193	139285	1513114	100.00

Table 6.4 : Foreign Tourist Traffic (2005)

Domestic Tourists Staying Overnight in Accommodation Units														
Destinations	*Months*												*Total*	*Contri.*
	Jan	*Feb*	*Mar*	*Apr*	*May*	*Jun*	*Jul*	*Aug*	*Sep*	*Oct*	*Nov*	*Dec*		*%*
Patna/Sonepur Maner/Hajipur/ Sasaram	2844	360	801	435	188	328	103	354	720	876	1632	2063	10704	16.70
Muzaffarpur	27	5	2	0	3	0	0	0	0	0	2	3	42	0.07
Gaya	220	261	108	1039	39	28	13	11	20	66	85	237	2127	3.32
Bhagalpur/ Sultanganj	10	0	0	0	0	2	0	0	0	0	0	0	12	0.02
Sitamarhi	0	0	0	23	348	120	79	120	42	319	110	207	1368	2.13
Darbhanga	99	61	170	830	165	19	0	70	100	118	0	0	1632	2.55
Pawapuri	0	0	0	0	0	0	0	0	0	0	0	0	0	0.00
Raxaul	221	22	716	515	280	259	245	78	95	123	90	78	2722	4.25
Munger	0	1	0	0	1	1	2	6	3	3	12	2	31	0.05
Madhubani	63	31	51	37	50	29	0	0	8	10	0	0	279	0.44
Madhepura/ Singheshwara	25	0	0	0	0	0	0	0	0	0	0	0	25	0.04
Saharsa	16	0	0	0	0	7	0	0	0	0	0	0	23	0.04
Overall in non-Buddhist destinations	3525	741	1848	2879	1074	793	442	639	988	1515	1931	2590	18965	29.58
Bodhgaya	7278	6489	2941	956	348	247	842	1266	1395	2902	7027	7080	38771	60.47
Rajgir	626	230	707	47	14	14	38	496	479	492	919	956	5418	8.45
Nalanda	0	93	93	11	0	8	60	55	2	0	181	305	808	1.26
Areraj	0	0	0	0	0	0	0	0	0	0	0	0	0	0.00
Vaishali	24	0	52	52	0	0	0	2	4	6	9	3	152	0.24
Kesaria	0	0	0	0	0	0	0	0	0	0	0	0	0	0.00
Overall in Buddhist destinations	7928	7212	3793	1066	362	269	940	1819	1880	3400	8136	8344	45149	70.42
Overall in Bihar	11453	7953	5641	3945	1436	1062	1382	2458	2868	4915	10067	10934	64114	100.00

Table 6.4 shows the foreign tourists traffic in Bihar (2005).

A total of 58,44,209 tourists were registered in the period January-December 2005. Out of all tourist traffic 26% were domestic tourists, 1% were foreign tourists, 14% were tourists who stayed with friends and relatives and 59% were day tourists. The peak in tourist traffic came in the fourth quarter. This rise can be attributed to the Sonepur cattle fair, which was attended by approximately 5,80,000 day tourists in the months of November-December. Tourists traffic dipped in the second and third quarters due to high temperatures in the summer months. There was a significant increase in the tourist traffic in September because of higher numbers visiting Gaya for Vishnu Puja and religious rites (Pind-dan). The months of January and December witnessed higher numbers of foreign tourist. (Fig. 6.2).

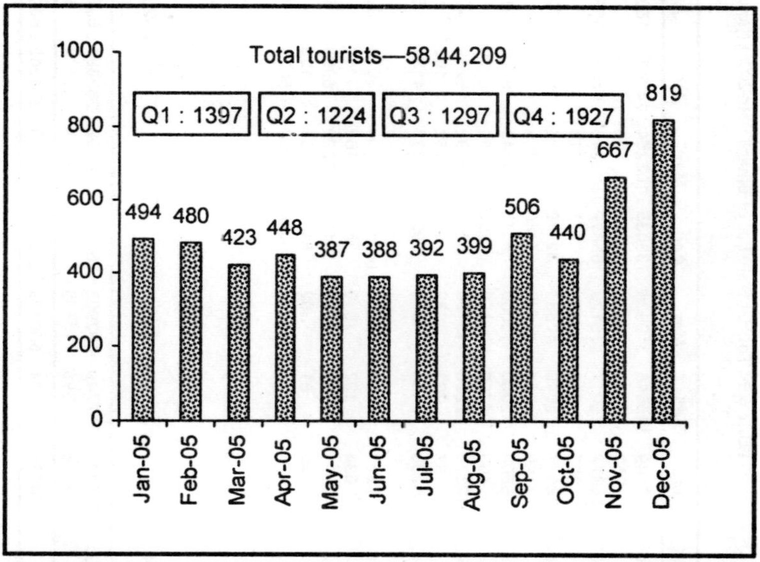

Fig. 6.2 : Month-wise Trend in Tourist Traffic in Bihar (2005)

Tables 6.5, 6.6 and 6.7 show that there is a steady increase in the number of Indian and foreign tourists to Bihar, the total of which increased from 107.76 lakh in 2006 to 112.19 lakh in 2008.

Table 6.5 : Tourist Statistics of Bihar (Year-2006) (January to December, 2006)

Place	*Tourist*	*Jan*	*Feb*	*Mar*	*Apr*	*May*	*Jun*	*Jul*	*Aug*	*Sep*	*Oct*	*Nov*	*Dec*	*Total*
Patna	Domestic	17809	145548	310936	133035	103254	143437	168346	153337	160247	183321	174610	148767	2008647
	Foreign	252	439	420	287	120	124	97	86	459	499	622	559	3964
Gaya	Domestic	65372	75017	75123	65652	66288	64635	308820	355009	41169	5748	6057	7795	1136725
	Foreign	202	216	1494	171	113	94	142	187	160	57	159	343	3338
Bodhgaya	Domestic	56577	75649	47889	32110	15588	16273	9661	17240	54216	36689	47220	55678	464790
	Foreign	7498	21284	11287	5440	689	81	160	221	229	1534	2052	2442	52917
Rajgir	Domestic	36500	22000	19000	8678	10748	9040	21500	340	20706	88400	37705	44000	348277
	Foreign	400	1000	300	200	50	30	200	1000	405	4000	1800	1500	10885
Raxaul	Domestic	12379	12226	13190	9306	9692	9289	10213	9623	10140	14510	15198	15781	141547
	Foreign	187	203	233	141	152	103	1226	247	191	273	348	265	2469
Munger	Domestic	6230	3404	4654	3993	3823	4134	5211	4604	4156	3131	4555	3683	51578
	Foreign													
Vaishali	Domestic	7853	4200	14200	100680	15400	5078	32278	51076	3279	7540	8116	8523	261223
	Foreign	634	192	1910	3860	168	117	566	2447	1442		125		11461
Muzaffarpur	Domestic	2991	9705	8001	5101	7209	6985	5207	1330	6109	3542	4739	4720	65639
	Foreign	35	61	92	8108	81	125	201						8703
Bhagalpur	Domestic				5449	4390	5020	17025	6300	7185	6501	5995	7077	64942
	Foreign													
Sonepur Fair	Domestic											4001000		4001000
	Foreign											709		709
Shrawani Mela Sultanganj (Bhagalpur)	Domestic							2020600	105300					2125900
	Foreign													
Total	**Domestic**	365711	347749	492993	364004	236392	269891	2598861	733819	310207	349382	4305235	296024	10670268
	Foreign	9208	23395	15736	18207	1373	674	1492	4188	2886	6363	5815	5109	94446
Grand Total		374919	371144	508729	382211	237765	270565	2600353	738007	313093	355745	4311050	301133	10764714

Source: Bihar Economic Survey, 2006-07.

Table 6.6 : Tourist Statistics of Bihar (January to December, 2007)

Place	Tourist	Jan	Feb	Mar	Apr	May	Jun	Jul	Aug	Sep	Oct	Nov	Dec	Total
Patna	Domestic	18706	159359	330945	139037	11424	162531	169754	163457	169229	192326	180621	159776	1857165
	Foreign	292	493	425	327	155	154	102	92	463	511	635	576	4225
Gaya	Domestic	67362	75987	77023	66058	67387	65130	318731	365028	47661	6021	6098	7875	1170361
	Foreign	241	292	1532	185	129	121	139	198	184	69	178	369	3637
Bodhgaya	Domestic	56947	76891	48492	33114	15689	16485	9896	17542	54884	36784	47985	56452	471161
	Foreign	7584	21986	11892	5998	721	120	189	265	288	1622	2102	2520	55287
Rajgir	Domestic	36702	23012	19089	8721	10811	9106	21613	398	20841	88789	37811	44958	321851
	Foreign	465	195	356	278	62	42	252	1059	478	4085	1867	1599	10738
Raxaul	Domestic	12415	12308	13239	9420	9745	9324	10098	9688	10201	14579	15241	15821	142079
	Foreign	219	287	299	183	187	165	1327	284	209	309	384	311	4164
Munger	Domestic	6297	3483	4751	4110	3909	4211	5269	4678	4184	3201	4598	3742	52433
	Foreign													0
Vaishali	Domestic	7902	4295	14248	100712	15468	5124	32293	51112	3297	7620	8198	8588	258857
	Foreign	695	228	1998	3909	211	201	631	2499	1493		184		12049
Muzaffarpur	Domestic	3021	9841	8121	51841	7269	7019	5289	1402	6178	3598	4810	47878	156267
	Foreign	84	98	121	8187	103	164	258						9015
Bhagalpur	Domestic				5486	4421	5110	17123	6387	7213	6589	6101	71123	129553
	Foreign													0
Sonepur Fair	Domestic											4111000		4111000
	Foreign											787		787
Shrawani Mela Sultanganj (Bhagalpur)	Domestic							2221300	155670					2376970
	Foreign													
Total	Domestic	11702	14462	24488	170135	27472	17618	2276894	217070	18181	17807	4131080	127589	7094498
	Foreign	11786	14560	24609	183808	31996	22892	4515575	379127	25394	24396	8248968	198712	1361823
Grand Total		23488	29022	49097	353943	59468	40510	6792469	596197	43575	42203	12380048	326301	20786321

Source: Bihar Economic Survey, 2007-08.

Table 6.7 : Tourist Statistics of Bihar (Year-2008) (January to December, 2008)

Place	Tourist	Jan	Feb	Mar	Apr	May	Jun	Jul	Aug	Sep	Oct	Nov	Dec	Total
Patna	Domestic	18789	159402	330987	139102	11469	162595	169802	163531	169333	192412	180784	159854	1858060
	Foreign	385	587	521	415	231	201	197	126	562	598	713	615	5151
Gaya	Domestic	67429	76589	77125	66542	67512	65222	318815	365578	47845	6158	6210	7923	1172948
	Foreign	319	345	1512	299	286	201	265	321	253	122	254	485	4662
Bodhgaya	Domestic	56998	76954	48685	33268	15745	16621	9999	17754	54983	36845	48745	56821	473418
	Foreign	7721	23101	12874	6210	906	224	287	402	365	1721	2189	2598	58598
Rajgir	Domestic	36884	23211	19152	8796	10985	9268	21758	521	20987	88869	37985	45874	324290
	Foreign	512	265	421	321	102	95	368	1214	641	4254	1998	1689	11880
Raxaul	Domestic	12524	12441	13270	9512	9809	9415	10208	9808	10921	14719	15361	16423	144411
	Foreign	301	359	368	234	251	214	1378	320	269	378	421	398	4891
Munger	Domestic	6389	3983	4896	4580	4109	4411	5329	4757	4268	3326	4721	3742	54511
	Foreign													0
Vaishali	Domestic	8054	4396	14587	100884	15869	5258	32369	51248	3365	7754	8248	8588	260620
	Foreign	789	333	2104	4098	369	452	784	2658	1698		414		13699
Muzaffarpur	Domestic	3157	9998	8458	52147	7301	7098	5321	1652	6321	3754	4987	48120	158314
	Foreign	152	175	241	8356	235	261	324						9744
Bhagalpur	Domestic				5524	4554	5211	17254	6258	7375	6700	6325	71365	130566
	Foreign													0
Sonepur Fair	Domestic											4115800		4115800
	Foreign											879		879
Shrawani Mela Sultanganj (Bhagalpur)	Domestic							2258970	157875					2416845
	Foreign													
Total	Domestic	210224	366974	517160	420355	147353	285099	2849825	778982	325398	360537	4429166	418710	11109783
	Foreign	10179	25165	18041	19933	2380	1648	3603	5041	3788	7073	6868	5785	109504
Grand Total		220403	392139	535201	440288	149733	286747	2853428	784023	329186	367610	4436034	424495	11219287

Source: Bihar Economic Survey, 2008-09.

Tables 6.8 and 6.9 and Fig. 6.4 and 6.5 shows that the government's efforts to rejuvenate and revitalize the once moribund sector have shown amazing results. The inflow of foreign tourists in Bihar saw a six-fold increase in 2008-09 as against 2005-06 to 3,56,446 in 2008-09.

Moreover, the number of domestic tourists touched an all-time high of 1.22 crore in 2008-09 from 86.87 lakhs in 2005-06.

The current growth in the number of foreign and domestic tourists has been attributed to state government's efforts to create a more conducive and secure environment. "People (tourist) are now feeling safe and secured in the new regime and this has resulted in a remarkable increase in the tourists inflow to the state", says an official of the tourist department.

Table 6.8 : No. of Domestic and Foreign Tourists in Bihar (2000-2009)

Years	*Domestic Tourists*	*Foreign Tourists*	*Total*
2000	5520589	73321	5593950
2001	6861168	85673	6946841
2002	5860207	112873	6105647
2003	6044827	60820	8173692
2004	8135574	38118	8750541
2005	8687220	63321	10764714
2006	10670268	94446	10530249
2007	10352887	177361	12235183
2008	11889657	356446	12246103
2009	12289528	417895	10907423

Table 6.9 : Budget : Allocation and **Actual expenditure** on Tourism Sector in Bihar Tourism

(Rs. in Lakh)

Years	*Amount Approved*	*Actual Expenditure*
2001-02	210.00	48.60
2002-03	500.00	75.10
2003-04	350.94	350.60
2004-05	957.73	957.00
2005-06	743.00	737.00
2006-07	1830.00	1823.34
2007-08	2679.72	2673.54
2008-09	2513.02	2512.78
2009-10	2978.00	2967.00

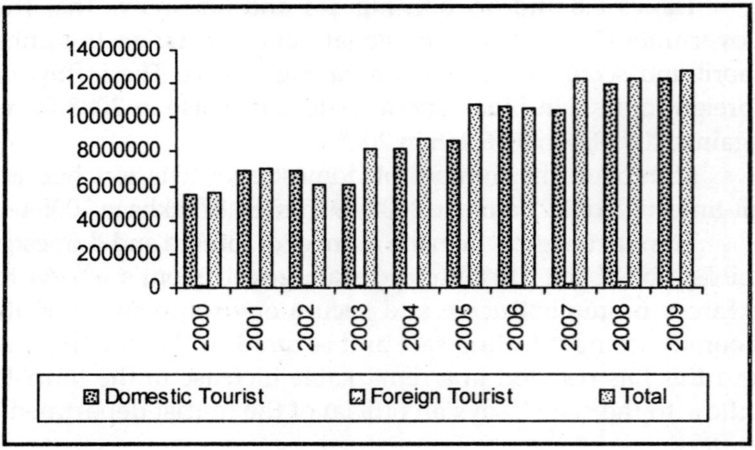

Fig. 6.3 : No. of Domestic and Foreign Tourists in Bihar (2000-2009)

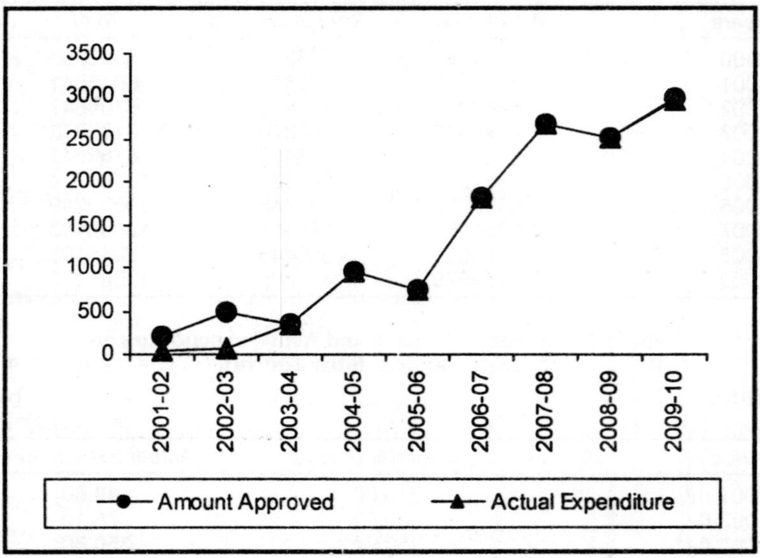

Fig. 6.4 : Budget : Allocation and Actual expenditure on Tourism Sector in Bihar Tourism (Rs. in Lakh)

Thus, Bihar is one of the oldest inhabited places in the world, with a history spanning 3,000 years. The rich culture and heritage of Bihar is evident from the innumerable ancient monuments spread throughout the state. Bihar is visited by scores of tourists from allover the world with around 9 million tourists every year. In earlier days, tourism in the region was purely based on educational tourism, as Bihar was home of some prominent ancient universities like Nalanda University and Vikramasila University. Bihar is one of the most sacred places for various religions like Hindusim, Buddhism, Jainism, Sikhism and Islam. Mahabodhi Temple, a Buddhist shrine and UNESCO World Heritage Site is also situated in Bihar. Mahatma Gandhi Setu, Patna, is the longest river bridge in the world.

Hospitality

The boom in India's tourism industry and the surge in tourist inflow to the country have percolated to other associated sectors like hospitality. The revenues for the Indian hotel and restaurant industry in the year 2006-07 exceeded US$ 118.85 million, an increase of nearly 22 per cent over the previous year. The industry is poised for rapid growth and is projected to be well worth over US$ 158.49 million by the year 2010. And with the continuing surge in tourist inflow, this sector is likely to offer tremendous opportunity for investors. For example, while the estimated number of required hotel rooms is around 2,40,000 the current availability is just 90,000 rooms—leaving a shortfall of 1,50,000 rooms to be provided.

India's hospitality sector is expected to see around 40 international hotel brands by 2011, according to a report by Ma Foi Management Consultants. Moreover, the sector is expected to provide over 4,00,000 jobs.

Along with these large-scale expansion plans international hotel asset management companies are also likely to enter India. Several global hotel chains see immense investment opportunities in the sector with global chains like Hilton, Marriott International, Berggren Hotels, Cabana Hotels, Premier Travel Inn (PTI), Inter Continental Hotels group and Hampshire amongst others having announced major investment plans in India with others likely to follow suit.

With land prices coming down and a huge opportunity for quality hotels in India, many global hotel players are announcing new projects in India.

According to Rashes Shah, analyst with brokerage firm, ICICI Direct, "International hotel majors have a long-term view of India. Most properties will become operational only around 2012 by which time the market is expected to bounce back. Most of them also have enough cash to buy land".

Thus, hotels are no longer satisfied with the plain-vanilla room concept but are now getting ready for alternate hospitality formats such as residential hotels, destination resorts, condo hotels, vacation ownership and private residents' club.

REFERENCES

Alan Trevithick (1949): *The Revival of Buddhist Pilgrimage at Bodh Gaya, Anagarika Dharmapala and the Mahabodhi Temple*, p. 36.

Badan, B.S. and Bhatt, H. (2007) : *Tourism and Economic Development*, Commonwelth Publishers, New Delhi-2.

Bhatia, A.K. (2007) : *Tourism Development : Principles and Practices*, 2nd Revised Edition, Sterling Publishers Private Limited, New Delhi-20.

http://drdapatna.bih.nic.in/patna_at_glance.html

http://www.tourism.gov.in/survey/BIHAR%20TOURISM%20ANNUAL%20STATISTICS%20%20REPORT%20Final.pdf Statics Tourism in Bihar on Indian Government's tourism website

http://www.indiaheritage.org/creative/creative_metal_work.htm

Omalley L.S.S. (2005): *History of Magadh*, Veena Publication, New Delhi, p. 31.

Pathak Prabhu Nath, (1988): *Society and Culture in Early Bihar (C.A.D. 200-600)*, Commonwealth Publishers, New Delhi, p. 6.

Patil, P.B. (2006) : *Tourism Development : Problem and Prospects*, Current Publications, Agra-10 (U.P.)

Waddell Austine L., (1993): *Report on the Excavations at Pataliputra (Patna)—The Palibothra of the Greeks*, Asian Publication Services, Calcutta, pp. 5-7.

Verma, S.B., Jiloka, S.K. and Thryambakam, P. (2006) : *Rural Tourism and Tribal Development*, Deep and Deep Publications Pvt. Ltd., New Delhi-27.

7

The Competitive Environment of Tourism in Bihar : Fairs and Festivals

Environment is constantly changing. It is this constant change that makes environment scanning important for leisure, tourism and other organizations. Organizations that remain static in a dynamic environment experience strategic drift are likely to fail. Fig. 7.1 illustrates the concept of strategic drift.

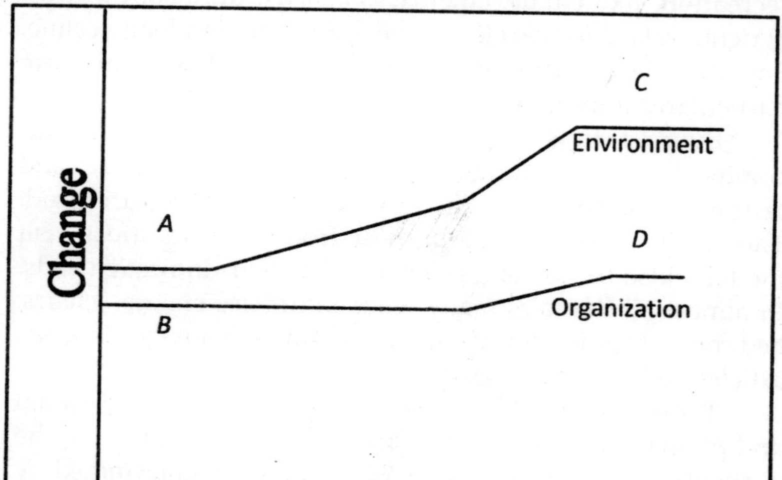

Fig. 7.1 : Strategic Drift

Between period t_0, and t_1, the operating environment is static, and the organization illustrated makes no policy change, so that by the end of the period, at t_1, organizational policy at *B* is in tune with the environment at *A*. However, the period t_1

to t_2 represents a period of dynamic change in the operating environment. The organization, however, undertakes only marginal policy change to that by the end of the period it is experiencing strategic drift, presented by the distance *CD*.

The purpose of the present chapter is to highlight the competitive operating environment and culture in the form of fairs and festivals which also attract the tourists in Bihar.

The Fair

The large number of annual fairs, whether due to religious tradition or economic reasons, have still a very great hold on the volume of trade and commerce within the state. Although most of the consumer goods are now available at any town or township, the fairs have not lost their hold. To the villagers and particularly to the women in the villages, the fairs have a strange fascination. With the provision for amusement and recreation, like circus, cinema, *nautankis*, dramas, theatres, agricultural exhibition etc., the fairs show no sign for a decline. For the sale of cattle and agricultural goods the fairs are particularly important.

Every fair is a great clearinghouse for trade and commerce. A large number of temporary shops crop up and articles of almost every description are sold and purchased. The visitors and particularly those from the rural areas visit the fairs also for making purchases for their domestic needs. In almost all the fairs many wooden articles such as chairs, bed cots, tables, iron goods, foodstuffs and other miscellaneous articles are sold in a large quantity.

These fairs may be divided into two parts, viz., seasonal and permanent. Seasonal fairs are those which are held in the particular season and the time of such fairs is determined by the lunar calendar, whereas permanent fairs those which are held throughout the year once or twice a week irrespective of the seasons and are locally known as *haats*. Seasonal fairs are basically religious in character, whereas permanent fairs are commercial in its composition. A large number of such fairs are held in various parts of the state, however, among these a few only are worth special mention by virtue of their significance and importance in the public life.

Harihar Kshetra Fair, Sonepur

Sonepur (Saran) is considered a place of exceptional holiness and the Ganga Asnan or ceremonial bathing in the Ganges is held by the orthodox Hindus to be unusually efficacious. But the great attraction of the place is the cattle fair, which is held during Ganga Asnan. It lasts for about a fortnight but is at its height for two days before and two days after the bathing in the Ganges on the day of the full-moon (Kartik-Purnima). Immense crowd assemble, the number of which is impossible to estimate with any degree of accuracy.

The roads leading to Harihar Kshetra or Sonepur are thronged for days and in spite of many special trains and buses being provided, they are crammed. Goods of a very great variety and origin are sold at the fair, and also a large number of cattle, horses and elephants; it is in fact one of the largest cattle markets of the world. The period of the inception of the fair like the temple is shrouded in obscurity. Previously, the fair was held at Hajipur (Ramchaura) and only oblation was offered to the deity at Sonepur. The fair at Sonepur appears to have come into prominence during the reign of Aurangzeb, as an European traveller Marshall had mentioned that even the traders of the far-flung Tatar Desh (country) used to come in the fair to deal in commerce.

In former years, the fair was the occasion of a large social and sporting gathering of Europeans. The Sonepur fair was much patronized by the European indigo planters of the nineteenth century. A large camp was held in a magnificent grove and the visitors amused themselves with racing, polo, gymkhanas, tennis, dances and visits to the fair, which presents Indian life under many interesting aspects.

Gulab Bagh Fair

Gulab Bag Fair was first held in the year 1919 within the limits of the Purnea Municipality and was sponsored by Raja P.C.

Lal of Nazarganj. Later it was shifted to the present site. Now this fair has gained a wide popularity and has become an important source of trade and commerce.

The fair is held annually in the month of December and lasts for a month. Lakhs of people visit this second largest cattle fair held in Bihar after the well known Sonepur fair.

Karhagola Fair

Karhagola Mela (fair) had been mentioned in the Riyazu-s-salatin (1788). It is held at Karhagola Ghat which is the terminus of the Ganga-Darjeeling Road, on the bank of the river Ganga every year on the Maghi Purnima, the full moon day of Magh as per Hindu calendar (corresponding with 15th or 16th February) and lasts for about a fortnight. The orthodox Hindus look upon the day as an auspicious one, being the day on which according to Hindu mythology Kaliyug began, and therefore, a bath in the sacred waters of Ganga is considered an act of virtue. A large concourse of people attend the place, and the fair was in the past an important institution from a commercial point of view. A brisk trade was carried on in spices, iron, ploughshares, knives, razors, brass and iron cooking utensils, blankets and durries. But now it has lost its trade importance and is only a religious fair.

Khagra Fair

Khagra Fair (Kishanganj) was started in 1883. The fair is held towards the end of December and lasts for about a month. Before the partition of India in 1947, the fair was very important from commercial point of view. Previously shopkeepers of Dhaka (now in Bangladesh) and other places used to come here. It is reported that the shopkeepers of Punjab also visited the fair. But after partition the shopkeepers of Bangladesh and West Pakistan have ceased to come.

Bettiah Fair

This fair is held at Bettiah (West Champaran) on the Dussehra Durga Puja and lasts for about fifteen days. It attracts a vast number of people from the neighbouring villages at the time of fair. It is estimated that their number does not fall much short of two lakhs or so. The most important feature of this fair is the organization of a cattle fair where several thousand cattles are bought and sold. The cattle fair also attracts sellers and purchasers from the neighbouring districts of Muzaffarpur and Saran as well as from Nepal. The cattle brought for sale here are generally of local breed and are poor in quality. All kinds of commodities required in daily use are sold at this fair. It is the largest fair in the district.

Behula Fair

Bhagalpur is famous for Behula Puja. There is a place at Champanagar known as Behula Asthan where snakes are worshipped on Bisahari Day or Mansa Puja. This Puja (worship) takes place in the month of July every year attended by thousands of persons. An important fair called Behula Fair is held on this occasion in Champanagar and Bhagalpur town.

Baunsi (Mandar) Fair

This fair is held at Mandar (Banka) on the occasion of Makar Sankranti, i.e., in the month of January of every year. It is the largest fair in the area that lasts for about a week and nearly one lakh of people of the district and outside visit the fair.

Malmas Fair

A triennial fair, known as 'Malmas Fair' is held in the leap years in the extra month of the Indian calendar. The Hindus attach a very great importance to bathe in the Saptadhara and Brahmkund and other time-honoured Kunds in the Rajgir hill. The popular belief is that during this month all the gods and goddesses of the Hindu pantheon congregate at Rajgir and thus to visit the place at that time is a rare opportunity of appeasing all gods and goddesses in one single act of worship. Though primarily of religious importance the fair also adds to the local economy. It draws people from allover the state. Shopkeepers and entertainers come even from outside. The total number of visitors is between 12 to 15 lakhs. The Fair lasts for full one month.

Another fair is held here annually on the occasion of Makar Sankranti for the last few years. Its duration is for 3 to 4 days.

Baisakhi Purnima Fair

The full-moon-day (Purnima) of the month of Baisakh is a very important date for the Buddhists. It is on this day that Lord Buddha had his birth, enlightenment and ascension (Mahaparinirvan). To mark this date, a big fair is held at Bodh Gaya where the famous Buddhist temple is situated. Thousands of Hindus from the neighbourhoods as well as from beyond the limits of the district join this fair. The temple is decorated and lit up and the Buddhists and the Hindus offer worship to Lord Buddha. The Buddhist scholars cite the sacred scriptures of the Buddhists. The Fair is marked by cultural shows and exhibitions of agricultural, handicrafts, cattle and art products.

Pitripaksha Fair

Gaya is one of the great places of pilgrimage in India and has special sanctity in the eyes of the Hindus. It is their belief that it is incumbent on every Hindu to visit there and make offerings for the souls of his ancestors. To save the spirits of the manes from the torments is the first duty of the descendants, and the performance of the *Shraddha* or funeral ceremonies at Gaya is regarded as a certain means to secure that end. The sanctity of 'Gaya Shraddha' is based on a legend contained in the *Gaya Mahatmya*, which forms part of the *Vayu Purana*. Hindus of all parts of India, Nepal and even abroad come to Gaya, especially during Pitripaksha, in the Bhadrapad (September-Full-moon day)-Ashwin (October-15th day of the Dark fortnight) months to perform *Shraddha* (offering oblation to ancestors) ceremony of their ancestors under the guidance of Gayawal Pandas (priests). Fair continues for one fortnight.

Brahampur Fair

This Fair or Mela is held at Brahampur (Bhojpur) village, which is at a distance of about 3 kms from Raghunathpur Railway Station. This fair is important for a very large transaction in cattle. It is held twice in a year (i.e. on the occasions of Phalgun-Shivaratri and Baisakh Shivaratri) and lasts for ten to fifteen days. There is a Shiva temple where people come to offer *Puja* (worship).

Saurath Sabha

Saurath is a village in the Madhubani district at a distance of about 29 kms north of Darbhanga town on the Darbhanga-Madhubani Road. Original name of the village, as mentioned in 'Tithi Nirnaya' is Saurashtra. The annual Saurath Sabha, that helds in the Hindu calendar months of Jyestha-Aasadh, is an important social congregation where the marriages of Maithil boys and girls are fixed up according to the reading of horoscope by the *Panjikars* (Registrars). Thousands of people congregate at Saurath on this occasion.

Other Hindu Fairs

- Gupta (Fair) Mela (Rohtas): Basant Panchami (February)—lasts for 15 days.
- Karaghar Fair (Rohtas): Thrice in a year. Cattle Fair, lasts for 7 days.
- Buxar Fair (Buxar) : Thrice in a year. Religious Mela (fair).
- Singheshwar Asthan Fair (Madhepura) : Shivaratri to Phalgun Purnima.
- Tribeniganj Fair : Begins from Ramnavami and lasts for 15 days.
- Kusheshwar Asthan Fair (Darbhanga) : In the month of Phalgun (February-March).

Some Muslim Fairs

Annual Urs of Phulwari Sharif (*Patna*)

Nearly seven kms from Patna junction Railway Station, Phulwari Sharif is an important Muslim pilgrimage. It has been always a favourite abode of Sufi saints in various times. Hazrat Pir Muzibullah Quadri was one of those in the 18th Century. The Khankah Muzibia founded by him at Phulwari Sharif is called the Bari Khankah. Sacred hairs of the beard of Paigamber Hazrat Muhammad Saheb is preserved here in the Bari Khankah that attracts throngs of his followers and a big fair is held every year.

Annual Urs of Khankah Emadia Mangal Talab, Patna Saheb

One of the off-springs in the family of prominent Sufi Saint Hazrat Pir Muzibullah Quadri had founded another Khankah during 19th Century near a tank called Mangal Talab that is situated in the Patna Saheb Chowk area. It is called Khankah Emadia that houses a Madarsa. An Urs is held here annually when throngs of devotees assemble and pay their respect to their beloved Sufi Saint.

Urs Chiraga of Mittan Ghat, Patna Saheb

A beautiful double storied mosque was built by Mugal Prince Azim on the banks of the Ganga at Mittan Ghat in Patna Saheb. The area was previously called Azimabad during the reign of Mugal Emperor Aurangzeb. This mosque was built for Mulla Mittan who was teacher of the Prince. It was the place from where the great Sufi Saint Hazrat Makhdum Muneem used to preach his disciples during the 18th century. The ancient mosque still exists and is popularly known as Dargah Sharif. Every year, after five days of "the Eid" festival, an annual Urs Chiraga is held here when devotees assemble at this Dargah Sharif in great numbers.

Annual Urs of Amjhar Sharif, Aurangabad

Amjhar Sharif is an important Islamic pilgrimage in the Aurangabad district. It is about 10 kms from Panchrukhia on the Daudnagar-Gaya Road (about 100 kms from Patna) under Haspura Police Station. There is an ancient *Mazar* (Grave) of a Muslim saint Hazrat Saiyadana Mohammad Jilani Amjhari Quadri. His Urs Mubaraq (Anniversary) is celebrated here in the first week of Rabi Allab (June) every year. Thousands of Muslim pilgrims visit this place from allover India on this auspicious occasion. Holy Hairs of the Saint, which is still preserved here, are put on Holy Display during the Annual Urs.

Annual Urs of Biharsharif

There is a hill called Pir Pahari, about 1 km to the north-west of the Biharsharif town. At its summit is the Dargah or mausoleum of the Saint Mallik Ibrahim Bayu, round which are ten smaller tombs. This tomb, which stands on the south bank of the river, is held in great veneration by the local Mohammedans, who assemble here on the 5th day of Sawan to celebrate the anniversary of his death. The Chhoti Dargah is the shrine of Badruddin Badr-I-Alam, famous saint who died here in 1440.

Annual Urs of Lakri Dargah (Gopalganj)

The village is situated about 24 kms north of Siwan and has apparently derived its name from a Muslim tomb that it contains. The tomb is that of a Mohammedan saint named Shah Arzan who hailed from Patna. It is said he was attracted by the solitude of the place and had performed a *chilla* or a religious contemplation of 40 days. He also set up a religious establishment, which was endowed by the Emperor Aurangazeb. The anniversary of the saint's death is celebrated on the 11th of Rabi-us-Sani every year that attracts a large crowd.

Hajipur Karbala

The Karbala was constructed 175 years ago by Shah Alam. A large number of Muslims visit this place of pilgrimage throughout the year.

Festivals

The festivals in Bihar can be divided as religious festivals and Tribal festivals. Known as the cradle of Buddhism, Bihar has an immense Hindu majority. So Hindu festivals are celebrated with great pleasure and enthusiasm. Bihar has a long list of celebrations among which Chhath puja, celebrated six days after the Deepavali is the most important. Observed mostly by the people of North Bihar, this puja is devoted for the worship of the Sun God. The other main festivals of Bihar include Kartik Purnima, Holi, Dussehara, Deepavali, Saraswati Puja, Bhaiya Dooj etc.

The months of Bhadon and Ashwin are marked by many religious observances and ceremonies. This is the most critical season of the year to the cultivator, when he must have rain. The end of the former month, he observes the fast of Anant-brat in gratitude for the ingathering of the *bhadai* harvest and in the hope of further prosperity.

Chhath Puja

Chhath, also called Dala Chath—is an ancient and major festival in Bihar. It is celebrated twice a year: once in the summers, called the Chaiti Chhath, and once around a week after Deepawali, called the Kartik Chhath. The latter is more popular because winters are the usual festive season in North India, and Chhath being an arduous observance requiring the worshippers to fast without water for more than 24 hours, is easier to do in the Indian winters. Chhath is the worship of the Sun God. Wherever people from Bihar have migrated, they have taken with them the tradition of Chhath. This is a ritual bathing festival that follows a period of abstinence and ritual segregation of the worshipper from the main household for two days. On the eve of Chhath, houses are scrupulously cleaned and so are the surroundings. The ritual bathing and worship of the Sun God takes place, performed twice: once in the evening and once on the crack of the dawn, usually on the banks of a flowing river, or a common large water body. The occasion is almost a carnival, and besides every worshipper, usually women, who are mostly the main ladies of the household, there are numerous participants and onlookers, all willing to help and receive the blessings of the worshipper. Ritual rendition of regional folk songs, carried on through oral transmission from mothers and mothers-in-law to daughters and daughters-in-law, are sung on this occasion for several days on the go. These songs are a great mirror of the culture, social structure, mythology and history of Bihar and eastern Uttar Pradesh. Chhath being celebrated at the crack of the dawn is a beautiful, elevating spiritual experience connecting the modern Indian to his ancient cultural roots. Chhath is believed to be started by Karna, the king of Anga Desh (modern Bhagalpur region of Bihar).

Among ritual observances, the month long Shravani Mela held along a 108 kilometre route linking the towns of Sultanganj and Deoghar (now in Jharkhand state) is of great significance. Shravani Mela is organised every year in the Hindu month of Shravan, that is the lunar month of July-August. Pilgrims, known as Kanwarias, wear saffron coloured clothes and collect water from a sacred Ghat (river bank) at Sultanganj, walking the 108 km stretch barefooted to the town of Deoghar to bathe a sacred Shiva-Linga. The observance draws thousands of people to the town of Deoghar from allover India.

Teej and Chitragupta Puja are other local festivals celebrated with fervor in Bihar. Bihul-Bishari Puja is celebrated in the Anga region of Bihar. The Sonepur Cattle fair is a month long event starting approximately half a month after Deepawali and is considered the largest cattle fair in Asia. It is held on the banks of the Son River in the town of Sonepur. The constraints of the changing times and new laws governing the sale of animals and prohibiting the trafficking in exotic birds and beasts have eroded the once-upon-a-time magic of the fair.

Apart from Chhath, all major festivals of India are celebrated in Bihar, such as Makar Sankranti, Saraswati Puja, Holi, Eid-ul-Fitr, Eid-ul-Adha (often called Eid-ul-Zuha in the Indian Subcontinent), Muharram, Ram Navami, Rath Yatra, Rakshabandhan, Maha Shivaratri, Durga Puja, Diwali, Laxmi Puja, Christmas, Mahavir Jayanti, Buddha Purnima, Chitragupta Puja, and several other local festivals as well.

Navaratri

Navaratri is one of the major festivals connected with the autumnal equinox, beginning on the first and ending on the tenth day of Navaratri. After the idol of Durga has been worshipped for mine preceding days, it is taken to the river and cast into it. Dussehra celebrates the victory of Rama over Ravana. Hence it is also called Vijayadashami. Huge colourful paper and wooden effigies of Rama's enemies, Ravana, Meghanada and Kumbhkaran filled with fire works are burnt during Dussehra.

Holi and Diwali are the other important Hindu festivals celebrated in Bihar.

Hindu women worship Lord Shiva at Jeth Amavasya to ensure the long life of their husband. At Mauni Amavasya they sit silently under a *pipal* tree on the day of a new moon, provided it is a Monday.

Nag Panchami is a festival observed on the fifth day of the bright half of Sravana. It begins with a fast. Bathing fairs are held on the banks of rivers.

Makar Sankranti is also observed as a festival among certain classes. On this occasion, the participants and believers eat rice flakes, curd and sweets made of til. Janmashtami is observed on the eighth day of the second fortnight in the month of Bhadrapada. Special meals are held and thousands of people visit the sacred places and temples.

Maha-Shivaratri is celebrated with great rejoicing and feasting. Other Bihari festivals are: Saraswati Puja which is celebrated in all educational institutions and images of goddess of learning are worshipped. Raksha Bandhan, Godhan,

Ramnavami, Chitragupta Puja are celebrated mostly by the Kayasthas and Viswakarma Puja is observed only by factory workers and workmen. The chief Muslim festivals in Bihar are the Muharram, the two Ids and Shab-i-barat.

Tribal Festivals

In tribal life, there is a succession of festivals throughout the year which are connected with agricultural operations. The important festivals among them are Sarhul, Karma and Soharai, Hindu festivals of Holi and Durga Puja are also celebrated with great enthusiasm by Hindu tribals.

Sarhul

Sarhul is the most popular of all tribal festivals. It is celebrated on the last day of Baisakh which corresponds to the month of April. It is observed at a time when sal trees are laden with flowers.

It resembles the Vasant-mahotsava of the Hindus and may therefore be described as the spring festival of the tribals. It is an occasion of great festivity and enjoyment for people of all ages. All night maidens and youths sing and dance to the accompaniment of the drum, while the old sit and enjoy the enchanting dances.

Soharai

Another festival among the aboriginals is Soharai or Banda Parab, which occurs is the month of Pausha, celebrated shortly after the harvest of the rice-crop of the year. It may be called the harvest festival of tribals. On this occasion domestic animals are worshipped, after being washed, anointed with oil and smeared with vermilion.

Karma Festival

This festival is observed by the tribals as well as non-tribals. On this occasion, the tribal youths spend the whole night singing ad dancing. The songs sung on this occasion are of legends of *Karma* and *Dharma*.

Folksongs and Music

Bihar has a very old tradition of beautiful folk songs, sung during important family occasions, such as marriage, birth ceremonies, festivals, etc. They are sung mainly in group settings without the help of many musical instruments, though Dholak, and occasionally Tabla and harmonium are used. Bihar also has a tradition of lively Holi songs known as 'Phagua', filled with fun rhythms. During the 19th century, when the condition of Bihar worsened under the British misrule, many Biharis had to migrate as indentured labourers to West Indian islands, Fiji, and Mauritius. During this time many sad plays and songs called *biraha* became very popular, in the Bhojpur area. Dramas on that theme are still popular in the theaters of Patna.

Dances of Bihar

Dance forms of Bihar are another expression of rich traditions and ethnic identity. There are several folk dance forms that can keep one enthralled, such as *dhobi nach, jhumarnach, manjhi, gondnach, jitiyanach, more-morni, dom-domin, bhuiababa, rah baba, kathghorwa nach, jat jatin, launda nach, bamar nach, jharni, jhijhia, natua nach, bidapad nach* and *sohrai nach.*

Cuisine

The staple food is *bhat, dal, roti, tarkari and achar*. It is prepared from rice, lentils, wheat flour, vegetables, and pickle. The traditional cooking medium is mustard oil. *Khichdi,* a broth of rice and lentils seasoned with spices and served with several accompanying items, constitutes lunch for Biharis on Saturdays.

Chitba and *Pitthow* which are prepared basically from rice, are special foods of the Anga region. *Tilba* and *Chewda* of *Katarni* rice also are special preparation of Anga.

Kadhi bari is a popular favourite and consists of field soft dumplings made of *besan* (gram flour) that are cooked in a spicy gravy of yogurt and *besan*. This dish goes very well over plain rice.

Bihar offers a large variety of sweet delicacies which, unlike those from Bengal, are mostly dry. These include *Anarasa, Belgrami, Chena Murki, Motichoor ka Ladoo, Kala Jamun, Kesaria Peda, Khaja, Khurma, Khubi ka Lai, Laktho, Parwal ka Mithai, Pua* and *Mal Pua, Thekua, Murabba* and *Tilkut*. Many of these originate in towns in the vicinity of Patna.

Several other traditional salted snacks and savouries popular in Bihar are *Chiwra, Dhuska, Litti, Makhana* and *Sattu*.

There is a distinctive Bihari flavour to the non-vegetarian cooking, as well, although some of the names of the dishes may be the same as those found in other parts of north India. Roll is a typical Bihar non-vegetarian dish. These are popular and go by the generic name roll Bihari in and around Lexington Avenue (South) in New York City.

REFERENCES

Badan, B.S. and Bhatt Harish (2007): *Tourism and Economic Development*, Commonwealth Publishers, New Delhi, pp. 233-34.

Bhatia, A.K. (2007) : *Tourism Development : Principles and Practices*, 2nd Revised Edition, Sterling Publishers Private Limited, New Delhi-20.

http://drdapatna.bih.nic.in/patna_at_glance.html

http://www.tourism.gov.in/survey/BIHAR%20TOURISM%20 ANNUAL%20STATISTICS%20%20REPORT%20Final.pdf Statics Tourism in Bihar on Indian Government's tourism website

http://www.indiaheritage.org/creative/creative_metal_work.htm

Nambisan Vijay (2000): *Bihar in the eye of the beholder*, Penguin Books, New Delhi, p. 14.

Pathak Prabhu Nath, (1988): *Society and Culture in Early Bihar (C.A.D. 200-600)*, Commonwealth Publishers, New Delhi, p. 6.

Patil, P.B. (2006) : *Tourism Development : Problem and Prospects*, Current Publications, Agra-10 (U.P.)

Verma, B.S. (1992): *Socio-religious Economic and Literary Condition of Bihar*, Munshiram Manoharlal, New Delhi, p. 21.

Verma S.B. et al., (2006): *Rurual Tourism and Tribal Development*, Deep and Deep Publications Pvt. Ltd., New Delhi, p. 3.

8

Marketing of Tourism in Bihar

Introduction

The tourism is one of the most important industries with a tremendous growth potentiality. It makes substantial contribution to the nation to generate income and employment. The tourism has its origin in the growth of human civilization development. In 1929, the revenue earned from World Travel and Tourism was $ 30 million which worked out just 2 per cent of the World Gross Product. Whereas, in 1990 it crossed to $ 2,000 billion forming 12 per cent of the World Gross Product. The tourism accounts for 6 per cent of employment in the organised sector and 7 per cent of the total capital invested in the World.

Although India has a late start in the field of tourism, it has recorded appreciable development over the years. In 1990, the country could receive 62.3 million domestic tourists and 1.71 million foreign tourists enabling the country to earn foreign exchange to the extent of Rs. 1440 crores. The foreign exchange earnings rose to Rs. 3,300 crores in 1991-92 and the industry was much ahead to others in earning foreign exchange. The total earnings from tourism rose to Rs. 73,660 crores in 1994-95. About 5.5 million persons got direct and 8 million persons indirect employment in the industry in 1989-90. The industry has a great potentiality to grow in India, as India is being considered as an important tourist destination which offers a mix of Eastern tradition and grace and the Western modernity. Cultural, historical and natural attractions abound in the country. John Prendergast in his book, *The Road in India,* has observed: "India can be exasperating and it can be lovable. It has yet to learn much about tourism and how to give as well as take... There will be moment when you curse the day our come, but all the time you are absorbing rich experience, so that instead of your once in a life time visit, you will thinking of another based on what you have learnt." India offers unique destination for diversity and homogeneity.

India has not taken big strides in attracting foreign tourists from overseas. It accounts for just 0.31 per cent of world tourism. The pattern of world tourism indicates that 82 per cent of the tourist movements are generated by 17 countries, i.e., 12 in Europe, 2 in North America, Mexico, Japan and Australia. More than 90 per cent of tourist traffic is between Europe and North America. Countries like India can aspire to get only a portion of the tourists left outside Europe and North America Circuit. Thus, India is one among a hundred or more countries vying for the travellers from the main generating countries. One healthy trend is that, the growth rate of tourism in India is more than double the growth rate of tourists in India, the average stay of tourists in India is 28 days, much higher than that of the most other countries, particularly south Asian countries. In spite of dismal role of the industry in global terms, it is the third largest industry in earning foreign exchange. By the end of the century, the tourism industry is poised to earn foreign exchange to the extent of Rs. 10,000 crores.

Although the tourism industry makes substantial contribution to generation of employment and earning foreign plan. The tourism never accounted for more than 1 per cent of the total plan outlay. It must be admitted that the tourism is one of the many activities which helps development without competing with more pressing demands from other sectors like industry, agriculture and social services. The investment made in development of infrastructure like road, railways, air transport, communication, electricity, etc., promotes developmental activities along with tourism. Its recent example is the huge investment made during Asiad on new hotels, stadia, imported cars, coaches and improvement in civil amenities, has made Delhi Asia's being convention centre and helped in the promotion of tourism.

The tourism is highly competitive business where more than 125 countries are engaged in attracting tourists. India has to be marketed as an important tourist destination. An image building exercise has to be carried out to correct the erroneous impression that the country is seething with dirt, squalor, mass poverty and destitution. The projection of India's vastness and a wide variety of tourist attractions would be a challenge to our marketing effort. India has not geared itself to the changing trends of tourist preferences. Even now India is viewed as the centre of cultural tourism only, no substantial effort has been made to build up base for the development of modern tourism such as leisure travel, beach holidays, wildlife tours, skiing, trekking, fishing, photography, yoga, mystique, conventions and incentive tours.

The tourism in India remained confined to golden triangle of Delhi, Jaipur and Agra during fifties, but now the whole country from Himalayas in the north to Kanya Kumari in the south and from Gir forest in the west to Kaziranga in the north-east emerging as the tourist destination.

Bihar as a Tourist Destination

In spite of mass poverty, social chaos, dirt, squalor and destitution, Bihar has a great potentiality to be one of the most important tourist destinations in the country. The potentiality is to be converted into tourist product by adopting proper marketing strategy. Bihar had been the centre of country's culture and civilization. For about 1000 years, the history of Bharat has been shaped by Magadh whose boundary extended to Kabul and Kandhar. Gautam Buddha attained enlightenment at Bodh Gaya, Bihar to get emancipation from the miseries of worldly life. Pataliputra today known as Patna had been the centre of power of Magadh empire. Jains' 24th tirthankar was born at Vaishali and got Nirvana at Pawapuri. His memorial standing in the middle of tank full of lotus flowers gives peace to our mind. Famous mathematician Arya Bhatt lived at Pataliputra. Mahatama Gandhi started his *Satyagrah* movement from Champaran in Bihar. Besides being sacred place for Buddhists and Jains, it is a place of pilgrimage for Sikhs as Guru Govind Singh was born at Patna.

The nature has bestowed precious gift to Bihar. Natural beauty of Chotanagpur catches our imagination. Kakolat, Jonha, Hundru, Dasham falls present fascinating scene and visit to these places is refreshing. Tilaya and Maithon water reservoirs have a good potentiality to be developed as centres for water sports. Hazaribagh and Betala National Parks are teeming with wildlives. Visitors get spell-bound to have a glimpse of roaring elephants, tiger, bison, sambhar and different species of deer in these parks. Valmiki Nagar, Bhimbandh and other wildlife sanctuaries are back in life after a decade of protection. Today there are altogether a dozen of sanctuaries where a variety of wildlife species thrive in their own habitat. Tourist lodges, rest houses, view towards elephant ride make a adventure holiday in the state a thrilling experience.

The historical and archaeological monuments have a wide scope in Bihar. Remains of Nalanda and Vikramshila reveal the educational and cultural attainment of the State in the 5th century A.D. Nalanda University founded in 5th Century A.D. had 10,000 students from many parts of Globe. The Chineses Chronicler Hiuen Tsiang spent many years here both as a student and teacher. Nagarjuna, the Mahayan Buddhist philosopher, Dinagra, the logician and Dharampala, the Brahmin scholar taught here.

The statue of Yakshini made of sandstone about 2000 years ago which attracted the world's attention at Indian festival at Moscow, Newyork, London and Paris, is spreading its grandeur at Patna Musuem. Sandstone pillars of Mauryan halls at Kumhrar (Patna), Ashokan pillars at Vaishali, Lauria and Nandan Garh and Mausoleum of Shershah at Sasaram are relics of rich cultural heritage of Bihar.

Bodh Gaya, Rajgir and Vaishali belong to Buddhist circuit where thousands of foreign tourists from allover the world particularly from south Asian countries visit every year. Located at the Bank of the river Niranjana, Bodh Gaya is one of the most sacred places for Buddhists. Here under Bodhi tree,

Shakyamuni Gautam attained supreme knowledge to become Buddha, the enlightened one. Such is the attraction of the Place that several international Buddhist communities from Burma, Tibet, Japan, China, Korea, Thailand and Vietnam have established their monasteries and displaying their own architectural styles, vying with each other to keep world alien.

Rajgir, another centre of pilgrimage for both Buddhists and Jains, has a great potentiality to be developed as the centre of religious tourism. It is the place where Buddha spent many months of retreat and used to meditate and preach on the Griddhkuta, the hill of vultures. Lord Buddha delivered some of his famous sermons here and converted king of Magadh, Bimbsara and countless others to his creed. Mahavir 24th Tirthankar of Jains spent fourteen years of his life at Rajgir and Nalanda. A Shanti Stupa built by a Japanese saint on the hill and connected with ropeway is a rare attraction.

Another place in Buddhist Circuit Vaishali is famous for world's first democratic republic Lichhavis. Lord Buddha visited the place and delivered his last sermon. Sandstone pillar of 60 feet height installed by the Emperor Ashoka in the third century B.C. is the testimony to the glorious heritage of the place. Lord Mahavir was born here. The place was visited by Chinese travellers Fa-hien and Hiuen Tsiang during 5th and 7th Centuries A.D respectively who wrote a lot about Vaishali. Thus, Bihar has a great potentiality and prospect for both cultural and modern tourism. This is also important from the viewpoint of economy.

Tourist Product

Tourism marketing, which involves marketing a tourist product, clearly means the proper development of the product as per the needs of the consumer by employing the techniques of direct sales, publicity and advertising. Table 8.1 and Figure 8.1, shows the total earnings from tourist in Bihar (2001-04).

Table 8.1 : Earnings from Tourists in Bihar (2001-04)

S.N.	*Earnings*	*2003-2004 (Lakhs)*	*2002-2003 (Lakhs)*	*2001-2002 (Lakhs)*
1.	Hotel (Self Run)	182	193	173
2.	Hotel (On Lease)	33	21	26
	Hotel Total (1+2)	**215**	**214**	**199**
3.	Transport	114	120	114
4.	Ropeway (On Lease)	52	56	61
5.	Others	15	18	23
	Total (3+4+5)	**181**	**194**	**198**
6.	Eng. Section	30	23	10
7.	H/Q (Interest)	51	82	39
	Total (6+7)	**81**	**105**	**49**
	Grand Total	**477**	**513**	**446**

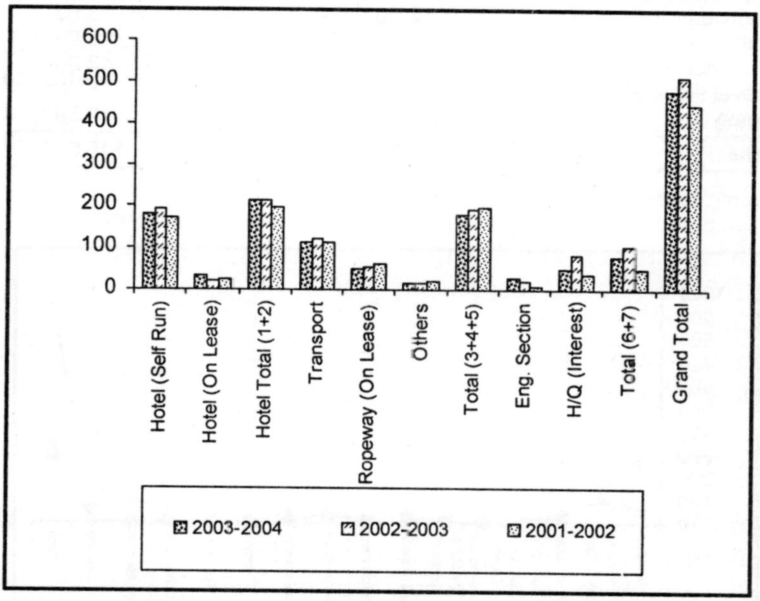

Fig. 8.1 : Earnings from Tourists in Bihar (2001-04)

The average per day expenditure of the domestic tourist was Rs. 286 while average per day expenditure of foreign tourist was Rs. 939. Domestic tourists spent the most of their money on food and beverages while the foreign tourists spent their money on accommodation, food and beverages, travel services, ornaments, textile products and on hiring. (Table 8.2 and Fig. 8.2)

Table 8.2 : Expenditure of Tourists in Bihar

Expenditure	*Domestic (Rs.)*	*Foreign (Rs.)*	*Overall (Rs.)*
Accommodation	53.17	275.70	73.49
Food and beverages	103.17	167.53	109.05
Food products	26.05	48.20	28.07
Alcohol products	3.64	12.40	4.44
Tobacco products	6.39	10.74	6.78
Medicinal product	4.63	9.92	5.11
Study material	10.41	37.43	12.87
Entertainment	7.02	3.52	6.70
Textile products	33.36	68.18	36.54
Durable goods	14.07	44.52	16.85
Footwear	2.80	10.78	3.53
Toiletries	7.19	17.10	8.09
Ornaments	6.90	74.36	13.06
Travel services	.28	92.60	8.70
Hiring	6.96	66.40	12.39
Total	286.04	939.38	345.67

Source: Bihar State Tourism Development Corporation

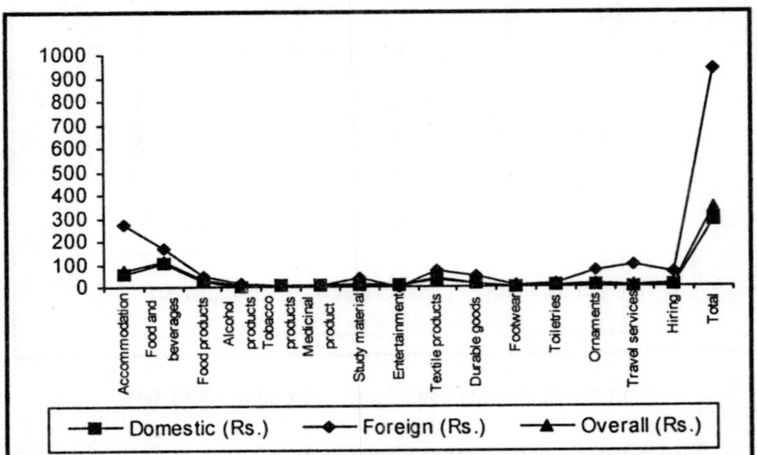

Fig. 8.2 : Expenditure of Tourists in Bihar

Tourism Marketing

Tourism marketing is a multidimensional activity. It is the marketing strategy planned to woo the consumer in the face of stiff competition. Tourism business can gain competitive advantage by:

(i) Product differentiation, that is, by providing quality service in a better way than the competitors;
(ii) Lowering the price in an appropriate healthy and attractive manner with malice towards none;
(iii) Serving particular segments or groups of customers in a more innovative and a worthy manner than the competitors.

Souvenir and Handicraft Shops in Bihar

There were a total of 89 souvenir and handicraft shops in Bihar. Bodh Gaya and Rajgir together accounted for 52% of the souvenir and handicraft shops in Bihar. Patna, Madhubani and Bhagalpur/Sultangangj were the other towns with a significant presence of shops. (Table 8.3 and Fig. 8.3)

Table 8.3 : Population of Souvenir and Handicraft Shops (2005)

Cities	*Shops*	*Emporium*	*Others*	*Total*
Patna and other adjacent towns	7	6	2	15
Muzaffarpur	1	—	—	1
Bhagalpur/Sultanganj	5	2	3	10
Sitamarhi	1	1	—	2
Madhubani	4	3	3	10
Madhepura	5	—	—	5
Bodhgaya	5	15	5	25
Rajgir	3	10	8	21
Total	**31**	**37**	**21**	**89**

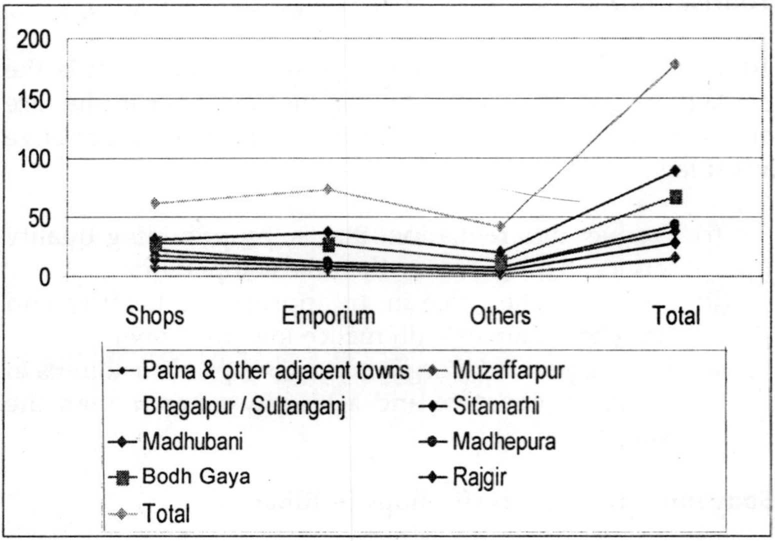

Fig. 8.3 : Population of Souvenir and Handicraft Shops (2005)

Employment Status

Average employment in accommodation units is given in Table 8.4 and Fig. 8.4.

Table 8.4 : Average Employment in Accommodation Units

Cities	*#*	*#*	*Departments*								*#*
	Accom. Units	*Rooms*	*Purchase and Stores*	*HR*	*Public Relation*	*Engg.*	*Telephone*	*Health Club*	*Laundry*	*Other*	*Employees*
Bodh Gaya	53	992	7	2	2	8	4	1	11	27	393
Rajgir	35	684	1	1	0	2	0	0	2	0	144
Nalanda	6	86	0	0	0	0	0	0	0	0	46
Vaishali	5	41	0	0	0	0	0	0	0	1	11
Areraj	2	29	0	0	0	0	0	0	0	0	3
Kesaria	2	11	0	0	0	0	0	0	0	0	0
Total	103	1843	8	3	2	10	4	1	13	28	597
Overall for Bihar	498	9596	92	22	10	32	9	9	52	119	4119

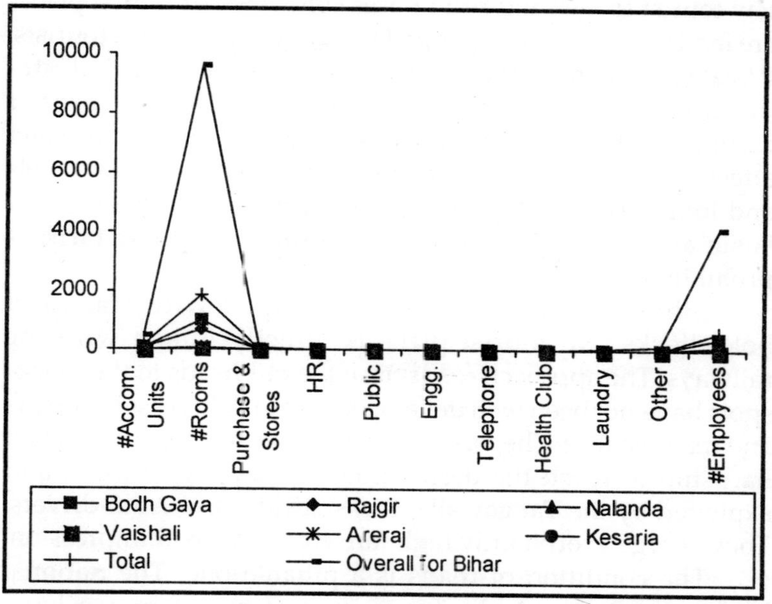

Fig. 8.4 : Average Employment in Accommodation Units

Constraints

Bihar is one of the poorest states with per capita income much lower than the national average and nearly 56 per cent of the population below the poverty line. This poses a great stumbling block in the way of growth of tourism. The stark poverty of the masses is visible at the tourist places where helpless and destitute flock around the foreign tourists wander with the begging bowls in their hands. A few kind-hearted and sensitive tourists get moved and leave the place in disgust. Some capture the abject poverty of the places in their camera and show it to the whole world. This does not augur well for the growth of tourism in Bihar. No efforts are being made to keep beggars away from the tourist spots.

Bihar has ample scope for cultural tourism, but the hinterland of the places of historical and religious importance are not developed. Parks and entertainment centres where tourists can take fresh air and relax are yet to be developed. A few tourist lodges and rest houses contracted at tourist places are inadequate and ill-equipped to cater to the modern tourists. Private sector entrepreneurs have not entered in this industry in any significant way. Non-availability of proper accommodation at tourist centres has become both cause and effect of the development of tourism in Bihar. A few hotels and lodges set up at Patna by the private entrepreneurs lack basic amenities and nicely in dealings and their tariff is prohibitive.

Bihar's tourist centres are gripped with transport bottlenecks. No tourist place is directly linked with the railways. The approach roads from the rail-heads to the tourist spots have not been well developed and lack necessary repairs and maintenance. The foreign tourists have to encounter a great hardship to reach the destination, as they are tortured and exploited by the Tangawalla, Rickshawala, and Auto-drivers. They charge exorbitantly high fare creating a bad impression.

The condition of roads is a pitiable one. The national highways due to lack of repairs and maintenance have developed pot holes which cause road accidents. Road jams on the national highway No. 2, which is used by the tourists from the Buddhist countries for visiting Sarnath from Bodh Gaya, are a normal feature. Government of Japan has given handsome assistance for the widening of roads connecting Bodh Gaya from Patna-Rajgir and Sarnath, but the progress is not satisfactory.

Social condition and environment have a great bearing on the growth of tourism. Simmering social discontents manifested through kidnapping, riots, road hold up, robbery, road blocks are affecting the inflow of tourists in Bihar. Foreign tourists visiting Bodh-Gaya get bitter taste of exploitation, intimidation and deceit. Their belongings are snatched in broad day light and the police does not come to their rescue.

Marketing Strategy

Marketing has a special significance for the promotion of tourism in the state which has so many constraints to overcome. The nature and dimension of marketing the tourist product are distinct. In manufacturing enterprises, a marketing policy was devised for the product which has already been produced. In tourism, the product is an amalgam of various elements, some of which are tangible and some intangible. The marketing strategy in this respect would be based on the consumer's needs, expectations, attitudes, likes and dislikes and the 'tourist product' which is to be development must suit the taste and pocket of the consumers. The tourism is a complex industry with multidimensional activities, which together turn out 'tourist-product'. Various sub-sectors, which are the constituents of the industry, are themselves independent industries e.g. hotel, transport and communication industries. Its marketing is also complicated, as it has to be directed at a large number of people in various lands of socio-economic structure having different tastes, habits, attitudes, expectations and behaviour pattern.

The raw materials for the tourist products are natural beauty, climate, history and culture and the people. The other things are facilities for the comfortable living such as water supply, electricity, road transport, communication and other essentials. The product may be entirely manmade or the nature's creation improved upon by man. All the components of the product are supplied by various individuals or group like hotel company, airlines or other suppliers directly to the tourists. A tourist combines these individual tourist products in a large number of ways. There would be many possible destinations, each with number of hotels, each reached number of airlines and buses. The selection of product is a difficult exercise. The different segments which constitute, the tourist product work independently, each one striving to maximize its gain from tourism. If the desperate efforts of the different segments are unified and consolidated, the marketing of Bihar as a tourist destination would be successful.

A survey has been conducted to identify and potential tourists visiting the state, as the needs of all the tourists are not uniform. American, European Japanese, Chinese, South East-Asian and Australian visit the state, but each needs distinct approach. The facilities are to be created at tourist places as per the customers' needs. The planning for the development of hotels and tourist spots need be based on the realistic needs of the consumers so that the investment to be made to meet the projected demand fetches good return. A study of foreign markets would enable the government and other concerned institutions to distribute the promotional expenditure equitable on those areas which have the biggest tourist potential. A properly conducted market research would cover the entire gaunt of the marketing function viz. product pricing, distribution and promotion.

The estimation of price at which the product is to be sold is quite important. A customer is price sensitive. The tourists expect to get maximum value out of each dollar spent. Foreign tourists are not always looking for convenient foods, perhaps they prefer Indian cuisine like tandoori chicken, kabab, mixed vegetables and *pakauras*. An innovative approach is required so that prices are competitive. Product differentiation is a must for price differentials. In case of hotel chains, each chain should have distinct product line and pricing. The Government should exercise some sorts of control over pricing and quality of the product. The coordinating agency may be Department of Tourist, Government of Bihar.

The distribution of tourist produce in Bihar is equally important. The product is mainly to be sold to foreigners. It is not enough to distribute posters, leaflets and guide books through tourist offices and foreign mission. An attempt should be made to establish personal contact with the potential travellers by a strong market presence and intensive selling campaign by our offices abroad. The state government can supplement the efforts of the Central Government in collaboration with travel agents and tour operators. First, Bihar should exploit its traditional market of Buddhist countries, particularly of South-East Asia and then it should move to new and emerging market across the globe.

The travel agents create market for the tourist product. They determine the source of business from where the tourists originate, the requirement of hotels and transportation and know the preferences of the customers. After determining the market needs, the travel agents apply various methods to achieve the objectives. A travel agent has a great scope to make improvement on the itinerary of the client whereby he enjoys his visit to the country and returns as a friend and ambassador of goodwill. The nationally and internationally known travel agents need be patronized to promote tourism in the state.

An important thing for the promotion of tourism in the state is that the tourist product must have a distinct image. The receptionists, the public relation officers, tourist information officers and the staff at restaurant must leave indelible impact on the tourists by their grace and decent behaviours. They should cherish the memory of their stay in the State. For this purpose human resources engaged in the marketing of tourist products must be harnessed by proper motivation. To establish direct link with the customers by own staff is the least expensive exercise. Staff should have a caring concern for the customer and should have a motto that the customer is always right. Proper motivation is possible when employers grant incentives to employees and create congenial atmosphere.

Thus, Bihar need well developed infrastructure coupled with proper marketing strategy for the promotion of tourism in the State.

REFERENCES

Badan, B.S. and Bhatt, H. (2007) : *Tourism and Economic Development,* Commonwealth Publishers, New Delhi-2.

Bhatia, A.K. (2007) : *Tourism Development : Principles and Practices,* 2nd Revised Edition, Sterling Publishers Private Limited, New Delhi-20.

Gupta Sunil and Bansal S. P. (2008): *Tourism Towards 21st Century,* Deep and Deep Publications Pvt. Ltd., New Delhi, p. 16.

Panigrahi Srikanta K. (2006): *Ecotourism in India,* Commonwealth Publishers, New Delhi, p. 62.

Patil, P.B. (2006) : *Tourism Development : Problem and Prospects,* Current Publications, Agra-10 (U.P.)

Singh K. P. and Prasad Alok (2008): *Marketing of Tourism in Bihar,* Deep and Deep Publications Pvt. Ltd., New Delhi, pp. 170-74.

Verma, S.B., Jiloka, S.K. and Thryambakam, P. (2006) : *Rural Tourism and Tribal Development,* Deep and Deep Publications Pvt. Ltd., New Delhi-27.

Wahab, C. R. (1976): *Tourism Marketing,* International London Press, p. 20.

9

Tourism Planning and Policy of India vis-à-vis Bihar

Planning

Tourism planning leads to tourism,development. In fact, tourism planning is the process for tourism development. In general terms, planning refers to methods and means used in making decisions about the future. Planning not only guides actions to be taken in future but also helps in problem solving and arriving at decisions which help planners in achieving desired objectives. Planning is not static but dynamic and guides future actions. Tourism planning process involves creating a future that is acceptable to the host community as also to others who would be part of the host community as tourists for a short period of time. Since tourism involves hospitality, the planning for various tourism facilities must be based on the needs of the guests.

The need for planning arises whenever some rational thinking is required to arrive at a choice among a set of limited means so that certain ends are satisfied especially when the means are substitutable among themselves. In other words, planning essentially attempts to allocate scarce resources between different competing uses with a view to maximizing output, income and employment and to ensure the balanced growth of different sectors. Such planning may be at an individual level or at a firm level or at an industry level or for the economy as a whole. There are broadly two economic systems prevailing—planned economy and market economy.

Planned economy is one in which each production unit (or a firm) uses only the resources of men, material and equipment allocated to it by simple order. On the other hand, a market economy is controlled by the forces of market, like demand, supply, prices, transport, etc. Plan can be applied to any type of economic system, whether centrally structured or built up of many units of purely market economy character. The different institutional frameworks will lead to compulsory planning under the first system and to indicative planning under the second.

Planning for Tourism

In the field of tourism, the need for planned development is of paramount importance. Many countries in the world, especially the developing countries, have lately realized the importance of tourism and the benefits which it brings out. The use of macro-economic planning techniques for tourism sector are, however, relatively new. The planning methods for national economic development, which have been largely utilized since the end of the World War II, did not always cover tourism development as a particular field. The increasing significance of tourism as a source of income, employment generating, regional development and as a major factor in the balance of payments for many countries has been attracting the attraction of many governments as well as others with an interest in economic development. Thus, tourism development became more and more a particular field of research in the economic planning undertaken by many countries. As far back as in the year 1962, the Secretary General of United Nations had declared : "Impressive unanimity has been achieved regarding the potential value of development planning."

The United Nations Conference on International Travel and Tourism held in Rome in 1963 emphasised the need for planning in tourism and made several recommendations. Some of the important recommendations that the United Nations Conference made in the area of planning in tourism were as follows :

(i) that the government of developing countries give high priority to projects concerning the development of tourism in their respective countries.

(ii) that the government of developing countries should consider the possibility of seeking the assistance of the United Nations Special Fund for regional and subregional survey of existing and potential tourist resources and for the preparation by experts of tourist traffic estimates and forecasts, with a view to the establishment of short-term and long-term plans for the development of tourist facilities and plants.

National Policy

The Ministry of Tourism had prepared a draft of National Tourism Development Policy with objective of positioning tourism as a major engine of economic growth and to harness its direct and multiplier effects for employment and poverty eradication in an environmentally sustainable manner. This draft was circulated to all the stakeholders in the Tourism sector—the Private sector, the Industry Associations, the State Governments, Departments and Ministries of Government of India. The draft on National Tourism Policy-2002 was also discussed at the three-day Tourism conclave comprising of—

(a) Meeting of all foreign and domestic officers of Tourism Ministry;

(b) Meeting of State Tourism Secretaries; and

(c) Meeting of the State Chief Ministers and Tourism Ministers.

I. Account should be taken of the fact that for the last four decades or so, a tourism revolution has been sweeping the world. In 1964, the number of tourists leaving their homes, worldwide, was 10 million. This number increased to 200 million in 1974, 500 million in 1992 and 700 million in 2001. And this number is likely to swell to 1.5 billion by 2020 and receipts from it are estimated to cross $ 2000 billion. If India has to partake in this revolution in a meaningful way, it must change its strategies as well as the techniques and tools of its machinery of implementation. In this connection, it has to be noted with concern that during the last decade or so, India's share of world tourist traffic has remained static at 0.38 per cent.

II. At the institutional level, a framework would have to be evolved which is Government-led, private sector-driven and community welfare-oriented. Government has to provide a legislative framework to regulate tourism trade and industry, ensure safety and security of the tourists and create basic infrastructure and health-care facilities. The private sector has to act as a mainspring of the activities and impact dynamism and speed to the process of development as well conservation. Both Government and private sector would be required to safeguard the stability and also the social and economic advancement of the local communities and the communities in the neighbourhood.

III. The deep-rooted relationship of tourism and our cultural assets should be fully recognized and provided for. Improvements and environmental upgradation of the protected monuments and the areas around them should be considered as linchpin of the tourism industry.

IV. Effective linkages and close coordination should be established with such Departments as Civil Aviation, Environment, Forest, Railways, Home, etc.

V. Sustainability should serve as a guiding star for the new Policy. The development and management strategies should be so worked out as to ensure that tourism largely acts as a smokeless industry and its ecological footprints remain as soft as possible. No one engaged, directly or indirectly, in the tourism industry should be allowed to secure short-term gains by resorting to what has been called the darker side tourism. Neither over-exploitation of national resources should be permitted nor the carrying capacity of the tourist-sites ignored.

VI. Greater emphasis should be laid on eco-tourism whose parameters should be broader than those of nature tourism alone. It must help in eliminating poverty, in ending unemployment, in creating new skills, in enhancing the status of women, in preserving cultural heritage, in encouraging tribal and local crafts and in proving overall environment and facilitating growth of a more just and fair social order.

VII. Special thrust should be imparted to rural tourism and tourism in small settlements, where sizeable assets of our cultural and natural wealth exist.

VIII. Due importance should be given to domestic tourism, particularly tourism connected with pilgrimage, and it should be so designed that the infrastructure created under it serves as a backbone of international tourism in times to come.

IX. A new class of young tourists with marked preference for adventure and distant destinations, in hills, caves and forests, is emerging. This class is not looking for 5-star accommodation but only for simple and clean places to stay. The requirements of this class of tourists should be met and guest tourism encouraged through Panchayats and local bodies and associations.

X. Special attraction of tourists for the Yoga, Siddha, etc., as well as for the Indian cuisine should be made use of and effectively encouraged.

XI. The tourist industry and travel agents should be persuaded to evolve and adopt voluntarily a Code of Ethics and its infringement should be firmly dealt with by Tour and Travel Associations.

XII. A section of the State Police should be imparted to it.

XIII. At the international level, India should play a dynamic role and make its presence felt at the World Tourism Organization, World Tourism and Travel Council and Earth Council. Its unique cultural values and spiritual heritage should be projected with dignity and elevation befitting a great nation, whenever suitable opportunity comes our way.

XIV. The civilizational issues as well as issues pertaining to civic administration and good governance must be attended to and made an effective part of the tourism policy. It should be ensured that good policies are not shipwrecked in the sea of halfhearted implementation.

The Policy Document seeks to enhance employment potential within the tourism sector as well as to foster economic integration through developing linkages with other sectors. Broadly, the Policy Paper attempts to :

- position of tourism as a major engine of growth;
- harness the direct and multiplier effect of tourism for employment generation, economic development and providing impetus to rural tourism;
- focus on domestic tourism as a major driver of tourism growth;
- India's position as a global brand to take advantage of the burgeoning global travel trade and the vast untapped potential of India as a destination;
- acknowledges the critical role of private sector with Government working as a proactive facilitator and catalyst;
- create and develop integrated tourism circuits, based on India's unique civilization, heritage, and culture, in partnership with States, private sector and other agencies;
- ensure that the tourist to India gets physically invigorated, mentally rejuvenated, culturally enriched, spiritually elevated and "feel India from within".

The Policy Document takes into consideration seven key areas that will provide the thrust to tourism development. These are: *Swagat* (welcome), *Soochana* (Information), *Suvidha* (Facilitation), *Suraksha* (Safety), *Sahyog* (Cooperation),

Sanrachana (Infrastructure Development), and *Safai* (Cleanliness).

Tourism Development Goals, Objectives and Strategies

The tourism industry, unlike many other industries, is a composite of several service providers. These service providers are generally in the private sector. In additions, public sector institutions such as the national or state department of tourism are involved in the planning, development and management of tourism. The participation of different private and public agencies makes tourism industry a complex phenomenon requiring a strong cooperation and coordination for it to be developed and expanded along lines that will contribute to the overall national development objectives. Lift to itself, the industry will develop naturally, but not necessarily optimally or sustainable, and without any clear links to the broad development objectives of the country. Uncontrolled tourism growth could damage India's socio-cultural structure, degrade its tangible and intangible cultural and natural heritage, and lead to adverse economic impacts such as high importation costs, and weakening inter-industry linkages. On the other hand, when the industry is properly planned, developed and managed at all levels of Government, in partnership with the private sector, it will strengthen India's socio-cultural structure. It would valorize its tangible and intangible cultural and natural heritage, and lead to positive economic impact, including enhanced employment and income opportunities in rural areas, lower importation costs and stronger inter-industry linkages.

The vehicle for achieving the positive benefits of tourism, mitigating the negative effects and delivering sustainable industry development framework, of India's national development priorities is the preparation and implementation of a comprehensive national tourism policy. The overall goal and strategy for the development of the tourism industry is to ensure that its development is closely tied to the national development priorities of the country. In this context, the

Government of India's vision for the development of the tourism sector is to achieve a superior quality of life for India's people through tourism, which would provide a unique opportunity for physical invigoration, mental rejuvenation, cultural enrichment and spiritual elevation.

Key Objective

To achieve the overall vision for the development of tourism, five key strategic objectives need to be achieved. They are:

1. Positioning and maintaining tourism development as a national priority activity;
2. Enhancing and maintaining the competitiveness of India as a tourism destination;
3. Improving India's existing tourism products and expanding these to meet new market requirements;
4. Creation of world class infrastructure; and
5. Developing sustained and effective marketing plans and programmes.

Positioning Tourism as a National Priority

1. Inclusion of tourism in the concurrent List of the Constitution of India. This will provide a constitutional recognition to the tourism sector, help in channeling the development of tourism in a systematic manner and enable Central Government to legislate for tourism development. The proposal for including tourism in the Concurrent List was circulated to the State Governments and discussed at the Chief Ministers' Conference. Majority of the States have agreed to the proposal.
2. To provide effective linkages and close coordination between Department, a Group of Ministers on Tourism has already been constituted.
3. Constitution of a Tourism Advisory Council with key stakeholders to act as a 'think tank'.

4. Prepare the basis for the adoption of the Tourism Satellite Account System based on SN3 protocol for the national accounts.
5. Plan and implement a professional managed integrated communications strategy to be called the 'National Tourism Awareness Campaign'.

Enhancing India's Competitiveness as a Tourist Destination

1. Visa-on-Arrival. Implement visa-on-arrival and consider strategies or the fast issuance of visas and permits, including electronic visa approaches, and improved processing of arrivals by customs and immigration officials.
2. Computerization of the system of issuance of visas by Embassies/High Commissions.
3. Air capacity available to India is woefully short during peak travel months ranging from October to March and specially from main tourism originating destinations like North America, Western Europe and South-East Asia. Additional seat capacity from the major destinations would provide a major impetus to tourism and economic development. An analysis by Indian Council for Research on International Economic Relations (ICRIER) reveals that the benefits of the additional seat capacity, whether provided by the national carrier or any other international carrier would have a significant benefits for national economy.
4. Improve the standard of facilities and services at the nation's international and major domestic airports by employing professional property management agencies to manage the physical premises on an out-source basis and speeding up the privatization/leasing of airports.
5. There is a need for creation of special Tourism Policy Force for deployment at major tourist destinations. This will provide travellers security through a spirit of courtesy and hospitality.

Improving and Expanding Product Development

In relation to the development of products that are related to the special interests of the target markets, the product development strategy should be to:

1. India has a unique cultural heritage. It has a vast array of protected monuments spread throughout the length and breadth of the country. India has 22 world heritage sites (16 are monuments). The conservation, preservation and integrated development of the area around these monuments provides a rare opportunity for growth and expansion of cultural tourism in India.
2. Development of sustainable beach and coastal tourism resort products based on a more flexible approach to development in the coastal zone. There is a need for identifying a series of government sites on the West Coast of India, free of encroachments, for the development of beach resorts by the private sector, with sites to be offered on long-term lease at preferential terms. These sites should primarily be in the regions of Goa, Kerala and North Karnataka for reasons of air access.
3. Develop and position Kochi and the Andaman & Nicobar Islands as international cruise destinations. This positioning is supported by their proximity to international cruise routes, their exotic appeal and the need for high quality, low impact, eco-tourism activities in the islands and develop a dedicated cruise terminal.
4. Capitalize by packaging India's unmatched variety of traditional cuisines that are today becoming increasingly popular in the world. The linkages and ripple effects created by a rapidly expanding restaurant sector can have dramatic implications for the Indian economy, implement private-public partnership of the Culinary Institute of India that will research and document ancient culinary traditions, create a highly skilled workforce of culinary professionals that can

populate not only hotels and catering establishments in India, but also internationally, serving to promote India internationally through a non-traditional medium, and encourage Indian entrepreneurs to establish restaurants of Indian ethnic cuisine internationally, by conceiving an innovative incentive scheme.

5. Actively promote the development of village tourism as the primary tourism product to spread tourism and its socio-economic benefits to rural and new geographic areas. Key geographic regions for the development and promotion of endemic tourism. The optimum locations appear to be: North Eastern States, Uttaranchal, Rajasthan, Ladakh, Kutch, Chhattisgarh and the Plantation (tea, coffee) Regions.
6. India has some of the greatest variety of fauna in the world that has perhaps not been exploited to its full potential for tourism. In this context, the wildlife sanctuaries and national parks need to be integrated as an integral part of the India tourism product and priority needs to be given to the preparation of site and visitor management plans for key parks, after a prioritization of parks. Tentatively, these would be: Corbett National Park, Kanha National Park, Bandhavgarh National Park, Ranthambhore, Mudumalai, Nagarhole, Kaziranga, Periyar, Bharatpur, Little Rann of Kutch, Chilika and Sundarbans. The quality of tourist facilities available at the parks should be enhanced, in particular, improve visitor information/interpretation centres and the tiger and the elephant should be the 'brands' in Indian wildlife tourism.
7. India perhaps has one of the greatest adventure tourism assets in the world in the form of the Himalayas as well as in its mighty rivers. Mountain-based adventure (soft and hard) activities in the Himalayas, creating the 'Himalayas' as the brand and an icon of Indian adventure tourism, should be developed and

promoted. White-water and more sedate great river rafting offer a unique tourism product, while regulations and certification for adventure tourism operators should be introduced so they meet minimum safety and conservation standards.

8. That the domestic tourism market is mostly local or regional in nature and prefers recreational pursuits and that recreation and leisure is a vital component of the quality of life, particularly in urban areas, and needs to be recognized.
9. India, despite its size, significance and attributes with world cities such as new Delhi and Mumbai, receives a minuscule proportion of the global meetings, incentives, convention and exhibition market. It is imperative not just for India's tourism development but also for the development of international and domestic trade and commerce that India constructs a world-class international convention centre in Mumbai.
10. India is the region of the world's greatest bio-diversity, with a variety of unique natural locales and is, therefore, a perfect candidate for eco-tourism. In this context, eco-tourism should be made a priority tourism product of India, with the focal points located in the Himalayas, North-Eastern States, Western Ghats, Jharkhand, Andaman & Nicobar Islands and the Lakshdweep Islands. Tour operators need to be encouraged to promote eco-tourism, which should also be made at grassroots, community-based movement through awareness, education and training of the local community as guides and interpreters.
11. India is today being 're-discovered' by the world at large for the depth of its understanding of physical, mental, emotional and spiritual. India has traditions that focus on the holistic healing of individuals and one elevating the individual to a higher plane of consciousness and awareness. This can be India's most unique tourism product—holistic healing and rejuvenation of the individual from every dimension—

physical, mental, emotional and spiritual, and in doing so, it will capture the essence of the best of Indian philosophy and culture for international and Indian visitors alike.

12. India has come to have a series of unique lodging products that can become one of India's immediate Unique Selling Propositions (USPs). In this context, step should be taken to establish a scheme for providing seed capital to entrepreneurs for the development of such unique accommodation products to be funded and administered at the State level, with adequate controls.
13. India is a veritable shoppers' paradise and the retail trade provides enormous forward and backward linkages throughout the economy. In this context, shopping should be recognized as an integral part of the tourism experience and a most valuable contributor to revenues. The development of dedicated shopping centres for traditional crafts, designed along the lines of ethnic village haats such as Dilli Haat and Shilpagram needs to be encouraged, the availability of information on where to procure specific craft and produce reliable, unbiased shopping guides enhanced, funding support to reputed NGOs promoting the handicrafts sector should be provided, a directory of traditional crafts persons should be produced and promoted, touring should be controlled through regulation and legislation and the 'Made in India' brand should be promoted.
14. Indian has unique events, fairs and festivals, some of which are well established such as Pushkar, Desert Festival at Jaisalmer, Kumbh Mela, etc. In this context, this sector should be promoted as a unique product of India, the 'Festivals of India' programme should be reintroduced in the top 12 future markets for India. Initially, there should be an annual event in UK and USA, followed by triennial events in each of the other markets.

15. Business travel is also a form of tourism and typically occurs in urban environments and should be recognized accordingly. Urban quality along the lines specified for regional and site master plans, including tourism interests and requirements in the urban planning process should be improved and New Delhi and Mumbai should be positioned as 'World Cities' and the level of physical infrastructure, urban ambience and public services developed befitting such a status.
16. A series of themed cultural attractions should be developed based on outstanding site planning and design, a National Register of key cultural sites for tourism should be prepared and published and developed and Delhi should be positioned as the cultural capital of India, supported by an on-going and vibrant calendar of cultural events.

The development of this recommended niche-based special interest product-mix will position India as a unique world-class destination.

Bihar Tourism Policy (2003)

The Government of Bihar is firmly committed to capitalize on its 'new State advantage'. The State has taken a conscious decision to do away with past legacies and to adopt a fresh approach to economic development. The Tourism Policy reflects the contemporary views of the Government of Bihar. It is not a modification of any earlier policy and has been developed based on a comprehensive analysis of best practices of other Indian States and counties in the region.

Transformation

Alec Bran and his wife Robyn are upmarket couple living in Tokyo. Both are working professionals with a penchant for travelling. They are also devout Buddhists. So it is not really a surprise to see them coming all the way to Bodh Gaya in Bihar.

Ask them about their yearly visits to the holy place and they are more than willing to share. "These visits to Bodh Gaya are a must for us; this place gives us mental and spiritual peace", says Alec. And how do these metropolitan people adjust in a place such as Bihar? "The hospitality shown by the people here is amazing. We feel as though we are spending time with our own people. The government accommodation is very good and the facilities extended to tourists are remarkable" gushes Robyn. "Last year we got along three more friends with us. We want to share this experience with all our friends and family."

They are just two of the three and a half lakh foreign tourists flocking to Bihar annually.

Gone are the days when the mere mention of Bihar was enough to elicit a weary response from people. Even though this state has a rich heritage and abundant natural resources, tourism had fallen prey to political machinations and administrative neglect over the last decade-and-a-half of misrule. But since around four years, the advent of a new and responsive regime has proved to be manna from heaven for this sector. The scope of tourism is unlimited in Bihar, and people are flocking to experience it firsthand.

The culturally-rich state of Bihar derives its name from 'Vihar', which means a recreational site by the side of a pool or pond. Endowed with a rich cultural heritage, Bihar was the seat of power of the great Magadh Empire, whose might put a check on the further onslaught of Alexander the Great. Bihar has been a cradle of civilization and the centre of religious activities of Boudh, Jain, Hindu, Sikh and Islam.

It has the Ganga river as its lifeline, besides many other rivers such as Kosi, Gandak in North Bihar, and Sone in South Bihar. The mighty emperor Ashoka wielded power from his capital Patliputra, now modern-day Patna. Herein lies the history of the young prince Sidhhartha, transforming himself into Lord Buddha by getting enlightenment through sheer penance under the Bodhi tree. Bihar is also the birthplace of the 24th Tirthankara of Jain religion, Lord Mahavir. Even during the reign of the Mughal rulers Bihar featured prominently. Later on, Gandhiji experimented 'Satyagraha' first time in Champaran, which is famous as the 'karmabhoomi' of Bapu. A home to the world's ancient university at Nalanda and Vikramshila and benevolent shrines that grant eternal salvation at Gaya, verdant virgin forests of Chotanagpur plateau to the intricate craftsmanship and play of colours a Madhubani painting, it is truly a place that asks to be explored. Or as Alec and Robyn would vouch, "Bihar is not the destination, but the journey itself."

Waking Up the Sleeping Giant

Tourism has established itself as a smokeless industry, and Bihar government is leaving no stones unturned to promote it. The state's budgetary allocation for tourism has been enhanced to exploit the potential of this sector. The fund earmarked for tourism in the budgetary proposal for the year 2005-06 was Rs. 7.43 crore, which was raised to Rs. 29.78 crore for the year 2009-10. Outlining the efforts of the state government towards tourism, sources said the state government is promoting tourism as an industry for which it has set up a council that would coordinate between the agencies linked with tourism.

The state government has also formulated and notified a new 'Bihar Tourism Policy 2009' under which it will provide capacity building programmes for guides, travel operators, hospitality, hotel management and catering services. The Bihar government has also outsourced the services required in the tourism industry.

Apart from this, prospective live stores in the tourism sectors would get rebates in land registration, electricity consumption and luxury tax, and other benefits.

Special facilities, including information centres, have been set up at airports, railway stations and other places for tourists coming to Bihar. In addition, the state government has also initiated the process of putting in place a 'tourist police' which would provide security, information and help in a tourist-friendly manner. This force is to be deputed at all the important places of tourist interest like Gaya, Bodh Gaya, Rajgir, Nalanda and Vaishali.

The department of tourism has also prepared a 'Media and Marketing Plan' to promote tourism in Bihar. Private T.V. channels and F.M. Radio have been roped in for publicity campaigns. Tourist map of Bihar, short film for tourists, a new user-friendly website of Bihar tourism, a tourists guide titled 'A journey through Bihar', a calendar of all tourist festivals are some of the initiatives taken by the state government. Luxury Volvo Bus service, online reservation of BSTDC hotels, computerized booking of tickets, outlets of Central Cottage Industries Corporation at BSTDC hotels, Ayurvedic wellness centres are some of the new schemes undertaken by the department of tourism.

Jain circuit package, Yoga circuit package, 'Pind-daan' package, Gandhian circuit, Eco circuit, Sufi circuit and 'Trace your root' package are innovation over and above the usual Buddhist circuit.

The state government has also approved plans to open 5-star hotels at Patna, Bodh Gaya and Rajgir under public-private partnership. Fresh proposals are being considered for promoting water tourism in the state.

With a view to making travel more convenient for all tourists including foreigners, steps are underway for broadening and strengthening roads linking to Buddhist, Jain, Sikh religious circuits.

Talks are also on with several aviation companies for increasing the frequency of international flights to and fro Bodh Gaya airport.

On a more specific note, the tomb of Sher Shah Suri, the emperor who built the Grand Trunk Road from Kolkata to Peshawar in the 16th century and thus laid down the foundation of the Indian highway system, is being refurbished at a cost of Rs. 94 crore so that it becomes one of Bihar's major tourist destinations.

Plans are also underway to spend over Rs. 4 crore to develop Patna's iconic Golghar into a full-fledged tourist center considering the historic importance of the beehive-shaped granary of the British era.

Revival of India's Greatest University

Nalanda University

Walking in the awesome ruins of this archaeological and academic masterpiece—past lecture halls, rooms for monks and temples—it is quite overwhelming to know that you are at a site where Hiuen Tsiang, the great Chinese philosopher, was a student for five years and taught for a year.

Nalanda is belived to be one of the ancient schools of knowledge that carved an enlightened niche during the 5th-12th century span. It derived its name from 'Na-alam-da', meaning 'insatiable in giving', one of the names by which Lord Buddha was known. The Nalanda Museum—maintained by the Archaeological Survey of India—still has an amazing collection of exquisite bronze sculptors of Pala dynasty dating back to 9th-10th centuries. Spread over 15 hectares are the ruins of six temples, 11 monasteries, the Sariputra Stupa built by Ashoka, and generous dotting of fresco work. This university housed 10,000 students, 2,000 teachers and had a curriculum including Buddhist studies, fine arts, medicine, mathematics, politics, astronomy and the art of war.

For an institution that was one of the finest universities in recorded history, the makers of the new Nalanda University have a tough act to follow. Undulating efforts are underway to bring about another Asian renaissance with the reconstruction of this grand academic wonder.

A short distance from the well-preserved remains of the old university, 500 acres of land is being acquired by the state government to rebuild the ancient seat of learning The project would cost Rs. 1,000 crore spread over the first few years, out of which, the state government has already provided Rs. 16 crore for the land and is committed to allotting more funds.

The Dalai Lama, Nobel Laureate Amartya Sen, British economist Meghnad Desai and economist Jean Dreze are the advisors to the Bihar government for setting up the university.

Drawing inspiration from Oxford and Cambridge—the English universities that came into being about the time Nalanda University was witnessing the end of its glorious days—the new university hopes to transform Nalanda into a university town.

The Bihar cabinet has already cleared the Nalanda Bill; it was passed by the state legislature on March 26, 2010.

The aim is to provide a novel curriculum—which strikes a balance between modern and ancient thought. While its seven schools will provide courses like Communication, Applied Sciences, Development Studies, International Studies, Languages and Natural Resources Management, it will also teach Theology, Astronomy, Culture, Ethics, Philosophy and Buddhist Studies.

The university will have an international character and attract students, faculty and research staff from different parts of the world. It will offer postgraduate and research degree programmes in engineering technology, fundamental and basic sciences, social sciences, conflict resolution, knowledge management etc. The School of Languages will be the only programme providing undergraduate courses in Persian, Korean, Chinese and Japanese etc.

The state government has received a formal intimation from Japan's department of economic affairs showing interest in the project, while Singapore and South Korea have also promised funding.

Founded under the Gupta Empire, Nalanda was destroyed thrice and rebuilt twice before it was finally burnt by marauding Turkish invaders led by Bakhtiyar Khilji. Its nine-storeyed library and priceless books, it is said, burned for days.

Resurrecting such a glittering academic past will not be easy, but that it is being revived is a fitting tribute to one of the finest universities of all time.

Vikramasila University

Vikramasila University was one of the two most important centers of Buddhist learning in India, along with Nalanda University during the Pala dynasty. Vikramasila was established by King Dharmapala (783 to 820) in response to a supposed decline in the quality of scholarship at Nalanda.

Atisha, the renowned pandita, is sometimes listed as a notable abbot.

A fortified Vikramasila was destroyed by Muslim invaders fighting the Sena dynasty along with the other major centers of Buddhism in India around 1200. The remains of the ancient university have been partially excavated at village Antichak in the Bhagalpur district, Bihar state, India, and the process is still underway.

Excavated remains represent the ruins of Vikramasila Mahavihara, the celebrated university founded by Pala king Dharmapala in late 8th or early 9th Century A.D. It prospered for about four centuries before it collapsed in the beginning of 13th Century A.D. It is known to us mainly through Tibetan sources, especially the writings of Taranath, the Tibetan monk historian of 16th-17th Century A.D.

Vikramasila was one of the largest Buddhist universities having more than hundred teachers and about one thousand students. It produced eminent scholars who were often invited by foreign countries to spread Buddhist learning, culture and religion. The most distinguished and eminent among all was Atisa Dipankara, a founder of the Sarma traditions of Tibetan Buddhism. Subjects like theology, philosophy, grammar, metaphysics, logic etc. were taught here, but the most important branch of learning was tantrism. Meticulous excavation at the site conducted initially by Patna University (1960-69) and subsequently by Archaeological Survey of India (1972-82) has revealed a huge square monastery with a cruciform stupa in its centre, a library building and cluster of votive stupas. To the north of monastery a number of scattered structures including a Tibetan and a Hindu temple have been found. The entire spread is over an area of more than one hundred acres.

The monastery, or residence for the Buddhist monks, is a huge square structure, each side measuring 330 metres having a series of 208 cells, 52 on each of the four sides opening into a common verandah. A few brick arched underground chambers beneath some of the cells have also been noticed which were probably meant for confined meditation by the monks.

The main stupa built for the purpose of worship is a brick structure laid in mud mortar which stands in the centre of the square monastery. This two terraced stupa is cruciform on plan and about 15 metres high from the ground level accessible through a flight of steps on the north side. On each of the four cardinal directions there is a protruding chamber with a pillared antechamber and a separate pillared mandapa in front. In the four chambers of the stupa were placed colossal stucco images of seated Buddha of which three were found *in situ* but the remaining one on north side was possibly replaced by a stone image after the clay image was somehow damaged.

The walls of both the terraces are decorated with mouldings and terracotta plaques which testify the high excellence of terracotta art flourishing in the region during Pala period (8th to 12th Century A.D.).

About 32 metres south of the monastery on its south-west corner and attached with the main monastery through a narrow corridor is a rectangular structure identified as a library building. It was air-conditioned by cooled water of the adjoining reservoir through a range of vents in the back wall. The system was perhaps meant for preserving delicate manuscripts.

The architecture of the stupa and the themes of terracotta plaques of Vikramasila Mahavihara are comparable to the contemporary Somapura Mahavihara, Paharpur (Bangladesh). On plan both are very much alike except that Vikramasila monastery is larger and has fort like projections on its outer wall.

A large number of antiquities of different materials, unearthed from this place in the course of excavation, are displayed in the site museum maintained by the Archaeological Survey of India.

Sonepur Fair

A traditional fair that has remained pristine in its charm through the ages, Sonepur Fair also happens to be the largest cattle fair in Asia. Legend has it that two brothers, devotees of

Lord Vishnu, one wily and the other honest, cast a spell upon each other making one an elephant and the other a crocodile. On a Kartik Purnima day, the honest elephant went to the confluence of the holy river Ganga and Gandak to bathe and was attacked by the wily crocodile. Lord Vishnu himself intervened and helped the good triumph over the evil. With Lord Vishnu's help the elephant prevailed over the crocodile.

Boats at the river banks, a large number of imposing Indian elephants, camels, horses, cows, buffaloes, oxen, goats, dogs, cats and birds for sale, loosely robed *sadhus* (holy men), freshly washed animals, shops on the pavements overflowing with goods, swirling crowds in colourful dresses and joyful moods, curious onlookers—such are the scenes that dominate this wonderful fair. The central draw of the fair is cattle trade.

The fair entertains visitors with 'nautanki'—a typical traditional musical drama performance. Other attractions are the circus, magic shows, fortune-telling parrots, and peddlers of fancy goods.

Eco-Tourism

Kakolat (Nawada): This waterfall is about 150 to 160 feet from the ground level. Just below the fall there is a deep natural reservoir. A legend is prevalent that in Treta Yuga a king was cursed by a sage and had to take the shape of python and lived here. The place was visited by the great Pandavas during their exile and the accursed king got salvation from the damnation. The king after getting rid of the curse proclaimed that one who would bathe in the waterfall will not take the *yoni* of snake and that is why a large number of people from far and near bathe in the river.

Bhimbandh (Munger): Bhimbandh Wild Life Sanctuary covers an undulating tract of Kharagpur Hills. The vegetation of these forests is rich with Sal, Kendu, Semal. A host of animals such as Tiger, Leopards, Sloth Bear, Nilgai, Sambhar, Barking deer, Wild Beer, four horned Antelope are found in these forests. In the valley portions and at the foothills are several hot springs of which the finest are at Bhimbandh, Sita Kund and Rishi Kund. Among them the Bhimbandh groups of springs have the maximum temperature (52°C to 65°C) and constitute the best area for the exploration of geothermal energy potential.

Madhubani Painting

It is an impressive work of art practiced in the interiors of Mithila region in Bihar that has found a pad in the international market. It entails arduous craftsmanship by the rural women of this virgin patch of land, offering a vibrant aroma of the folk life. The tradition, which dates back to the aegis of Lord Rama, was originally used to decorate the freshly plastered mud wall of huts, but now has found its demeanour in paper, cloth and canvas. The paintings show symbolic motifs, the religious Gods and Goddesses such as Durga, Radha and Krishna, Shiva and Parvati. The colours range from strong primary colours such as vibrant red, yellow and green to ochre, brown and black. The pigments are taken from spices, minerals, charcoal, vegetable matter, flowers and plants depicting special events and aspects of everyday life. These paintings are now professionally produced on paper, canvas and textiles for international and national exhibitions etc. They can be bought straight from the artisan's house or government emporia that dot the cities.

Buddhist Circuit

Bihar bracketed the moment when Lord Buddha attained enlightenment and founded Buddhism. The religious itinerary could be started from Vaishali, the place where Buddha delivered his last sermon before reaching Kushinagar, connoting his impending departure from the modern world. There is no scope of missing the huge lion pillar built by Emperor Ashoka to commemorate the demise.

Rajgir (100 km from Patna), is where the teachings of Buddha were recorded in writing for the first time. It is said that it was at Rajgir that physicians treated Buddha to Jivak after he was injured by his cousin Devdatta. Among the many historical and archaeological sites and edifices, Ajatshatru's Fort deserves a mention. It has an impressive structure of 'Parinirvana' (the great cessation); Lord Buddha lying with his right hand resting under his head to commemorate the final salvation of the great founder of Buddhist creed. Nalanda, the most renowned university in ancient India, is the next stoppage. The divine itinerary comes to an end at Sarnath, the holy place where Buddha preached his first sermon called the 'Dharmachakra Pravartana' in the deer park, that now contains impressive ruins, a couple of monasteries and the beautifully polished Lion Capital of Ashoka.

Bodh Gaya

It is here that Prince Siddhartha achieved Enlightenment under the Bodhi tree and got the name 'Buddha', meaning omniscient and the 'all compassionate one'. Bodh Gaya, nestling on the banks of river Niranjana, is the spiritual home of Buddhists from allover the world. Many a weary souls have relaxed in the light of Buddhism under the stems that have now found their place in the world heritage site list. The Mahabodhi Mahavihara complex is another sacred delight. It has a 2 m high image of Buddha in 'Bhumisparsha mudra' (seated cross-legged with one hand touching the earth) carved in black stone and adorned in gold. The 80 ft high statue of Buddha in the town together with the 152 m high statue of Maitreya in the outskirts are a must see. Bodh Gaya today is a bustling place and there are numerous monasteries and meditation centres run by Tibetan, Burmese, Thai and Vietnamese communities that offer short-term courses on meditation and yoga.

Jain Circuit

Pawapuri

This sinless town is also known as "Apapuri". A great pilgrimage centre of Jains where Mahavira the greatest propounded of Jainism delivered his last sermon, took Mahaparinirvana and was cremated. It is also famous for the two beautiful temples—Jalmandir and Samosharan.

Rajgir

It is one of the most important tourist places in India. Being located in a valley, Rajgir is a very scenic, with lush green forest. Rajgir was the capital of the Magadh Mahajanpad (State) when Patliputra was not formed. In those days it was called Rajgrih, which means the home of Royalty. Apart from being a place for worship, Rajgir has also come up as a health and winter resort with its warm water ponds which are said to contain medicinal properties. The added attraction of Rajgir is the ropeway which takes you uphill to the Shanti Stupa and monasteries built by the Japanese devotees on top of the Ratnagiri hills.

Parasnath

Parasnath, the highest hill in Bihar (height of 4,480 ft), is an abode of both Swetamber and Digamber Jains. 23 out of 24 Tirthankaras are believed to have attained salvation here. Parasvanatha, the 23rd Thirthankara was very popular among the tribal population of Chotanagpur. He is identified by the snake king Dharanendra whose many hoods protect the meditating Thirthankar.

Bisram

It is said that Lord Mahavira, the last Jain Tirthankar took rest for some time at this place during his wanderings. Hence this place is called *Bisram* or rest.

Strategic Intent and Approach

Bihar, situated in the heart of India, is endowed with a rich cultural heritage and attractive natural diversity. The State is abundant with ancient monuments and exquisitely carved temples, Buddhist sites, palaces, water falls, cave and hills plateaus. Most of these sites are untouched and unexplored and offer a unique and alternate experience to tourists compared to traditional destinations which have become overcrowded.

Tourism has very important linkages with other sectors, including industry, trade, transportation, hospitality, etc. the Government of Bihar recognized these vital linkages as well as the importance of tourism for creating large scale employment and for promoting social integration.

The tourism Policy is focussed on creating a unique image for the State and to position it as an attractive destination. The specific objectives of this policy are to:

- Promote economically, culturally and ecologically sustainable tourism in the State;
- Strengthen the quality and attractiveness of the tourism experience in Bihar;
- Preserve, enrich and showcase the rich and diverse cultural and ecological heritage of the State;
- Increase the contribution of tourism to the economic development of interrelated sectors;
- Encourage and promote private sector initiatives in developing tourism-related infrastructure;
- Transform the role of Government to that of facilitator;
- Promote new concepts in tourism such as time-share, eco-tourism, village-tourism, adventure-tourism;
- Respect the intellectual integrity and rights of local communities.

To meet these objectives, the State has identified specific initiatives, which can be broadly classified as under :

- Infrastructure and Institutional Development,
- Tourism Product Offering,
- Marketing.

Tourism Policy of Bihar Government

Infrastructure

Arranging accommodation for increased number of tourists, building of highways on tourist circuits, international level airport, local transport, rail routes linking tourist spots, vital telecommunication link and adequate and quality supply of electricity. Preparing an area based Master Plan for the same.

Accommodation

Arranging for differentiated accommodations ranging from economy class (halls and dormitories) to luxury class (5-star hotels and resorts).

Heritage Hotels

Identifying heritage buildings and mansions and converting them into Heritage Hotels.

Paying Guest Scheme

Identifying the houses, house owners and families interested in this stream of tourism development.

Way Side Facility

Comfortable rest houses fitted with basic amenities flanking the highways along the fuel filling stations.

Land

The department of tourism, in conjunction with the revenue department and local district administration, simplify the rules and regulations for land allotment in order to create tourism infrastructure.

Tourism as Industry

Special facilities, rebates and incentives would be given to entrepreneurs who invest in or promote the tourism industry.

Road Transport

Road construction, their maintenance and proper availability of tourist vehicles would be given due importance, apart from packaging the tour programmes on the inter-state and intra-state bus routes interlinking the tourist spots.

Air Taxi and Helicopter Services

On the basis of demand creation by value tourists, air taxi and helicopter services would be provided.

Fairs and Festivals

Organising the cultural and religious fairs and festivals in systematic way and developing scheduled package tours to coincide with the fairs' timings.

Tourist Information Centres

These would be modernized to provide timely and accurate information about tourist places, hotel bookings, transport facilities and package tours etc.

Handicraft and Cottage Industry

Establishment of Shilp Gram (craft villages) and handicraft markets near tourist places, in order to exploit the full potential of this sector.

Weekend Tourism

Developing tourist spots with an aim to attracting tourists from the neighbouring states creating shopping malls, eating outlest and entertainment centres etc.

Tourism with Wildlife

Developing wildlife sanctuaries, crocodile parks, snake parks, theme parks, etc. in a bid to attract domestic and foreign tourists.

Guides

Selection of guides, training and grooming, and granting them licence.

Aqua Tourism

Construction of floating restaurant and river cruises, and promotion of water sports.

Beautification, Light and Sound System

Effective light and sound system at historical sites and places of tourist interest, renovation of old heritage buildings.

Publicity and Extension

Participating in national and international exhibitions for exposition of its tourist sites, advertising in newspapers and magazines, and binging out tourism-related features.

Rural Tourism

Efforts to promote rural tourism in Bihar as majority of people live in villages here. This would also provide excellent employment opportunities for the local people.

While implementing this Policy, the State will promote only those initiatives that support sustainable development of the sector and maintain ecological balance. Moreover, the State Government will encourage the involvement of local communities and will specifically elicit their cooperation in preserving, enriching and promoting the State's rich cultural heritage.

Towards this end, the State will enact suitable legislation and set up a State Tourism Promotion Board as the nodal agency for implementation of this Policy and for the sustained development of the sector.

Infrastructure and Institutional Development

To harness the true potential of tourism, it is necessary to undertake large-scale development/improvement of infrastructure and create a conducive investment climate. Accordingly, the State will take the following measures:

Integrated Development of Special Tourism Areas and Constructive Collaboration between Government and the Private Sector

The Government will adopt a selective and integrated approach for development of tourism areas. Tourism development will be primarily driven by the private sector with the role of Government being that of a facilitator and a catalyst. Towards this end, the State will take the following steps :

- Identify and prioritize important tourism area/circuits, which have potential for tourism and investment inflow. For example, wildlife and pilgrimage tourist circuits would be linked to heritage properties to exploit geographical congruity.
- Prepare a Perspective Master Plan for tourism development in consultation with experts. Focus will be on integrated/intensive development of tourist destinations after assessing the tourism potential, local aspirations and likely local economy benefits.
- Integrate spatio-economic development plans with tourism planning agencies in the State.
- Provide world-class tourist facilities, amenities and landscaping of areas around important monuments in a phased manner.

- Assess carrying capacity and promote ecologically, economically and culturally sustainable tourism in the State.
- Make it mandatory for specified class of hotels and resorts to provide 2% of their built-up area at nominal charges to the State Government for allocation to set up 'Gift Centre' to sell handloom, handicrafts, food and herbal medicines and such other products of the State.
- Work with Bihar Infrastructure Development Corporation to identify and prioritize specific infrastructure projects, which would help in creating linkages and development of tourist circuits. Towards this end, the State would, in line with the Draft National Tourism Policy, look at the feasibility of creating a special fund for Tourism Development, which would help in bridging the gap for funding critical infrastructure requirements and also support (as equity) specific tourism related projects. This would, in turn, promote collaboration of the Government with the private sector.

Incentives to the Private Sector

- Give tourism 'industry status', so that the facilities and benefits available to the industry for the purpose of infrastructure development/mega projects, applicability of electricity tariffs, etc., are also available to tourism projects.
- Create nucleus infrastructure in the initial stages of development to demonstrate the potential of the area. Towards this end, the State will give 15% investment subsidy for capital costs on tourism projects in special tourist areas, subject to maximum of Rs. 20 lakhs.
- Make tracts of Government land available either through sale, lease or as Government equity in case of a joint venture for the purpose of promoting private investments in the development of tourism infrastructure.

- Rationalize taxes with reference to developmental needs of tourism sector. The Government will consider providing exemption from luxury and entertainment tax to projects with investments beyond a certain threshold value in special tourist areas.

Develop Infrastructure Linkages and Human Resources

In order to improve accessibility, promote connectivity and develop the requisite skills to serve the tourism industry, the State will take the following steps:

- Improve arterial roads in tourist locations.
- Enhance the number of tourist coaches and provide wayside amenities along with filling stations or otherwise on all the highways connecting important tourist centres.
- Encourage operation of charter flights and work on upscaling aviation infrastructure. Give impetus to helicopter services to areas not serviceable otherwise.
- Evaluate the feasibility of launching a tourist train in collaboration with the Indian Railways on identified tourist circuits.
- Set up prepaid counters at airports, railway stations and bus stands in major cities in the State.
- Increase the number of metered taxis, conducted tours in all places of tourist interest.
- Undertake a training needs assessment study for tourism and related industries as part of the Perspective Master Plan for tourism development.
- Encourage the setting up of a wide array of HRD institutions, including vocational training institutes, hotel management training institutes etc. Private participation would be encouraged by making land available at concessional rate to prospective private sector promoters.
- Streamline and strengthen training of guides and other grassroots level workers.

Strengthen the Institutional Mechanism

To provide a conducive and responsive institutional framework for sustained development of the tourism sector, the Government of Bihar will take the following steps:

- Set up the State Tourism Development Board (STDB) as the nodal agency for formulating strategic plans, decision-making, coordinating with various bodies and agencies involved in tourism, providing necessary assistance for setting up tourism projects, including an escort service to investors. The Board would ensure inter-departmental coordination, i.e. between tourism, forests, arts and culture, etc., for collaborative development of the tourism sector. The composition of the Board will include government officials as well as representatives from the private sector.
- Set up a Paryatan Bhavan at Bodhgaya in line with the requirements of the Draft National Tourism Policy as a one-stop tourist reception centre. This would cater to various needs of travellers, foreign as well as domestic, offer air and train reservations, foreign exchange counters and information about all tourist centres.
- Set up District Tourism Promotion Councils to decentralize tourism development. People's participation including Panchayati Raj institutions, cooperatives and local communities will be encouraged to achieve a wider spread of tourist activities.
- Enact a Tourism Trade Regulation Act for improving services and regulating tourism trade in line with the proposed model guidelines to be circulated by the Ministry of Tourism, Government of India.

Improve Tourism Product Offering

In order to position the state as a unique multi-attraction tourism destination, the State has identified the following potential areas for development:

- **Eco-tourism:** The State will actively identify opportunities to promote nature-based tourism with increased local participation. Wildlife area, camping grounds and trekking facilities would be few of the prime attraction facilities. Gaya, Rajgir, Nalanda and Sasaram will be promoted as destinations for nature and wildlife tourism, respectively.

  As part of its drive to promote eco-tourism, the State will leverage on its wealth of medicinal plants to encourage development of herbal gardens and natural health resorts of Yoga and Ayurveda as places of tourist attraction.
- **Culture, Heritage and Village Tourism:** In order to showcase its rich heritage, the State will identify and develop villages and heritage properties, i.e., old palaces, havelis, Darbargadhs as places of tourist interest. These will be integrated with eco-tourism circuits to ensure that tourism development across the State is focussed. This product offering will also showcase local art and craft and provide fillip to rural employment. The State will ensure proper maintenance and professional site management of important heritage site/monuments. Bhoramdev, Rajim, Sirpur, Tala, Malha and Shivrinarayan will be promoted as prime sites for heritage tourism.

  The State will periodically organize fairs and festivals to promote its rich culture. An artisan village-cum-craft park, i.e. 'Urban Haat' will be set up at Madhubani. Financial assistance and training will be provided to artisans and craftsmen to revive local art and handicraft products.
- **Adventure Tourism:** The State will promote adventure sports such as trekking, rock climbing, canoeing, water rafting, bungee jumping, etc. The State Government shall make efforts to provide training to youth so that they are able to take up these activities on commercial basis and ensure the enforcement of safety standards. Ganga river, Gandank, Koshi dam, will be developed to cater to the needs of adventure tourists.

- **Pilgrim Tourism:** The State will also focus on the development of pilgrimage centres by creating necessary facilities like Dharmasalas. The State will also develop sites for Buddhist pilgrims and become part of the wider Buddhist circuit.
- **Business-cum-Entertainment Tourism:** The State will encourage setting up of business-cum-recreation centres to cater to the needs of business travellers to exploit the potential of business tourism. Setting up state-of-the-art convention centres, seminar halls, etc., for corporate events will be encouraged. In order to cater to the entertainment needs of business tourists with high purchasing power, facilities such as hotels, entertain parks, multiplex theatres, health spas, shopping centres, golf courses would also be set up.

Effective marketing

In order to improve tourist perception and project the State as a unique and desirable State to visit, the Government would implement a marketing strategy in collaboration with industry stakeholders and local populace. The Government will:

- Identify and promote anchor project to precipitate the emergence of local attractions.
- Develop a tourism portal, touch screen information kiosk, multimedia CD-ROMs for dissemination of tourism related information.
- Carry out market research at regular intervals to monitor tourist trends, conduct satisfaction surveys and adapt marketing strategies accordingly.
- Implement tourist friendly initiatives like metered taxis, introduction of computer-based information and reservation systems, setting up a chain of exclusive shops for sale of souvenirs, distribution of brochures, leaflets and other local items at all important tourist places.
- Organize fairs for promoting local cuisine, art and craft, folk songs and dances and participation in national/ international fairs, trade shows.

PLATE XXV

Nalanda University

Plate XXVI

Vikramasila University

Plate XXVII

History Stone Vikramasila

PLATE XXVIII

Kakolat (Nawada) Waterfall

- Form joint tie-ups with the tourism development boards/corporations of various Indian States and international bodies for reciprocal sales and marketing of each other's travel and tourism products.
- Institute monetary and non-monetary awards to promote excellence in tourism.
- Facilitate the participation and buy-in of the local people, Panchayati Raj Institutions, local bodies, religious trusts, cooperatives and other community-level institutions to promote cross-selling of the unique experience to visitors.
- Hire professional advertising agencies and public relations companies as well as involve private sector in planning and executing the promotional campaigns.

The government's efforts to rejuvenate and revitalize the once moribund tourism sector have shown amazing results. The inflow of foreign tourists in Bihar saw a six-fold increase in 2008-09 as against 2005-06. The number of foreign tourists increased from 63,321 in 2005-06 to 3,56,446 in 2008-09.

Moreover, the number of domestic tourists touched an all-time high of 1.22 crore in 2008-09 from 86.87 lakhs in 2005-06.

The current growth in the number of foreign and domestic tourists has been attributed to State government's efforts to creat a more conducive and secure environment. "People (tourists) are now feeling safe and secured in the tourists inflow to the state", says an official of the tourism department.

Cruise Control

It is indeed a novel experience for the people of Bihar to cruise around the sacred river while having delectable food. MV Ganga Vihar is the floating restaurant now operating on the River Ganga from Gandhi Ghat, Patna, in the state of Bihar. Some quick facts about this floating restaurant are :

- Inaugurated by Chief Minister Nitish Kumar on July 20, 2009.
- 48 persons can dine at a time.
- Non-vegetarian food available at Rs. 500 and vegetarian food available at Rs. 350.

- A bar and a recreation room is also available.
- Operated by the Bihar State Tourism Development Corporation twice a day.
- Also available on rent at Rs. 20,000 for four hours to celebrate social and family gatherings like birthdays, marriages.
- Cabinet meetings are also planned to be held in the floating restaurant to promote public awareness about the restaurant.
- As an inaugural offer, the floating restaurant was permitted to the public to view solar eclipse on July 22, 2009 with an entry ticket of Rs. 100.

The government is planning to operate more vessels with private operators now.

REFERENCES

Badan, B.S. and Bhatt, H. (2007) : *Tourism and Economic Development*, Commonwealth Publishers, New Delhi-2.

Bhatia, A.K. (2007) : *Tourism Development : Principles and Practices*, 2nd Revised Edition, Sterling Publishers Private Limited, New Delhi-20.

http://drdapatna.bih.nic.in/patna_at_glance.html

http://www.tourism.gov.in/survey/BIHAR%20TOURISM%20ANNUAL%20STATISTICS%20%20REPORT%20Final.pdf Statics Tourism in Bihar on Indian Government's tourism website

http://www.indiaheritage.org/creative/creative_metal_work.htm

Patil, P.B. (2006) : *Tourism Development : Problem and Prospects*, Current Publications, Agra-10 (U.P.)

Patil P. V. (2006): *Tourism Development: Problems and Prospacts*, Current Publications, Agra, pp. 221-23.

Pearce, Douglas (1988): *Tourism Today : A Geographical Analysis*, London Scientific and Technical Publishing Divn., p. 22.

Rai, Lajipathi H. (1993): *Development of Tourism in India*, Printwell, Jaipur.

Seth, P.N., (1978): *Successful Tourism Planning and Management*, Cross Section Publishing, New Delhi, p. 25.

Verma, S.B., Jiloka, S.K. and Thryambakam, P. (2006) : *Rural Tourism and Tribal Development*, Deep & Deep Publications Pvt. Ltd., New Delhi-27.

10

Conclusions and Suggestions

Conclusions

Tourism is a socio-cultural and economic event for the traveller and the host. Part of travel's attraction is the opportunity to see different areas of the world and observe foreign cultures and ways of life. Tourists are a major factor of socio-culture change.

Tourism has many positive social impacts. It increases communication with the people, improves self-image of the community, enhances employment opportunities, educational opportunity, develop motivation for learning and moderation of the tourist infrastructure.

An increase in development of tourism affect the size of population. It creates new jobs, slow out migration and attract new workers to the areas. Better occupational opportunities may also strengthen family ties in area. Other social changes may stem from development of tourism.

The prospect of good jobs in the tourism industry may increase the desire for educational attainment. Employment opportunities in tourism may draw workers from the other sectors of economy. Domestic jobs may then become income earning if performed in hotels. This may not only improve the status of the workers but also increase the income of workers.

Tourism may help to revive the local people's interest and pride in their culture, traditions and values. The homogenizing influence of mass media and the hegemonic culture generally tend to push the local folk traditions into oblivion. Tourism may certainly help in re-establishing in traditional skills and values.

Tourism also provides ample opportunities to study the religious and ritualistic services. These aspects of a culture have always fascinated the strangers. These aspects of a culture have public performances which provide inputs to symbolic qualities of tourism.

The major factor that should be borne in mind by any community involve with tourism is that the only constant is change. It is a highly competitive business. Tourism depends on many external factors over which a destined area has little or no control. Success can be influenced by the weather, changing consumer taste, economic cycles and government policies. Tourism development has a great appeal for many communities because of anticipated economic benefits, such increased income and employment. Low capital production, low employment, lower income are major constraints in the development of areas. So there is a greater need for intensive tourism planning. Tourism development can change economic scenario of the area economy and highly desirable to most communities. By tourism development area community can earn more income from other parts of the country and globe. Hence, the importance of tourism as a contributor to economic growth of a particular area has been accepted in recent years. The flow of money generated by tourism will find its way into the overall tourism economy through the multiplier effect.

Tourism, which has the potential to become India's key foreign exchange earner within the foreseeable future, has, of late, shown signs of steady rise in the inflow of foreign tourists. Statistics with the Union Government's Department of Tourism, which is responsible for promotional, developmental and regulatory functions in the tourism sector, show that tourist arrivals could mean that the violence in some parts of the country does not have a bearing on the tourism industry, as a whole.

For a number of years, stress is being laid on marketing India as a cultural destination. Now it has been decided to market Indian tourism. Tourism industry sources say that the major impediments holding down the growth of the industry are many, including the lack of proper infrastructure, inadequately maintained roads, absence of a railway system that can cater to the needs of the tourists, very high taxation, lack of good communication facilities, good middle-class accommodation, pollution, unsafe drinking water at most tourist spots and the non-availability of hygienic foodstuff.

Domestic tourism also needs special attention considering the increase in income levels and emergence of an urban middle-class that can afford a holiday and is willing to spend. However, there are no precise estimates of the total domestic tourist traffic in the country. Officials said to have provided budget accommodation for foreign and domestic tourists, Yatri Nivases are being provided at a number of places. These will have clean and functional accommodation available to the budget travellers at reasonable tariffs.

Tourism in India vis-à-vis Bihar was once a way of life. It is now in the process of being turned into an industry with emphasis mainly on earning foreign exchange. The driving force behind promoting tourism, so far the official policy is concerned, is to provide attractive opportunities to foreign tourists, especially the tourists from the developed countries, who, given the right incentives and stimulants, are expected to come to exotic India with loads of money to spend. Since the tourist industry is also proposed to be developed further essentially as a private enterprise, the incentives and stimulants for the foreign tourists are bound also to be such as to earn quick returns on investment and maximize profits by the tourism industry. This has its own wide-ranging implications. Given the paucity of resources for long-gestating investment, there will be either a need to attract foreign investment in the tourism industry or to look around for quick fixes by smart Indian business interests to make fast buck by ways not always above board or dignified. The drive to promote tourism in India, in these circumstances, is bound to be associated with many undesirable features such as have been witnessed elsewhere in many other countries, in which too, a healthy social and economically sustainable infrastructure for the tourism industry was missing.

So far, however, foreign tourism in India is still on a rather limited scale. It is also associated in the main with Five-or four-Star hotel industry, which obviously is not geared for the promotion of the mass tourism on a grand scale. The tourism and hotel industry is already the third largest foreign exchange earner, which fact may seem to be a very impressive achievement. But it reflects poorly on the total foreign exchange earnings of the country, especially on the trade account. In absolute terms, the foreign exchange earnings of India from tourism and hotel industry are still very small compared to many other countries.

It may, however, be well argued that since the Indian economy has shown in recent years a distinct shift towards the service sector as a major source of employment generation, tourism and the infrastructure for its promotion have a great potential to grow. The service sector, it has been estimated, may actually generate nearly 65 per cent of the increase in the total jobs in the coming years. Tourism and allied sectors alone can generate 0.35 lakh jobs per year, that is, more than the entire manufacturing sector. The Tata Economic Consultancy Services (TECS) reported sometimes ago that for every job created in tourism sector, 2.57 jobs are created elsewhere, mainly in supporting services and craftsmanship levels. The implications of the emerging pattern in the future expansion of employment opportunities in the economy needs to be further studied.

Suggestions

The following recommendations has been made in the 11th Five Year Plan to improve the tourism sector :

Creating awareness globally about the immense eco-tourism/adventure tourism potential in our country. Considering that the major chunk of Himalayas is in India, the perception worldover that Himalayas means Nepal has to be changed. A marketing and promotion strategy needs to be undertaken and can include:

- Road shows to showcase eco-tourism/adventure possibilities in India.

- Promotional films and advertising through electronic media.
- Detailed brochures/maps can be placed at the disposal of our overseas tourist offices.
- Familiarization trips for our officers overseas for eco-tourism/adventure tours in India.
- There is an urgent need for a National Policy on adventure tourism and there is need to revive an already existing national eco-tourism policy. At present, there are different safety and ecological rules in different States. Greater synergy between the Centre and the Himalayan states can lead to a national policy, which would help the industry tremendously. Uniform rules throughout India, especially with regard to safety and ecological guidelines, would go a long way in boosting this sector.
- The biodiversity found in our national parks is truly incredible. It is recommended that the Ministry of Tourism work in tandem with the State Ministries of Environment and Forests in twenty-five of our most popular National Parks. The wildlife experience has to be more ecologically friendly, educative and sustainable. Having interpretation centres in the parks with basic and clean amenities, informative films at park entrances on the Do's and Don'ts in wildlife parks will help sensitise visitors to our natural heritage. The Tourism Ministry should take the lead in this and get experts from overseas (like wildlife park officials from South Africa) to help us devise a strategy for better management of our parks which would focus on conservation, carrying capacity, improving the visitor experience, sustainability and inclusion of local communities in the preservation/conservation process.
- The Ministry of Tourism run/sponsor institutes to offer Adventure and Eco-Tourism as subjects in their syllabus. Government run mountaineering institutes like The Nehru Institute of Mountaineering (Uttarkashi) and The Himalayan Mountaineering

Institute, Darjeeling can offer adventure guide courses. This will ensure that country has a pool of trained adventure/Eco-tourism personnel, who will carry this sector forward professionally.

- Safe adventure tourism requires excellent adventure equipment and as of today, this has to be imported. The Ministry of Tourism recognized adventure tour operators should be allowed every year to import duty-free equipment up to 20 per cent of their annual turnover.
- Adventure tours/eco-tours were operated in wild areas where communication/medical facilities are not available. In this scenario, allowing the use of satellite phones and Global Positioning System (GPS) will go a long way in ensuring that safety standards in India are at par with international standards. Recognized adventure tour operators should be allowed to import/use satellite phones and global positioning systems.
- Soft loans be arranged for entrepreneurs for manufacture of adventure equipments.
- Contour maps of adventure areas/national parks need be prepared to help in better operations and selling in the global market.
- Waiver of service tax charged on adventure tours will give an impetus to this sector. Considering adventure tours are operational only a few months of the year, this will not be a major setback to the national exchequer and will give the necessary fillip to this sector.
- India has the maximum amount of red tape involved in giving clearances for organizing an overseas mountaineering expedition to India. The security concerns of the fifties and sixties perhaps warranted this. The Government needs to simplify procedures urgently to give a boost to this important segment of adventure tourism. There is need to open more trekking peaks in the country with simple application procedures. The nodal agency should be kept as the

Indian Mountaineering Foundation (IMF) and local State Governments should not have their own rules and regulations and instead should make a harmonious procedure in conjunction with the IMF.

- The condition of a minimum of four persons travelling together in remote areas like Arunachal Pradesh, Ladakh etc. should be done away with so long as they travel with Government approved operators.
- For all sectors of the Industry such as tour operators, hoteliers, airlines, transporters, lodge owners etc., a detailed environmental pledge has been formulated and is contained in the Environment and Eco-tourism handbook published by the Ministry of Tourism. It is suggested that all State Governments and the Ministry should encourage the different stakeholders to sign this pledge and thus, offer a commitment. Also, through the Ministry's communications such as brochures and websites, it be suggested, "Travellers/Tourists give preference to using services of those stakeholders who have displayed this environmental commitment."
- For all diverse topographical regions in India from mountains, beaches, forests, deserts, fragile areas etc., suggested building guidelines need to be drawn up which are in harmony with their immediate environment, like using local materials and reflecting the local culture. This will prevent pollution and over-building of places as has happened at hill stations like Mussoorie, Manali, Nainital and Shimla. Landscape architects should be involved at Government and Private level and these notes should be put in the "Call for investment brochures" published by State Governments.
- It is suggested that carrying capacity studies be undertaken for popular trekking trails, national parks, rivers, etc. so that a low environmental impact is maintained and sustainable practices are in place by the Industry. 'Honey pot areas ' need to have pressure relieved by opening closed areas and by publicising

lesser-known regions so that traffic is dissipated from popular zones.

- It is suggested that we create a Tourism and Environmental law weekend course for all stakeholders as well as Government to know their Rights and Duties as a citizen, specially as all operations will impact on nature, environment and built heritage cultures etc. Ministry of Tourism in conjunction with Industry and organisation like the WWF India can put this up.
- There is a requirement to have trained nature guides, naturalists, mountain trek leaders, etc. who have safety and environmental knowledge. Such courses could be initiated at tourism institutes, vocational study institutes as well as outdoor training institutes.
- Effective steps at the State level be carried out for garbage disposal through Municipal bodies, use of incinerators to be re-looked at, and NGO models like Kovalam Zero Waste to be studied. Industry to partner State Governments and NGOs to keep cities and towns clean in conjunction with local authorities.
- Environment education should be included in the curriculum of schools and colleges with a special component of Eco-tourism to make an eco-sensitive population of tomorrow.
- Good initiative by Ministry of Tourism for genuine experiences through village home stays in architectural dwellings that reflect local culture and have the use of local materials and through this, enhance the encouragement of handicrafts and arts of remote and fragile areas. This should be encouraged.
- The Himalayan Tourism Advisory Board (HIMTAB) has been doing good work on promotion of Adventure and Sustainable tourism and the Ministry of Tourism needs to have regular meetings of this board.

Thus, tourism is a service which is fast growing. To ensure the growth of this, in an orderly manner, one can ill-afford to ignore its managerial implications. For one looking for respite from the busy life, activity, speed and no leisure, hurried breakfast or more apt-skipped breakfast, timed sleep and all that make up the urban chaos, the tourist craves to be away from these modern abominations, to get away to those remote destinations where the joy of solitude and leisure can be relished. How far one can quench his thirst for leisure hours largely depends to what extent adequate infrastructure and imaginative package is provided by the tourist industry. India vis-à-vis Bihar could be a destination of the future tourists only if it plays its cards right.

QUESTIONNAIRE

Tourism Development and Marketing of Tourist Services in Bihar

---

Date:/ /2008 Location: ____________

1. Survey Point (RECORD BY TICKING ONE OPTION)
   (1) Railway Station (2) Airport (3) Bus Depot
   (4) Hotel (5) Tourist Site
2. Name: ____________________ Telephone No. (With STD/ISD Codes) _____
3. Age : ____ Yrs.
4. Record Gender. (i) Male (ii) Female
5. Are you? (i) Single (ii) Married
6. When did you arrive here? Date: ________
7. When you are scheduled to depart? _______
8. Number of days stayed for. ________
9. Which country do you belong to? ________________________
10. Is this your first visit to India? (i) Yes (ii) No
11. Are you an NRI? (i) Yes (ii) No
12. Which state of India do you belong to? ___________________
13. Do you live in this city?
    (i) Yes (ii) No
14. Have you travelled to Bihar before?
    (i) Yes (ii) No
15. How have you travelled to Bihar? READ OUT OPTIONS and TICK (SINGLE RESPONSE)
    (i) Train (ii) Bus (iii) Air Flight
    (iv) Personal Car (v) Taxi

16. Have you travelled to this city before?
    (i) Yes (ii) No
17. What is your occupation? READ OUT OPTIONS and TICK (SINGLE RESPONSE)
    (i) Business/Industrialist/Pretty Trader/Shop Owner
    (ii) Self-Employed Professional (Chartered Accountant, Cost Accountant, Doctor, Lawyer, Engineer, Consultant, Proprietor of a Firm Institute)
    (iii) Government Service (iv) Private Service
    (v) Student/Researcher (vi) Politician/leader
    (vii) Agriculturist (viii) Social Worker
    (ix) Retired (x) Monk/Priest
    (xi) Housewife
    (xii) If any other, Please specify __________
18. What is your educational qualification? READ OUT OPTIONS and TICK (SINGLE RESPONSE)
    (i) Illiterate(ii) Up to HSC/SSC
    (iii) Higher Education (Graduate and above)
    (iv) Technical Education
    (v) If any other, please specify __________
19. What is your approximate annual household income? READ OUT OPTIONS and TICK (SINGLE RESPONSE)
    (i) Less than 60,000
    (ii) 60,001-1,00,000
    (iii) 1,00,001-2,00,000
    (iv) 2,00,001-5,00,000
    (v) Above 5,00,000
20. How often do your travel? READ OUT OPTIONS and TICK (SINGLE RESPONSE)
    (i) Once a week or more often
    (ii) Once a fortnight (v) Once a month
    (iii) Once in 3 months (vi) Once in 6 months
    (iv) Once in a year (vii) Less often
21. What was your main purpose of visit? READ OUT OPTIONS and TICK (SINGLE RESPONSE)
    (i) Business (ii) Official Work
    (iii) Conference (iv) Employment

(v) Education (vi) Sports Meet
(vii) Pilgrimage (Buddhism)
(viii) Pilgrimage (others)
(ix) Historical tourism
(x) Adventure tourism (xi) Family/Friends visit
(xii) Recreation/leisure (xiii) Wildlife tourism
(xiv) Health tourism (xv) Sightseeing
(xvi) Shopping (xvii) Transit
(xviii) Social and Religious Function

22. Are you travelling ...? READ OUT OPTIONS and TICK (SINGLE RESPONSE)
(i) Alone (ii) With Family
(iii) With Friends (iv) With Family and Friend

23. How many people have travelled with you? ____________

24. Are you a part of an organized group/package tour?
(i) Yes (ii) No

25. Please give the information about sex and age of people, who have travelled with you? ASK and RECORD

Male	Age	Female	Age

26. How did you make your travel arrangement? READ OUT OPTIONS and TICK (MULTIPLE RESPONSE)
(i) Self (ii) Office/Employer
(iii) Travel Agent (iv) Tour Operator
(v) If any other, please specify ____________

27. (Where did you stay? READ OUT OPTIONS and TICK (MULTIPLE RESPONSE)
(i) 5 Star Hotel (ii) 4 Star Hotel

(iii) 3 Star Hotel (iv) 2 Star Hotel
(v) 1 Star Hotel (vi) Non-star Hotel
(vii) Private Guest House/Inn
(viii) State Government-owned/managed hotel
(ix) Government managed/owned circuit house
(x) Dharamshala/Sarai
(xi) Monastery (xii) Gurudwara/Temple
(xiii) Friend and Relatives (xiv) Motel
(xv) Youth/YMCA Hostels
(xvi) If any other, please specify ________

28. Pease tell us how much you are likely to spend here? Indian Rs/US $ ____ CIRCLE CURRENCY
29. Which mode Payment did you use mostly? READ OUT OPTIONS and TICK (SINGLE RESPONSE)
(i) Cash (ii) Credit card
(iii) Travellers' cheques
30. Please tell us, how much have you spent yesterday on ....?
Read Out Options and Tick (Multiple Response)

S.No.	*Accommodations*	*Amount (Rs.)*
1.	Hotels	
2.	Private Guest Houses	
3.	Tourist Guest Houses	
4.	Govt. Guest Houses	
5.	Dharamshala/Sarai	
6.	Rented	
7.	Relatives	
8.	Any other	
9.	Total (Post Code)	

31. Please tell us, how much have you spent yesterday on...?
Read Out Options and Tick (Multiple Response)

S. No.	*Food and Beverages*	*Amount (Rs.)*
1.	Railway Station, Bus Stand, Train	
2.	Hotels	
3.	Private Guest Houses	
4.	Tourist Guest Houses	
5.	Govt. Guest Houses	
6.	Dharamshala/Sarai	
7.	Restaurants	
8.	Cafeteria	
9.	Snack Bars	
10.	Lunch Counters	
11.	Refreshment Stands	
12.	Canteens	
13.	Milk Bars	
14.	Bars/Pubs and other drinking places	
15.	Mela, Fairs, Picnic	
16.	Any Other	
17.	Total (Post Code)	

32. Did you find your visit to Bihar better than or worse than or as per your expectations? ASK and RECORD (SINGLE RESPONSE)
   (i) Much better than expectation
   (ii) Somewhat better expectation
   (iii) As per expectation
   (iv) Worse than expectation

33. Which of these Buddhist site have you visited?
   (i) Areraj (ii) Aurangabad
   (iii) Bodhgaya (iv) Guneri
   (v) Kesaria (vi) Lauria
   (vii) Nalanda (viii) Rajgir

(ix) Vaishali (x) Vikramshila
(xi) Ajanta and Ellora (xii) Kalgaon
(xiii) Khandiri (xiv) Kaushambi
(xv) Kushinagar (xvi) Nagarjunakonda
(xvii) Ratnagiri (xviii) Sanchi
(xix) Sravasti (xx) Sarnath
(xxi) Udaygiri (xxii) Vidhisha
(xxiii) Any other, please specify ____________

34. Expenditure occurred for this trip prior to entering this centre/town.
Only expenditure attributable to this trip should be recorded.
How much you spent on?
(a) Accommodation Services __________
(b) Food and Beverages Services _______
(c) Transport Equipment Rental (Hired Taxi/Car/Jeep/Tractor etc.) _______
(d) Travel Agencies and Similar _______
(e) Other recreational and entertainment services ___
(f) Clothing and Garments ________
(g) Processed Foods ________

35. Visitors from:
(i) Within India ________________
(ii) NRIs ____________________
(iii) North America (USA, Canada, Mexico, Cuba...) ____________________________
(iv) South America (Brazil, Argentina, Chile, Guyana, Peru...) ______________________
(v) Europe (U.K., France, Spain, Italy, Germany...) ____________________________
(vi) Africa (Egypt, Libya, Algeria, South Africa, Nigeria...) ______________________
(vii) Asia (China, Korea, Japan, Philippines...) ____________________________
(viii) Middle East/Arab Countries (Iran, UAE, Yemen, Oman...) ______________________
(ix) South-East Asian Countries (Thailand, Malaysia, Indonesia...) ______________________

(x) Australia/New Zealand ____________

(xi) If any other countries, please specify ____________

____

36. Type of Organization: (OBSERVE and RECORD)
    (i) Travel Agency
    (ii) Tour Operator
    (iii) Adventure Tour Operator
    (iv) Tourist Transport Operator
    (v) Transporter
    (vi) If any other, please specify ______
37. Name of the Contact Person: ____________
38. Name of the Company: ____________
39. Address: ____________
40. City: ____________
    Telephone No. ____________
41. Ownership: (ASK and RECORD)
    (i) Central Government
    (ii) State Government
    (iii) Private Limited
    (iv) Proprietorship/Partnership
    (v) Public Limited
    (vi) If any other, please specify______
42. In which year it was established?
    Year: ____________
43. Membership:
    (i) TAAI
    (ii) IATO
    (iii) ATOA
    (iv) ITTA
    (v) IATA
    (vi) Local Association
    (vii) Regional Association
    (viii) If any other, please specify ____
    (ix) None

44. Total number of employees: ______ (permanent and temporary)

Departments	*Number of Permanent employees*	*Number of casual or temporary*
Administration		
Ticketing		
Foreign		
Accounts		
Tours		
Sales and Marketing		
Total		

45. Type of Organization: (OBSERVE and RECORD)
    (i) Shop (ii) Emporium
    (iii) If any other, please specify ____________
46. Could you please tell me that how much here you spent on...?

S. No.	*Expenditure Heads*	*Amount (Rs.)*
1.	Accommodations	
2.	Food and Beverages	
3.	Tea and Coffee	
4.	Alcohol Products	
5.	Tobacco Products	
6.	Medicinal Products	
7.	Study material and Stationery	
8.	Recreational and Entertainment	
9.	Textile Products	
10.	Durable Goods	
11.	Footwear	
12.	Toiletries	
13.	Gem and Jewellery	
14.	Travel Services	
15.	Transport Equipment (Rental)	
16.	Transport	
	Total	

47. How can the tourist services at the destinations, that you visited, can be improved?
Suggestions Please:

PLATE - XXIX

Gandhi Maidan, Patna

Kumhrar, Patna

Pathar ki Masjid, Patna

Old Fort Near Ganga River Bank, Patna

Padri ki Haveli, Patna

PLATE - XXX

Hajrat Makhdum Shah Daulat Maneri Saheb,Gandhi Maidan,
Patna, Maner Sharif

Jain Temple, Bhagalpur

PLATE - XXXI

Maha Bodhi Temple
(Bodhgaya Temple)

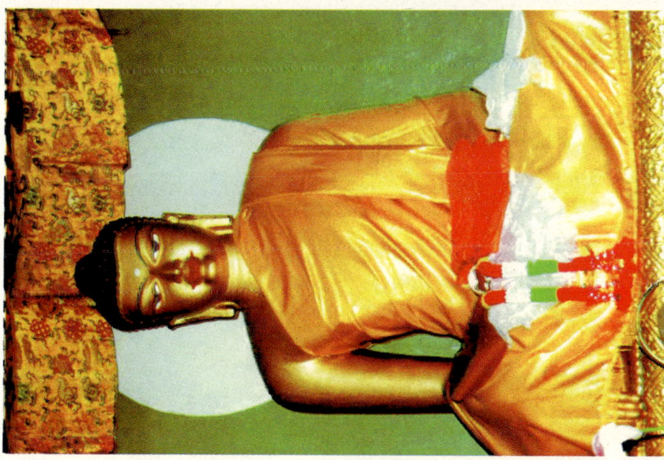

The main Image of Lord Buddha
(Bochgaya Temple)

Boddha Walkway
(Bodhgaya Temple)

PLATE - XXXII

Mandar Parwat, Baunsi, Banka

Lord Shiva Temple, Munger

PLATE - XXXIII

Old Secretariat, Patna

High Court, Patna

Shaheed Smarak, Patna

PLATE - XXXIV

Maha Bodhi Tree, Bodhgaya

80 feet high Buddha Statue, Bodhgaya

PLATE - XXXV

Mundeshwari Temple, Kaimur

Jain Mandir, Pawapuri

PLATE - XXXVI

Bhutan Temple, Bodhgaya

Monastery of Bodhgaya

Vishnupadi Temple, Gaya

Muchlund Sarovar, Bodhgaya

Index

Aalok Dhanwan, 120
Aboriginal communities, 40
Academic International de Tourism, Monte Carlo, 15
Accessibility, 31, 253-54
Accommodation, 17, 34-36, 55, 248
 Units, 95-96
Advantages and gains, 50
Adventure tourism, 30, 53, 85-86, 92, 95, 255-56
Afghan, 107
Africa, 26
Agamkuan, 140
Age of Tourists, 181
Agara Heritage Project, 84
Agra, 43, 53, 210
Agriculture, 13, 19, 209-10
Agro-Industries, 113
Agro-tourism, 15
Airports, improvement of, 48
Airport Authority, 95
Ajanta and Ellora, 77
Ajatshatru, 139, 245
Ajatshatru Stupa, 145
Akbar, 102, 140
Akhara, 145
Alexander the Great, 236
All India Kishan Sabha (AIKS), 103
Amartya Sen, 239
America, 20, 23, 24, 26
Amjhar Sharif, 200
Ancient Vajrasan, 148
Andaman and Nicobar Islands, 53, 83, 231, 233
Anga region, 119, 129, 203
Angika, 100
Angika Arts, 117
Annual migration, 20
Annual Plan, 88
Annual Tourist composition, 180
Annual Urs, 200
Anti-corruption wave, 110
Anugarh Narayan Sinha, 104
Approaches, 40
Aqua Tourism, 250
Areraj Pillar, 157
Archaeological Museum, 143
Archaeological Survey of Inda, 241
Arya Bhatt, 210
Aryan, 107
Arts and Crafts, 117-18
Ashoka (Mauryan Emperor), 101, 139, 157, 236, 246
Ashoka Group, 84
Ashokan Inscription and rock-cut cave, 153
Ashokan Pillar, 150, 156
Assistant for the Development of International Tourism (ADIT), 84
Atithi Devo Bhava, 41
Aurangabad, 117, 151
 tourist places in, 152
Aurengzeb, 120, 135, 201
Australia, 87, 93-94
Austria, 21
Ayurveda, 54
Azim-Ush-Shan, 139
Azimabad, 139, 200

Baba Nagarjun, 120
Baby Boomers, 93

Bachelor Degree in Tourism, 57
Badruddin-I-Alam, 200, 201
Bakhra Pillar, 157
Bakhtiyar Khilji, 240
Baikuntha Shukla, 103, 105
Bandhavgarh National Park, 232
Bangladesh, 242
Barabar Hills, 154
Baradari, 153
Bargain, 143
Bari Patan Devi, 141
Basham, A.L., 101
Basokund, 156
Battle of Buxar, 102
Bawan Pokhar Temple, 150
Beach and Coastal Tourism, 54
Belgiums, 21
Benefits, 40-41
Berggren Hotels, 191
Berneckar, 15
Betala National Park, 211
Bhagalpur, 72, 73
Bhargava, 48
Bharatiya Janata Party, 112
Bharatpur, 232
Bhojpuri films, 132-33
Bhookhi Peedhi, 120
Bhubaneshwar, 57, 87
Bhumihar Brahmins, 110
Bihar, 99
    agrarian movement, 103
    artisans of, 118
    Buddhist places in, 84-85
    cinema industry, 131-32
    cities and districts of, 109
    climate, 105
    cuisine of, 129-30
    culture of, 117-120, 255
    cultural heritage of, 135-36
    dances of, 119-206
    deciduous forests, 109
    demography of, 106-10
    domestic and foregin tourist in, 189-90
    earning from tourists, 213
    economic development, 100
    economy of, 112
    education system in, 114-15
    forest types of, 105
    foreign tourists in, 136, 185
    Gross State Domestic Product, 113-14
    handicraft shops in, 215-16
    Hindi writezrs in, 120
    hospitality in, 179-190
    identity of, 110
    Indian freedom struggles in, 164
    judiciary of, 109
    Knowledge Centre, 116
    languages of, 100
    literacy rate, 107, 115-16
    marketing system in, 43-44
    population growth of, 106-08
    religion in, 130-31
    sweet delicacies, 129
    tourists centres in, 218-19
    tourists places in, 135-59
    tourists points of, 107
    tourists services in, 272
    tourist statistics of, 186-88
    tourist traffic in, 182-83
Bihar e-Governance Services and Technologies (BeST), 116
Bihar Government, Tourism policy of, 248-49
Bihar Provincial Kisan Sabha (BPKS), 103
Bihar Rajya Home Stay Scheme, 182
Bihar Tourism, budget: allocation and actual expenditure, 189-90
Bihar School of Engineering, 114
Bihar Sharif areas, 118, 201
Bihar State Tourism Development Corporation (BSTDC), 137
Bihar Tourist Policy, 231, 235
Bihar Yoga Bharti, 157
Bihari festivals, 204

Bihari languages, 119
Bihari migrant workers, 20, 104, 107
Bihari Non-Vegetarian dish, 129
Bihul-Bishari Puja, 203
Bimbisar Jail, 144
Bisram, 246
Bodh Gaga, 131, 135, 147, 210, 211, 218, 235-36, 238, 245
Bodhi Tree, 147-48
Boost tourism, 71
Brajkhoonsi, 92
Brazil, 93
British Raj, 102
Buddha, 149-52
Buddha Stupas, 151-52
Buddhism, 101-03, 133, 191, 241, 244
Buddhist circuit, 244
Buddhist Vaishali, 212
Buddhist Monasteries, 135
Buddhist Pilgrimage Centre, 92
Buddhist places, 84
Buddhist Vihara, 97
Budgetary allocation, 238
Budhi Gandak, 104
Business-cum-Entertainment Tourism, 256
Business Tourists, 16, 73
  categories of, 32-33
Buxar Fair, 199

Cabana Hotels, 191
Cambridge University, 239
Canada, 21, 26
Capacity Building programmes, 56-57
Central Sector Tourism Plan, 84
Centrally sponsored schemes, 52
Chamberlain, 46
Champaran Satyagraha, 103
Chanakya National Law University, 116
Chandragupta Maurya, 139
Chaudhary, Malay Roy, 129
Chaumukhi Mahadev, 151
Chatterjee, Upamanyu, 120
Chhath Puja, 202-03
Chhattisgarh, 232
Chhoti Patan Devi, 140
Chiragdan, 153
Chitragupta Puja, 203
Chota Nagpur plateau, 104, 237
Chilika and Sundarbans, 232
China, 26, 93, 149
Cinema, 131-32
Colombo, 87
Commercialization, 44
Communication, 21, 35
  facilities, 54
Competitive market, 57
Computerization, 230
Concurrent list, 229
Constraints, 217-18
Construction, 19
Corbett National Park, 232
Coronation Tank, 151
Corruption, 100, 111, 112
Craft and Culture, 19
Craft melas, 59
Cross-sectoral synergies, 19
Cruise control, 251
Cruise Tourism, 93, 95
Cuisine, 129-30, 206-07, 220
Cultural destination, 264
Cultural environment, 19
Cultural exchange, 44
Cultural heritage, 76
Cultural Tradition, wealth of, 77
Cultural tourism, 15, 30, 195, 217, 231
Culture, 117-120, 255
Cunningham, 146, 156
Custom duties, 102

Dalai Lama, 239
Dargah Sharif, 200
Dariya Sahib, 131
Dasham falls, 211
Delhi, 43, 210
Detailed Project Reports (DPRs), 63

Destinations, 53
  development, 52-53
Develop infrastructure link-ages, 253-54
Dhabas, 56-57
Dharma Chakra Pravartana, 245
Dharamdas, 131
Dictionnaire Universal, 14-15
Dilli Haat, 54, 234
Discrepancies, 49
Domestic campaign, feature of, 58-59
Domestic Jobs, 263
Domestic promotion, 58-59
Domestic Tourism, 17, 20-21, 29-32, 34, 50-52, 73, 94-95, 226, 233, 265
Domestic Tourists, 19, 73
  movements, 25
  traffic, 183
Domestic and Foreign Tourists, 181
Drugs, 29
Dubai, 60

East India Company, 102
Eco-tourism, 15, 36, 85-86, 233, 243-44, 255, 267
  promotion of, 53
Economic advantage, 46
Economic benefits, 63
  development, 18, 478
  goals, 264
  liberalisation, 85
  system, 222-21
Economy, 112-13
Education, 114-15, 159-60
Educational development, 44
Eid-ul-Adha, 204
Eid-ul-Fitr, 204
Eighth Five Year Plan, 78
Eleventh Five Year Plan, 266
  tourism development, strategy for, 92-93
Emergence, 20
Employment, 28, 48, 50, 208
  avenues, 40
  generation, 18-19, 35, 70, 209, 266
  opportunities, 263
  potential, 50, 227
  status, 216-17
Enhancing India's Competitiveness, 230-31
Entertainment activity, 13
Entrepreneurship development programmes, 36-37
Environmental regeneration, 20
Expanding Product development, 231-32
Expenditure, 94

Fahien, 135, 145
Fairs, 59, 195-99
  Baisakhi Purnima, 197
  Behula, 197
  Bettiah, 196-97
  Brahampur fair, 199
  Gulab Bagh, 195-96
  Harihar Kshetra, 195
  Karaghar, 199
  Karhagola, 196
  Khagra, 196
  Malmas, 197
  permanent, 195
  Pitripaksha, 198
  Saurath Subha, 199
  Seasonal, 194
Fairs and festivals, 194-97, 234
Family income, 159
Federation of Hotel and Restaurant Association, 83
Festivals, 59, 203-04, 234
  Chhath puja, 202
  Navratri, 204
Fifth Five Year Plan, 89
Fiji, 93
Final phase, 39-40
First Five Year Plan, 86-87

5-Star accommodation, 226
Five Year Plan, 86-88
Focus on Tourism, 47
Folksongs and Music, 206
Food Craft Institute (FCI), 56
Foreign cultures, 263
Foreign currency, 14
Foreign exchange, 13, 18-20, 28, 34-35, 49-50, 62, 65-66, 77, 86, 208, 254, 264-66
  earnings, 67-68, 181-82
Foreign Tourist, 17, 64-65, 81-82, 181-82
  traffic, 184
Foreign Tourists Arrival (FTAs), in India, 64-65, 81-82, 181-82
Fortification Walls, 145
Fourth Five Year Plan, 88-89
  tourist facilities, 88
Four-point Journey, 92
Frankfurt, 60, 87
France, 21
Freight equalization policy, 100
Future Brand, 179

Galiti, 49
Gandhian circuit, 238
Ganga Asnan, 195
Ganga Darshan Complex, 157
Ganga river, 101
Ganga tributories, 104
Gautama Buddha, 130
Gaya, 43, 73
Gaya Shraddha, 198
Gazetteer, 146
Germany, 21, 87
Global chains, 111
Global Positioning System (GPS), 268
Global Tourism, scale of, 27-28
Global Tourists arrivals, 61-62
Goa, 43, 48
  tourism in, 48
Gods and Goddesses, 244
Golden Age, 101
Golghar, 139
Griddhakoot Hill, 144
Gross Domestic Product (GDP), 179
Gross revenue, 18
Group Tourists, types of, 29
Guide Training programmes, 57
Gulmarg, 89
Guru Govind Singh, 102, 135, 211
Guru of Sikhism, 102
Gwalior, 53

Haats, 54, 194
Hajipur Karbala, 202
Han Dynasty, 101
Handicrafts, 19
Harihar Kshetra fair, Sonepur, 195
Harmandir jee, 140
Heritage, 255
  cities, 53
  hotels, 248
  tourism, 53
Hill station, 269
Hilton, 191
Himalayas, 232-33
Himalayan Mountaineering Institute, Darjeeling, 268
Himalayan Tourism Advisory Board (HIMTAB), 270
Hindi writers, 120
Hindu deities, 117
Hindu fairs, 199-200
Hindu festivals, 131-32, 204-05
Hindu Monestary, 149
Hindu Temples, 241
Hinduism, 102, 107, 191-92
Hiuen Tsiang, 135, 142, 146, 156, 211-12, 239
Hiuen Tsiang Memorial Hall, 143
Horticulture, 19
Hospitality, 191-92, 230
  industry, 85
  programme, 59-60

Hot Water Springs, 146
Hotels, capital/interest subsidy for, 63
Hotel Management and Catering Education, 56
Hrishikesh Sulabh, 120
Human Resource, 253-54
  development, 55-57
Hyderabad, 53
Hypotheses, 71

Improve Tourism Product Offering, 254-55
Inbound tourism, 32, 34
Incredible India, 28
  campaign, 97
Incubating Tourism Entrepreneurs, 37-38
India,
  foreign tourist arrival in, 79-80
  global tourist arrival in, 80-82
  trends in, 81-82
India Tourism, scale of, 28-29
Indian adventure tourism, 54
Indian Institute of Public Opinion, 47, 49
Indian Institute of Tourism and Travel Management (IITTM), 57
Indian Mountaineering Foundation (IMF), 269
Indian National Congress, 112
Indian Wildlife Tourism, 53, 232
Indian Tourism Policy, 36
Indira Gandhi, 109, 110
Information Centres, 237
Information Technology, 58, 63-64
Infrastructure, 251
  development of, 209-10
Institute of Hotel Management (IHMs), 56
Institutional Mechanism, 254
Integrated development, 251-52
Intangible elements, 14
Inter Continental Hotels, 191
International Buddhist Communities, 212
International Tourism, 17, 21, 29-30, 32, 93-94
  revenues, 93-94
  source markets, 93
International Tourism Development Corporation (ITDC), 43, 83-84, 88-89
  programmes of, 88-89
International Tourists arrivals, 23-25
International Tourist Destinations, 26-27
International Union of Official Traval Organization (IUOTO), 22
Intra-regional Tourism, 25
Islam, 191
Islamic culture and food, 130

Jain circuit, 245-46
  package, 238
Jain temples, 135, 140
Jainism, 100-01, 191
  Tirthankara of, 131
Jaipur, 43, 53, 210
Jaisalmer, 234
Janata Dal, 110, 111
Janata Party, 110, 111
Japan, 93, 149
Jarasandh ki Baithak, 145
Jayaprakash Narayan, 104, 109
Jean Dreze, 239
Jewel Walk Shrine, 148
Jharkhand, 53, 85, 100, 111, 114
Job creation, 20
John Prendergast, 208
Joint advertising, 60
Jose Ignacio De Arrillaga, 14

Kabir, 131
Kabul and Kandhar, 210
Kamaldah, 140
Kanha National Park, 232

Karaghar Fair, 199
Karan Chaupar Cave, 154
Karmabhoomi, 237
Karma festival, 205
Karpoori Thakur, 110
Kashmiri Muslims, 30
Kaziranga, 232
Kesaria, 156
Khajuraho, 87
Khankah Emadia Mangal Talab, annual Urs of, 200
Khawa, 48
Khuda Bakhsh Oriental Public Library, 139
Khudiram Bose, 104
Kidnapping, 218
King Bimbisara, 130
King Dharmapala, 155, 240
Kisan Sabha Movement, 103
Konark, 87
Kovalam Zero waste, 270
Kukkul-pada-giri, 146
Kulu-Manali, 89
Kumbh Mela, 234
Kurkihar, 146
Kurt Krapf, 18
Kusheshwar Asthan Fair, 199
Kutch, 232

Labour-oriented industry, 56
Ladakh, 232
Lakri Dargah, 200
Lakshadweep Islands, 53, 233
Lakshmi Narayan Mandir, 130
Lalu Prasad Yadav, 108-12
Land allotment, 248
Land of Contrasts, 77
Large revenue generating projects, 55
Lauria Nandangarh, 156
League of Nations, 17
Leisure tourism, 30, 73
  categories of, 32-33
Lexington Avenue, 129
Lichhavies, 212
Little Rann of Kutch, 232
Lok Janshakti Party, 112
Lomas Rishi Cave, 154
London, 60
Lord Buddha, 101, 120, 150, 212
Lord Mahavira, 135
Lucknow Session, 103
Luxambourg, 21

Ma Fai Management Consultants, 191
Madhubani painting, 237, 240, 244
Madurai, 53, 87
Magadha, 100, 101-03, 210-13
Mahabalipuram, 87
Mahabharata, 154
Mahabodhi Temple, 147, 191
Mahajan, 48
Mahatma Gandhi, 102, 109, 210
  Setu, 191
Malaysia, 47
Maner Sharif, 141
Maniar Math, 144
Manjusha Kala, 117
Marital Status, 181
Mark Twain, 77
Market Research, 61-62
Marketing, 41-43, 57-58
  perspective, 41-42
  plans, 60
  promotion, 48
  strategy, 48, 218-19
Married couples, 29
Marriott International, 191
Mathura, 92
Media and Marketing Plan, 238
Meghnad Desai, 239
Meticulous excavation, 241
Meyer, R. de, 15
Ministry of Tourism and Culture, 35
Ministry of Tourism and Civil Aviation, 52, 54, 56, 58, 63, 88, 224, 267, 269-70
Mishra, Lalit Narayan, 110

Mithili community, 120
Modern Bihar, 115
Modern marketing techniques, 42
Modern Tourism development, 35, 210
Montague, 46
Monuments/Heritage Building and improvement, 55
Mosques, 153
Motivated Tourist, 30
Motivation, 48
Muchalinda Tank, 148
Mudumalai, 232
Muhammad Bin Bakhtiar Khilji, 102
Multi-billion-dollar industry, 15
Multi-stage random sampling technique, 72
Mumbai, 43
Munger, 72-75
  fort, 157
  monuments of, 157-58
Musical instruments, 118
Muslim fairs, 200-202
Muzaffarpur, 72, 73
Mysore, 43

Nagarhole, 232
Nagarjuna, 100, 142, 154, 211
Nagarjuna Hill, 154
Nalanda, 100, 135, 141, 238
Nalanda University, 102, 114, 158, 191, 211, 237, 238
National Council for Hotel Management and Catering Technology (NCHM&CT), 56
National Image Building and Marketing Plan, 91
National Institute of Pharmaceutical Education and Research (NIPER), 116
National policy, 224-25, 267-68
National priority, 229-30
National tourism, 32
National Tourism Awareness Campaign, 230
National Tourism Development Policy, 224
The Netherlands, 21
Nautankis, 194
Nav Nalanda Mahavihar, 142-43
Navaratri, 204-05
Nehru, Jawaharlal, 77
Nehru Institute of Mountaineering, Uttarkashi, 267
Nepal, 100, 104
New market requirement, 95
New York, 60
Nitish Kumar (Chief Minister, Bihar), 104, 108, 111, 261
Non-Governmental Organizations (NGOs), 14, 38
Non-Tourism categories, 32
Non-Traditional areas, development of, 91
North-America, 25, 230
North-Eastern States, 53

Oberai Hotels, 48
Objectives, 71-72, 228-29, 248
Observation, 40
Occupations, 159
Occupational opportunities, 263
Olympic Games, 16
Ongoing scheme, 55
Organizational policy, 193
Outbound Tourism, 32
Outreach training programmes, 56
Overseas Promotion, 60
Oxford English Dictionary, 14
Oxford University, 239

Pacific Air Travel Association (PATA), 83
Padri-ki-haveli, 141
Pandit Nalin Vilochan Sharma, 120
Pandit Karyanand Sharma, 120

Pandit Yamuna Karjee, 125
Pankaj Raj, 120
Parasnath, 245
Partition of India, 107
Patal-Ganga, 155
Pathar-ki-Masjid, 140
Patliputra, 100-03, 135-38, 40, 236
Patna, 73
  College of Arts and Crafts, 118
  Open 5-Star hotels, 38
  National Institute of Technology, 114
  Tourist places in, 138-39
Patna Saheb, 135, 200
Patna College, 114
Patna Museum, 139, 146, 211
Patna Qallam, 117
Patna School of Painting, 117
Patna University, 114, 241
Pawapuri, 245
Performing arts, 118-19
Perspective plans, 61-62
Phool Mahal, 153
Phulwari Sharif, annual Urs of, 200
Pilgrim tourism, 256
Pilgrimage, 212
  centres, 54
Pind-daan package, 238
Pippala Stone House, 145
Plans and programmes, 97
Planning Commission, 93
Planning and policy formulation, 62
Pleasure tourism, 30
Pleasure Travel, 16
Policy, 34-35, 222-50
  documents, 227
Political machinations, 236
Pollution, 265
Positioning Tourism, 229-30
Post-World War II, 20-21, 42
Potential, 34-35
Poultry, 19
Poverty alleviation, 19
  elimination, 20
  eradication, 50
Private Sector, incentives to, 252-53
Product/infrastructure, 50-52
Premier Travel Inn (PTI), 191
Primary phase, 35-36
Private hoteliers, 49
Private Sector Service Providers, 19, 55
Professional tourism, 30
Professionalism, 48-49
Promotion, 57-58
  strategies, 61-62
Promoting business activities, 13
Promoting tourism, 182
Promotional offices, 87
Prospect, 34-35
Public sector partnership, 19
Publicity, 59-60
Pushkar, 234

Rabri Devi, 108
Rahul Sankrityayan, 103
Rajasthan, 232
Raja Ben Chakrabarty, 156
Raja Vishal Ka Garh, 151
Rajendra Prasad (former President of India), 93, 103, 104, 109
Rajgir, 135, 143-44, 211-12, 238, 244
Ramayana, 117, 149
Ranbhum area, 145
Rangmala, 153
Ranthambhore, 232
Rashes Shah, 192
Rashtriya Janata Dal, 111
Raychoudhury, Samir, 129
Recreational Tourist, 30
Religious Tourism, 30

Revenue generating potential, 78
Rich historical heritage, regions of, 43
Rivers, 136
Riyazu-s-Salatin, 196
Robbery, 218
Rock-cut images, 155
Rohtasgarh, 153
Roll Bihari, 129
Rupee and Custom duties, 102
Rural Tourism, 33, 49, 53, 95, 250

Saharasa, 105
Saiva Temple, 155
Sanjay Gandhi Biological Park, 141
Saptaparni cave, 145
Sarhul festival, 205
Sasaram, 152
Satyagraha movement, 210
Seasonal fairs, 194
Seasonality, 94
Second Five Year Plan, 87
Second World War, 20, 28, 46, 223
Secondary phase, 37-38
Security and Intelligence Services (SIS), 114
Sepoy mutiny, 102
Service providers, capacity building of, 97
Seventh Five Year Plan, 92
Seventh-Tenth plan, tourism development in, 90-91
  objectives of, 90
Sex ratio, 158-59
Sharda Sinha (Padma Shri), 118
Sharat Chandra Chattopadhyay, 120
Sheesh Mahal, 153
Sher Shah Suri, 102, 111
Shilpagram, 54, 234
Shraddha, 198
Siddha, 226
Sikh Gurudwaras, 135
Sikhism, 191
Silao, 143
Singapore, 47
Sinha, S.N., 104, 105, 106, 111
Sir John Sargent, 46
Sita World Travels, 83
Sixth Five Year Plan, investment in Tourism, 89-90
Soharai festival, 205
Sonepur fair, 203, 242-43
South-East Asia, 230
South-Africa, 93
South Korea, 92
Souvenir, 215-16
Soveignties, 14
Special Tourism Areas, 84
Sports Tourism, 30
Sri Lanka, 47, 87
State/Union Territories Government, 55
State Tourism Development Corporation, 55
Stone railing, 148
Strategies, 228-29
Sudama Cave, 154
Sufi circuit, 238
Sufi Shrines, 135
Sun temple, 143
Sustainable human development, 19
Sustainable Tourism, 85-86
Swami Shahjanand Saraswati, 103-05
Swami Shivananda, 157
Swarn Bhandar Caves, 144

Taj Mahal, 77, 179
Tang Dynasty, 101
Tapodharma, 130
Tara Chandi Hill, 153
Tara Devi Temple, 149
Tata Economic Consultancy Services (TECS), 266
Taxation, 265

Technological advancement, 20
Tenth Five Year Plan, 51, 56-58, 60-64, 82, 92-93
  investment in, 91-92
  planning and policy formulation, 62-63
  promotion, strategies for, 61
  schemes and activities, 50
Thailand, 47, 149
Third Five Year Plan, 87-88
Tibet, 149
Tibetan Temples, 241
Tirthankara, 131, 236
Tokyo, 60, 235
Tomb of Shershah, 153
Tombs, 153
Tour and Travel Association, 226
Tourism, categories of, 29-30
  competitive environment of, 193-207
  characteristics of, 18
  components of, 30-31
  development of, 51, 76-77, 83, 138, 218, 222, 227, 272
    goals, 228-29
  entrepreneurship development programmes, 35-38, 40-41
  expenditure on, 19-20
  geographical components of, 31
  importance of, 18-19
  infrastructure, 33-36
  investment in, 78-79
  marketing of, 47, 208-220
    strategies of, 42-43
  meaning and concept of, 14-15
  objectives of, 71-72
  organisations, 42
  promotion of, 221
  role of State, 33-34
  sector, share in, 68-70
  types of, 28-29
Tourism under Five Year Plan, 86
Tourism after World War II, 28-29
Tourism industry, 15, 19, 33-34, 39-40, 56, 86, 136, 209, 253-54
  private sector in, 78
Tourism circuits, integrated development of, 51-52
Tourism Development Corporation (TDC), 38, 84
Tourism Needs Aggressive Marketing Strategy, 49
Tourism planning, 222-256
Tourism policy, 35, 243
Tourism policy force, 230
Tourism projects, classification methods of, 87
Tourism Satellite Accounting (TSA), 179, 230
Tourism Trade Regulation Act, 254
Tourists, 17-20
  circuit, 138
  destination, 54, 210-11, 230-31
    competitiveness, 96
  expenditure of, 214
  features of, 29-30
  generating countries, 21-22
  kinds of, 34
  movement, 209-10
Tourists centres, 86-87, 92
  developments of, 88-89
Tourist police, 237
Tourist product, 212-13
  distribution of, 219-20
Tourist Reception Centres, 54
Trace your root package, 135, 238
Transformation, 235-36
Transparency International India, 112
Transportation, 19, 35, 48
  system, 14
Travel, basic motivation for, 30
  expenses, 58
Travel Agents Association, 83

Travel Corporation of India, 83
Trends in the Nineties, 81-82
Tribal fetivals, 205-06
  Karma, 205
  Sarhul, 205
  Soharai, 205
Tribeniganj Fair, 199

Uncontrolled Tourism growth, 228
UN World Tourism Organisation (UNWTO), 180, 182
UNESCO World Heritage, 191
Unique Selling Propositions (USPs), 234
United Nations, 21
United Natons Conference on International Travel and Tourism, 223
United Nations Special Fund, 224
United Technologies Corp (UTC), 114
University complex, ruins of, 143
Unsafe drinking water, 265
Upanayanam, 117
Urs Chiraga of Mittan Ghat, 200
Ustad Bismillah Khan, 118
Uttar Pradesh, 99, 110, 203
Uttaranchal, 232

Vagishwari Temple, 146
Vaishali, 149, 211, 238
Varanasi, 92
Vardhaman Mahvira, 131
Vayu Purana, 198
Venuvan Vihar, 145
Vikramshila, 102, 155
Vikramshila University, 102, 114, 158, 191, 211, 237, 240
Village Tourism, 255
Visnu Jhopri Cave, 154-55
Vishnu Shanti-Stupa, 150
Vishnu Puja, 182
Visit India Tourism year, 46

Walter Hunziker, 18
Western culture, 48
Western Europe, 230
Wildlife tourism, 85-86, 92
Wildlife Sanctuaries and National Parks, 85-86
Working group, recommendations of, 95
World Bank, 111
World class infrastructure, creation of, 96-97
World Foreign exchange, 66-67
World Gross Product, 208
World Travel Tourism Council (WTTC), 27, 179-80
World Tourism Organization (WTO), 17, 18, 23, 27, 30, 226
World Tourist arrivals, 21
WTM London, 60

Yakshini, 211
Yatri Nivases, 265
Yoga, 54, 226
Yoga Bharti, 157
Yoga circuit package, 238
Yoga Vedanta Forest Academy, 157
Yogendra Shukla, 104
Yogic education, 158

Zamindari System, 103